John Hill

for the State of Texas

John Hill
For the State of Texas

My Years as Attorney General

BY JOHN L. HILL JR.

With Ernie Stromberger

Foreword by John Cornyn

Introduction by Elizabeth B. Lacy

Texas A&M University Press College Station

First edition
This paper meets the requirements
of ANSI/NISO Z39.48-1992
(Permanence of Paper).
Binding materials have been chosen
for durability.

LIBRARY OF CONGRESS CATALOGING-IN-PUBLICATION DATA

Hill, John L., 1923–2007.
John Hill for the state of Texas : my years as attorney general / By
John L. Hill Jr., with Ernie Stromberger.
p. cm.
Includes bibliographical references and index.
ISBN-13: 978-1-60344-072-1 (cloth : alk. paper)
ISBN-10: 1-60344-072-0 (cloth : alk. paper)
1. Hill, John L., 1923–2007. 2. Attorneys general—Texas—Biography.
I. Stromberger, Ernie, 1939– II. Title.
KF373.H465H55 2008
340.092—dc22
[B]
2008020183

Contents

A gallery of illustrations follows page 115.

Foreword, by Sen. John Cornyn vii
Preface xi
Acknowledgments xv
An Introduction to My Mentor, by Justice Elizabeth B. Lacy xvii

1. Riding Sharpstown to Victory 1
2. Reforming Consumer Protections 17
3. Cleaning Up the Houston Ship Channel 34
4. Beating the Southwestern Bell Goliath 58
5. Corralling Maverick Child Care Home Operators 89
6. Attacking Corruption in Duval County 116
7. Fighting California and Nevada for Howard Hughes's Estate Taxes 141
8. Defending the Death Penalty 165
9. Managing the Reform of Prisons and Youth Detention Schools 191

Appendix 1. Staff Leadership Team in the Texas Attorney General's Office, 1973–1978 215
Appendix 2. Key Dates in the Life of John L. Hill Jr. 218
Notes 223
Bibliography 249
Index 251

List of Illustrations and Photographs

Photographs

1. Hill's junior college portrait
2. John and Bitsy's 1946 wedding
3. Hill poses with Braniff crash client during 1962 trial
4. Governor Connally congratulates Hill as new secretary of state in 1966
5. Justice Greenhill administers Hill oath of office in 1975
6. Hill's environmental protection staff in 1973
7. Hill congratulates new First Assistant in 1973
8. Hill faces off with Southwestern Bell officials in 1975.
9. Hill's 1975 news conference rallies support for public utility commission law
10. Hill takes Bell rate increase fight to Texas Supreme Court in 1975
11. Hill confers with Duval County corruption task force head in 1975
12. Texas Rangers join Hill staff on Duval County task force
13. Hill discusses Duval County investigation with local prosecutor in 1975
14. Governor Briscoe signs Deceptive Trade Practices Act in 1973
15. Governor Briscoe signs 1975 law to curb mobile home sales abuses
16. Hill's efforts in 1976 to license evangelist's schools ignite protest rally
17. Brother Roloff, Bible in one hand and bullhorn in the other, rallies his flock.
18. John, Bitsy and grandkids greet Laredo parade crowd in 1977
19. Hill prepares to enter U.S. Supreme Court to argue 1978 Howard Hughes case.
20. Tax lawsuit against Willie Nelson triggers "Impeach Hill" banner at 1974 concert
21. Hill dons Uncle Sam suit for July 4 celebration
22. Hill's family at ranch near Dripping Springs
23. Bitsy, Melinda, Graham and Martha Hill at the ranch
24. John and Bitsy celebrate his 1978 victory over Governor Briscoe.

25. Hill lugs a football at 1975 college charity event
26. 1978 Hill family portrait
27. Hill with Larry York, John Odam in 1978
28. Hill's official portrait his first year in office

Illustrations

1. Southwestern Bell finds an unexpected obstacle blocking path to rate increase.
2. A page from the bizarre Howard Hughes activity log introduced as trial court evidence
3. Hill's gubernatorial campaign spurs jokes about political motivations in Hughes case.
4. Hill's 1977 proposal to beef up crime-fighting powers draws gibes.
5. Business lobbyists skewered for 1977 attempts to strip Hill's antitrust authority
6. Hill, Lieutenant Govenor Hobby, and Comptroller Bullock are ribbed for gubernatorial ambitions.
7. A Superman sendup is used to josh Hill's campaign for governor.
8. Comptroller Bullock taunts Hill, to the delight of Governor Briscoe.

FOREWORD

Twenty years after he served as attorney general, John Hill's legacy remained so singular that he was at the top of my list of resources to contact when I decided to seek election to that office in 1998. Although he was a Democrat and I was hoping to become the first Republican attorney general of Texas since Reconstruction, the luster of competence and dynamism his administration gave to that somewhat dowdy office created a level of respect throughout the legal profession strong enough to easily eclipse political partisanship. I hoped to live up to the standard he set. I wanted to model my administration after his.

His advice to me was simple: Play it straight. Do it by the book. Turn aside all the suggestions and requests from people who want you to bend the law, to cut some corners, to help them solve a problem with the state or a litigant. If you ever cave in to that pressure, it's almost impossible to get back on track. Decide what you believe the law and good public policy dictate, then stick with it—even if it means you lose on the issue.

When I won my race and was confronted immediately with the temptations Judge Hill had warned me against, my respect for his core integrity and fairness deepened. As I waded into the broad array of responsibilities of the office, I gained a firsthand appreciation for his decades-old accomplishments.

One of those accomplishments involved a process most nonlawyers would term arcane: issuing written interpretations of statutes. It's the type of law book spadework I would guess might appeal to a law professor but certainly not to a courtroom lawyer like Judge Hill, who was renowned for captivating juries with folksy aphorisms. Yet one of the innovations he is most proud to claim is his elevation of the opinion-writing process to a top priority.

He reviewed (and usually returned, often with copious scribbling in the margins, prompting follow-up exchanges) every draft prepared by his staff. His predecessors had selected different staff lawyers to form the committee that wrote an opinion; each opinion was credited to the assistant who drafted it. He replaced that procedure with a standing opinions committee chaired by David Kendall, a veteran generalist from a large

Houston law firm, and he directed that every opinion be signed only by him, his first assistant, and Kendall. He also installed a quasi-judicial approach by publicizing requests to alert all interested groups and by inviting them to file briefs advancing their interpretations.

This wide-open approach defied conventional wisdom at the time, which held that opinion requests often were an insider's game best played with minimal outsider input. The opinions were expected to be more attuned to political than legal considerations. Judge Hill rejected this approach not only because it offended the sense of dignity he believed the attorney general's office should command but also because he saw those opinions as the heart of his administration's legacy. He chafed at the thought of future legal researchers dismissing one of his opinions as the work of a political hack. That would have undercut his lifelong devotion to enhancing the profession he had loved from the minute he stepped into his first class at the University of Texas School of Law, where he displayed such mastery of legal cases when called upon by his law professors that he was accused by one of reading from an outline. He graduated near the top of his class, earning membership in the school's most prestigious honorary society, Chancellors. As a practicing lawyer, he won commendations from the State Bar of Texas for his success in pushing the corporate lawyer–dominated organization to expand its education offerings to include trial advocacy seminars—often organized and taught by John Hill.

The opinion-writing reforms he installed became doubly important when the Texas Legislature in 1973 enacted the Open Records Act, which assigned to the attorney general's office the resolution of disputes involving public access to governmental records. Judge Hill and Kendall interpreted that role to require for every open record request a written decision accompanied by an explanation of the legal reasoning. Because the new law's first five years of interpretive decisions occurred during Judge Hill's administration, these 220 rulings created a significant legal foundation that vastly simplified this job for me and his other successors. And, their unfailing thrust toward openness in cases where statutory discretion left the issue unclear created a much-needed basis for greater transparency in government.

The motivations that drove Judge Hill's insistence on exhaustive research for every legal opinion also promoted an expansive view of his office's powers and responsibilities. One of his most important organizational innovations was the creation of regional offices to assist in enforcing the new Deceptive Trade Practices Act, which his office successfully championed in the legislative session of 1973. Offices were opened in San Antonio, El Paso, Lubbock, Dallas, and Houston, and they were also assigned to support environmental and law enforcement cases. These offices vastly enlarged the impact of the new consumer protections and increased cooperation between the attorney general and local law enforcement, pollution control advocates, and prosecuting attorneys' offices. I used them to good effect, and they are still operating today.

These regional offices were the most visible evidence of the creative energy Judge Hill brought to the attorney general's office and imbued in his staff. His freewheeling style was a fortunate good fit with the tumultuous 1970s, when scandal-fed political turmoil in Austin and Washington, D.C., interacted with fallout from the social and cultural upheavals of the 1960s to banish the status quo. Judge Hill filled that governmental vacuum with a vibrant blend of activist advocacy and pragmatic progressivism that would have struggled for traction even five or ten years earlier—and that certainly would not have prospered in the antigovernment environment of subsequent decades.

The biggest contribution Judge Hill made to the image of the attorney general's office was a dimension few of his predecessors or successors could offer: a unanimous recognition among his peers as one of the state's best trial lawyers, an exceptionally talented advocate in the courtroom. My legal career began after his had already peaked, but I knew him by reputation. Colleagues a decade my senior still considered his 1958 *Texas Bar Journal* article on how to select a jury in personal injury cases an indispensable touchstone they kept handy in their briefcases for ready access. Colleagues two decades my senior told of sitting in on one of his trials as a learning experience, so legendary were his skills.

The facile mind, focused intensity, glib manner, and theatrical flair that charmed almost every one of the hundreds of juries he faced as a plaintiff attorney were traits all litigators hoped to claim. The confidence and élan he enjoyed and projected as attorney general in the courtroom, whether in the small and remote Duval County courthouse or the rarefied air of the Supreme Court building in Washington, dazzled his staff, frustrated his opposing counsel, and convinced the presiding judges they were witnessing a rare legal talent playing his case like a fiddle.

It was these intangible attractions that brought to the attorney general's office a bright and eager group of young lawyers who, inspired by their unflinching leader, boosted the stature of the state's law firm. Judge Hill's tenure coincided with an explosion of law student fascination with harnessing the law and legal research to address societal ills through the new strategies demonstrated by Ralph Nader. The Hill administration welcomed these nascent reformers with young faces—most of his top assistants were in their early thirties—as well as an aggressive but measured leadership on public policy issues of the day and a freedom to try new ideas, all overlaid with Judge Hill's demand for a quality work product. I was so impressed with the job he did in assembling such a stellar staff that I chose one of Judge Hill's young turks to help me replicate his success by leading my transition team when I won my election as attorney general. That young turk was Larry York, who at thirty-two was Hill's first assistant during 1973–74.

Texas was fortunate to benefit from Hill's leadership, and so were those of us who enjoyed the exceptional example he set for us.

John Cornyn, U.S. Senate
Washington, D.C.
October 2007

Preface

Had he not died unexpectedly in July 2007, John Hill would have written this preface with my help. Sadly, it now bears only my name.

John wanted to write this book about his years as attorney general because he considered those the most exciting and fulfilling in his long and active life. Those years, to John, meant more than his success in the 1950s and 1960s as one of the state's most respected trial attorneys, his two campaigns for governor, his service as chief justice of the Texas Supreme Court, or his service to and friendships with governors and presidents.

The attorney general's office offered greater opportunity for doing good for more people than any other state office, he believed, and the many good results he achieved validated the wisdom of his determination to provide Texans with first-class legal advocacy. His goal was a book that would demonstrate that these types of accomplishments—as well as his commitment to enforcing the law without fear or favor, a standard to which he believed too many in government did not adhere—were within the grasp of any public official who simply refused to cut corners for political expediency.

We agreed that I would write the book in his voice. To reconstruct the events and decisions that shaped his administration's destiny, the book would meld together his recollections shared during several interviews with me, his three oral histories, published references, and my thirty interviews of his former assistants and others in and out of government who were involved. To help readers imagine conversations conducted in private meetings where comments were not recorded, we relied on the memories of living participants to create dialogue. Quotations in the text lacking a source citation were derived using this technique. Each chapter was reviewed for accuracy by the principal assistants and others who served as my sources. John, of course, had the last say, with his edits of my manuscript. We submitted it to Texas A&M University Press in January 2007, five months before he died.

John chose depth over breadth in directing content. Among the dozens of knotty issues engaged by his staff but passed over for inclusion in the book were deep involvement in a massive constitutional revision process ultimately rejected by voters; critical advice on wording of government reform laws defining open records and open meetings criteria and strengthened ethics laws affecting officeholders' financial disclosure and lobby registration requirements; contentious legislative redistricting lawsuits that traveled to the Supreme Court of the United States and back several times before finally requiring single-member districts for the first time in all urban counties; and devising implementation strategies for state agencies after the landmark *Roe v. Wade* decision in 1973.

Another casualty of the content selection process was two mammoth sets of litigation caused by a shortage of natural gas the year he took office. One involved lawsuits filed against thirty oil and gas companies to force them to adjust their royalty payments from production on state-owned lands to reflect natural gas price increases that often reached 400 percent. The other involved refereeing the flurry of lawsuits caused by the collapse of Oscar Wyatt's natural gas delivery system, which was essential to Austin and San Antonio gas buyers.

In the state's royalty cases, Hill's staff recovered more than $1 billion in additional royalty income for the state's permanent education fund by forcing natural gas producers to pay royalties based on the value of the state-owned gas on the unregulated intrastate market, where soaring demand and supply shortages produced prices much higher than interstate market prices, which were kept lower by federal regulators.

The demise of Wyatt's Lo-Vaca Gathering Company, a subsidiary of his Coastal States Gas Producing Company, generated lawsuits against Lo-Vaca and Coastal States by Austin, San Antonio and its public utility, the University of Texas, and the Lower Colorado River Authority seeking millions in damages suffered when Wyatt's companies failed to provide gas in volumes mandated in purchase contracts. Hill and his staff took commanding roles in steering the case as it swirled through the courts and the Texas Railroad Commission for five years, producing several precedents in natural gas public policy later incorporated into federal law.

The process of winnowing the book's content left eight issues for comprehensive development. They are a mixture of legislative and judicial accomplishments and frustrations that reflect the overriding cultural and political turmoil of the 1970s, when the upheavals of the 1960s were being fitfully assimilated into all levels of government with varying degrees of acceptance.

Few attorneys general of Texas could claim as diverse a range of challenges as John. He lacked the high-visibility cases of some of his predecessors, such as Price Daniel's successful challenge in the 1950s of federal claims to a ten-mile-wide swath of offshore territory along the Gulf of Mexico coastline, Will Wilson's closure of Galveston gambling casinos in the late 1950s, and Waggoner Carr's investigation of the John F. Kennedy assassination. But none of his predecessors matched or even approached his five appearances before the Supreme Court of the United States, on cases ranging from a dense Louisiana boundary dispute to an emotional defense of the death penalty statute.

Because John was elected as an agent of change in one of the state's historic electoral upheavals, and because he seized this opportunity immediately, forcefully, and relentlessly, his early years as attorney general presented an image of a reformer and crusader. Public policy issues that languished under the desultory state government leadership booted out of office in the election of 1972 were jerked to life by his aggressive staff and shoved to the forefront of the polity's priorities. The state's first meaningful consumer protection law was enacted, Houston Ship Channel polluters were forced to comply with clean-up laws for the first time, the virtual monopoly operating the state's telephone service and its unregulated intrastate rate increases were successfully challenged in court for the first time, and Texas lost its status as the only state without a public utility commission.

Although John's crusader image persisted throughout his tenure—despite the fact that most of the reforms he championed were resolved in the first two years of his administration—he prided himself and his office more on "good lawyering" and "doing what's right" than in challenging political orthodoxy. That is why the content selected for this book includes several issues that bear no connection with his early reform initiatives: the child care litigation against Brother Lester Roloff that was legally principled but politically disastrous; his defense of the Texas death penalty statute before the Supreme Court of the United States; his cleanup of political corruption in South Texas; his unsuccessful defense of the state's young offender detention facilities and adult prisons against federal court challenges; and his successful challenge of the Howard Hughes estate's plans to avoid multimillion-dollar Texas inheritance taxes.

John wanted to help readers understand how these disputes fit into—and helped shape—the political, social, and governmental fabric of the Texas of the 1970s, how the Hill administration marshaled its resources to fashion a strategy, and how that strategy fared in the crucibles of the legislature, the courts, and public opinion. He sought a balanced history that avoided the one-sided self-aggrandizement often associated with political memoirs.

The result is an insider's view of some of the most contentious issues that grabbed the attention of state government in the 1970s, the people who engaged them, and the forces that tested him and his staff as they maneuvered through often uncharted public policy cross-currents.

Acknowledgments

John was indebted, as am I, to all of the assistants who worked for John whose names appear in the book, and several whose names do not appear. Their ready cooperation as sources and manuscript reviewers reflects their respect for John as an inspirational leader, a supportive boss, and a phenomenal lawyer.

I single out Larry York, John's initial First Assistant and afterward a lifelong friend and admirer, for his several roles: a source of essential information on several major cases, an always-available and cheerful advisor on many aspects of the book ranging from perceptive copy edits to capturing the tone of John's management style, and the donor of one of the book's most interesting photos. Virginia Supreme Court Justice Liz Lacy, the first female division chief in any state attorney general's office in the nation—a fact of which John often bragged—deserves thanks for taking on the job of representing the insights of his former assistants in a thoughtful introduction. Joe K. Longley provided office space, frequent and entertaining counsel, and the help of his legal and administrative assistant, Amy Weappa.

U.S. Sen. John Cornyn's contribution of a foreword, providing perceptions from a successor in the attorney general's office, is a significant addition. Former Lt. Gov. Bill Hobby was indispensable in reconstructing several key events in two of the book's major stories. After John's death, his daughter, District Judge Martha Jamison, gathered family photos for the book and coordinated family involvement.

Several former journalism colleagues with books to their credit or in progress offered valuable guidance: Dave McNeely, Bob Bullock's biographer and a fellow former John Hill staffer; Mike Cochran, Clayton Williams' biographer and a fellow former Associated Press reporter; Saralee Tiede, who is assisting Bill Hobby in writing his memoirs; and Carolyn Barta, Bill Clements' biographer, whose suggestions as a Texas A&M University Press manuscript reviewer were especially helpful. David Anderson, a University of Texas law professor and fellow former capitol press reporter, helped me maneuver through legal research issues; and *Austin American-Statesman* editorial cartoonist Ben Sargent, also a former capitol press colleague, generously provided the cartoons that greatly enhance the book's illustrations.

Generous assistance also was offered by Locke Liddell's Austin office manager, Edna Diaz, who provided office space and steered me to my faithful audio tape transcribers, Jenaya Farley and DeAnn Caylor; and by John's assistants, Brenda Reed and Dee Williams. Former Texas Public Utility Commissioner Dennis Thomas pointed me quickly to the resources I needed in researching the history of the telephone industry. Sandra Burrell at Liberty's Sam Houston Regional Library and Research Center, Mike Miller at the Austin History Center, Sherry Adams at the *Houston Chronicle,* Allison Ehrlich at the *Corpus Christi Caller-Times,* Beth Andresen at the Dallas Public Library, Laura Saegert at the State Archives, Hank Bass at the State Bar of Texas, and Joel Draught at the Houston Public Library all expedited my research.

Our thanks to Texas A&M University Press Editor-in-chief Mary Lenn Dixon, who accepted the book for publication; Maureen Bemko, who improved the text with deft copyediting; and Thom Lemmons, who guided the book through the publishing process at Texas A&M University Press.

Ernie Stromberger
Austin, Texas
November 2008

An Introduction to My Mentor

My first day on the job for John Hill was also his first day in office. I reported to his seventh-floor conference room for the kickoff meeting of all division chiefs and assistant chiefs—I was assistant chief of the then Consumer Protection and Anti-Trust Division—only to find my way blocked by the guardian of the inner sanctum, a veteran employee who had parlayed her job as switchboard operator into the enforcer of public decorum in the attorney general's office. She backed against the double doors to the conference room, spread her arms, and barked at me, "You can't go in there. They're having a meeting of division chiefs." After I persisted in requesting that John settle this dispute, he was summoned and assured her it was all right, that I belonged in the meeting. She grudgingly allowed me through the doors.

That incident reflects the culture of the attorney general's office, and much of the state, in 1973. The switchboard operator, in her years at the attorney general's office, had never seen a female attorney in an administrative position, much less a female attorney in a pants suit. There had been only a handful of female attorneys on the 100-member staff, and most had been much older than I. I was just three years out of the University of Texas law school, where I was one of only 18 females in a graduating class of 309.

I was not the only symbol of the many changes John's administration brought to the attorney general's office, a place generally considered a typical low-key state agency with career employees not infrequently hired because of their sponsorship by a powerful legislator or major political donor. Of the eleven division chiefs at that meeting in January 1973, five were new faces. The staff was brimming with freshly minted lawyers, male and female alike, who went on to lead divisions and eventually law firms. However short on experience some of us were, we all were long on enthusiasm and anticipation to work with the new attorney general of Texas. John's recruiting spanned both sides of the legal aisle, plaintiff and defense attorneys alike, some of whom he had met as adversaries and others, like myself, through word of mouth.

As he gathered us together in that first staff meeting in his seventh-floor conference room, his directions were clear. He would take care of the politics and support us publicly, but in return he expected us to work together, keep him informed of our activities, and never lose a matter because we were less than fully prepared or outsmarted. And he did not care how much we talked to the press (a big issue in those days of the Sharpstown banking scandal); he would only hold us accountable for what was printed in the newspaper or repeated on radio or television.

For the next six years, John stayed true to his word, and we all did our best to live up to his challenge. He sent us to court to litigate complex and important cases, to the Texas Legislature to "assist" that body with consumer protection legislation, ethics reform, revision of the state's constitution, and even impeachment proceedings. While he clearly took some risks in unleashing us twenty- and thirty-somethings as defenders of the State, he was never far removed from or unaware of what was happening under his watch. John not only roamed the halls of each floor in that Supreme Court building, his door was always open and he was always available to review strategy, a brief, or a legal position on any subject. Staff meetings were more than droning updates of the activities of each division. John probed and prodded and pushed, giving us the benefit of his experience and canny legal instincts as well as his disapproval when we were not sufficiently prepared or informed on an issue.

Actual involvement in litigation can be dangerous for an attorney general because official duties constantly demand time and attention and because there was always the specter of an embarrassing loss. John's love of the courtroom would not be denied, however, and he could not stay away from it. John personally participated in five cases before the Supreme Court of the United States, perhaps a record for an attorney general.

Such participation was always a source of consternation for the legal staff involved in whatever case was at hand. I remember an original jurisdiction case involving the boundary line between Texas, Louisiana, and the United States as it continued into the Gulf of Mexico. Texas claimed a nine-mile seaward limit, and the case was affectionately known as "who gets to drill for oil where." John designated himself as lead counsel, and although the rest of the trial team (Larry York, John Odam, Danny Goforth, and I) prepared the case, it was John who took the lead in the federal court in New Orleans.

We assistant attorneys general feared that the attorney general may not have been sufficiently familiar with the intricacies of the case to do legal combat with well-versed representatives of the Interior Department and the State of Louisiana. Our fears were quickly put aside as we marveled at John's way of making the international law of the sea sound like a simple West Texas theory. John practiced what he preached: always do your homework.

John's impact as attorney general was felt beyond state lines. He was recognized by his peers as a leader and took an active role in the National Association of Attorneys General. Often in charge of his briefing book, I had the opportunity to see John challenge attorneys general from around the country, including Arkansas's attorney general–elect, Bill Clinton, to use their positions as tools to improve the legal system and the people's access to that system, just as he did at home.

Working for and with John Hill and learning from him was a unique opportunity. But that opportunity does not tell the story of why the atmosphere in that attorney general's office was so positive and compelling. The enthusiasm for doing the job was the direct result of the fact that the attorney general knew who you were, cared about you, and thought life, even a lawyer's life, should be enjoyed. At the very first full office staff breakfast John went around the room and introduced each person by name and where they were from. We were not faceless litigators supporting a politician's platform. We were people with lives and interests. And John was interested in each of us on a personal level. He reveled in our happy times and fretted when things were not going well.

John encouraged us to "have a life" outside the office and to enjoy each other on a social level. Staff parties at his ranch were great events. His love of family was a model for all of us. His children were not strangers to the office, and his wife was always gracious and warm to staff. Only John could say "Bitsy" in a way that conveyed that devotion and respect he so clearly had for her.

One cannot speak of John Hill or working in his office without commenting on his sense of humor. Indeed, John's ability to laugh, and make others laugh at himself as well as at the rest of us, contributed to the pure fun of practicing in that office. "The Sayings of Chairman John," compiled by then first assistant Larry York, is a good example of our ability to combine work with play. I will indulge with two examples and their presumed meaning. The first is "We're up to our ass in bass." York defined that as used "synonymously with being in a 'lot of trouble,' although somewhat of a non-sequitur, since most fishermen would regard this as a pleasant state." The other is "Anyone with a head as big as a grape knows that," which was defined as "often used by the Chairman to support a proposition which cannot be supported otherwise, either by logic or legal authority." These idioms, whether used to break the tension or relax after a full day's work, reflect the good nature and shared responsibility that John Hill invested in us as members of his attorney general's office.

This easy-going side of John was paired with a capacity for deep-seated intensity. The legendary facility with words that made John a formidable trial attorney also made him a master of the tongue-lashing. One of his most famous occurred when a political rival, Comptroller Bob Bullock, decided to confront John personally after several weeks of news media sniping at our office's handling of lawsuits against merchants delinquent in sales tax remittances to the state. Bullock, who also harbored a ferocious intensity and sharp tongue, more than met his match. Hill's chewing-out convinced Bullock he needed to beat a hasty retreat. His anxiety jumped another level when he reached for a door handle to escape Hill's wrath—and opened the door to the executive washroom instead of the door to the hallway.

Long before terms such as "mentor" or "citizen lawyer" came to connote aspirations for members of the legal profession, John Hill was living them. As a public citizen for eleven years, with more than half of those years as attorney general of Texas, John was a "citizen lawyer." He used his legal knowledge and skill, along with the power and prestige of his office, to enhance the quality of government and its role in the life of Texas citizens. His causes ranged from the environment, consumer protection, ethics in government, regulation of public utility monopolies, and the very constitution of the State. Whether these causes arose in the courtroom, the legislature, or on the ballot, John was willing to devote his best efforts and resources to advancing the issue. By his actions, he mentored many younger lawyers along the way. And I was one of those lucky ones.

Elizabeth B. Lacy
Justice, Supreme Court of Virginia
Richmond, Virginia
May 2007

John Hill

for the State of Texas

(1)

Riding Sharpstown to Victory

In 1972, I knew I could rebuild the Texas attorney general's office into a legal powerhouse by attracting sharp young lawyers eager for a new challenge. The only obstacle standing in my path was an attorney general who wasn't ready to retire.

Running against an incumbent holding a statewide office in Texas is always difficult. That is particularly true in a race for an office not well understood by voters, which the attorney general's office always will be. Most of its responsibilities involve providing legal advice to state agencies and taking action in courts to implement a law or defend a state agency from legal challenge. Large businesses subject to far-reaching regulatory laws and rules kept a close watch on the attorney general's office, but the average citizen seldom was touched directly by it. That's why candidates for attorney general usually used the campaign theme "I'm tough on crime." Even though the attorney general's powers directly impacting law enforcement are minimal and it is only a small part of the officeholder's role, law enforcement is the only area of responsibility that may have a direct impact on most voters.

To win the election, I would need two circumstances to occur: a one-on-one race against the incumbent and a strong issue that would neutralize the incumbent's natural advantage. Both of these circumstances were beyond my control. On the first item, I could only wait until the filing deadline to determine who the candidates would be. On the second item, I was blessed with an epic influence-peddling scandal that tainted all Austin officeholders.

This scandal was quite a spectacle. The man responsible for this political turmoil was one of my fellow Houstonians but one whom I had never met. His name was Frank Sharp, and his misdeeds gave me my most effective campaign issue. What Sharp intended to do was to sucker the Texas Legislature into helping him stiff-arm federal bank examiners. The examiners' diligence threatened his diversion of huge chunks of his bank's funds into questionable investments. But he made a big mistake. He overestimated the amount of grease he needed to apply to the wheels of government to achieve his goal.

Like the comic-strip bank robber who unwittingly leads the cops to his location because his getaway car was billowing dollar bills from leaky cash bags, Sharp led investigators right to his door. The paper trail created by his disastrous political payoff scheme was so incriminating, it turned a normally low-profile federal investigative agency into a prosecutorial gorilla. The Securities and Exchange Commission (SEC) nailed Sharp and his political beneficiaries with a lawsuit so complex it took the news media a week of slogging through the morass of tangled information to begin grasping the scope of the evidence.[1]

The news of the SEC lawsuit broke as the legislature was beginning its biennial session in January 1971. The politicians who were beneficiaries of Sharp's largesse decided to stonewall. Unfortunately for them, the legislative session offered almost weekly opportunities for their antagonists to repeat the SEC charges and demand an explanation. All of this was dutifully reported by the news media—over and over and over again. And it definitely was not a pretty sight.

The picture that emerged was an image of wheeler-dealers in both the business and political worlds operating openly and increasingly in concert. Texas' growth in the 1960s was centered in Houston. The city became home to the astronauts when the Manned Space Center opened in 1961, and in 1965 it built the world's first indoor baseball and football stadium, the Astrodome, for the city's two new professional sports teams, the Astros and the Oilers.

Sharp capitalized on this growth by developing a four-thousand-acre plot of bald prairie west of Houston into a huge housing and retail subdivision, along the way creating one of the state's largest banks.[2] A better homebuilder than banker, Sharp's profligate lending practices and self-dealing were flagged by federal bank examiners. He faced loss of federal deposit insurance for his depositors—a critical consumer protection—if he failed to meet the examiners' demands for boosting his bank's capital base. His solution was to create a state version of the federal deposit insurance program, ridding him of the federal bank examiners' oversight.

With help from Gov. Preston Smith, who allowed Sharp's proposals to be considered in a special legislative session, and from House Speaker

Gus Mutscher of Brenham, who eased the proposal's quick four-day trip through the legislature, Sharp's well-disguised plan to allow banks to use privately provided bank deposit insurance caught the banking lobby and regulators off guard until it was on Governor Smith's desk.[3] They mounted a campaign to persuade Smith to veto the bill, which he did on September 29, 1969.[4]

The SEC's lawsuit revealed that between the bill's passage on September 9 and before it was vetoed, Mutscher, Smith, and five other capitol leaders earned a combined total of about $300,000 by selling stock in a Sharp-owned insurance company. They had purchased this stock with loans that Sharp provided through his bank. Six of the stock sales were made at an identical above-market price to a Catholic priest whose financial matters were under Sharp's influence.[5] It was a complicated story that later revealed, after Sharp testified as part of a plea bargain with federal prosecutors, that Sharp and Mutscher had agreed to a deal providing the stock profits in return for passage of the legislation.[6]

I was watching this drama unfold with heightened interest. My political ambitions were sidetracked after I had lost a race for governor in 1968, but they had not subsided.

My love affair with campaigning began when I was in high school in Kilgore. During the summer months between high school and college in 1940, my sister Laverne and I made political speeches all over East Texas on behalf of Olin Culberson, a successful reform candidate for the Texas Railroad Commission. Along the campaign trail, I met Gerald Mann, the state's attorney general and a candidate for the U.S. Senate. Knowing I was interested, even at age sixteen, in the law and public service, he told me, "Young man, there are two ways to get into politics in Texas as a lawyer. You can either go into politics early in life and ride it as high and hard as you can and hope to get out while you are still respected and can go full time back into the law practice, or you can go forward with your law practice and make a success of it and hope to get a break later on that will allow you to get into politics." I never forgot his advice, which I followed by choosing the second path he suggested.

Some people love politics for its intrigue. Others view it as a chess game of strategy and tactics. Still others see it as a vehicle to press an ideological agenda. For me, going into politics was always rooted in a sincere desire to serve and a love of campaigning and selling myself to the voters, just like I sold myself and my client to people serving on juries. At the University of Texas, I ran for (and won) the first opening I could find, which was a campaign for head yell leader, several months after I arrived on campus in 1941. I was elected president of my fraternity, Sigma Alpha Epsilon. I won a race for chairman of the Judiciary Council and was elected foreman (president) of the Texas Cowboys, an honorary service organization.

The most prestigious political prize at the university was the presidency of the student body, which was the political starting point for a future governor, John Connally, and a future congressman from Austin, Jake Pickle, who held the position in 1938 and 1937, respectively. I ran for that post in 1944, with backing from the social fraternities. I lost, polling 47 percent of the vote in a runoff against an independent who campaigned on academic freedom issues in response to critical comments about the university from the governor and legislators.[7]

That defeat was the end of my political activities for almost two decades. My first priority out of law school was to launch my career and start earning income to support my new bride and our first child. I had married a wonderful and beautiful coed I met at UT, Elizabeth Ann "Bitsy" Graham, in her northwest Texas hometown of Olney after I returned from two years as a navy officer in the Pacific at the close of World War II. I finished law school a year after we were married, graduating as a Chancellor because I was among the six with the highest grades in my class. Our daughter Melinda was born shortly thereafter. Politics was a luxury I was forced to delay until my practice was established.

Building a law practice from scratch consumed almost every minute of every day in the early years. Those time pressures began to abate when the cumulative effect of my courtroom successes over ten years allowed my practice to blossom into a prosperous law firm. I was eager to jump into the political game, but I could not find a promising team to join. Of the political figures of the time, I admired Pres. Dwight Eisenhower the most. But his political party had no local roots—Democrats held all state and most county elective offices in Texas—and Houston Republicans were a country club set closed to outsiders, particularly to trial attorneys.

The Democratic Party options for involvement centered on the organizations of our three leading officeholders: Senator Lyndon Johnson, whose role as majority leader made him the banner carrier for the national Democratic Party; our conservative governor, Price Daniel; and a liberal U.S. senator, Ralph Yarborough. Becoming a participant in Houston Democratic Party politics required choosing one side in the incessant turf battles among these three politicians' supporters. It was an investment of time I viewed as pointless.

The fresh face and energizing personality I was seeking to whet my political appetite arrived on the scene in 1961. John Connally was appointed secretary of the navy when his mentor LBJ became vice president after the Kennedy-Johnson ticket won the presidential election in 1960. But Connally resigned his post after less than a year so that he could challenge Price Daniel's bid for a fourth term as governor.

A strikingly handsome and articulate leader with a University of Texas beauty-queen wife and a whiff of the Kennedy administration's Camelot star power, Connally brought innovations to campaigning, to party politics, and to government. During the early and mid-1960s, he used his charisma and contacts with the Johnson organization to build a formidable political force that kept at bay a growing Republican Party and the liberal, and always persistent, anti-establishment Democrats.

I met Connally at a fund-raising reception in Dallas during his gubernatorial campaign in 1962 and immediately became a financial supporter. The campaign was a scramble among two tired retreads from the 1950s (Price Daniel and Atty. Gen. Will Wilson) and two newcomers: Connally, from Fort Worth, and Don Yarborough, a Houston lawyer with liberal Democrats' support seeking to capitalize on the similarity of his name to that of Senator Ralph Yarborough. The newcomers prevailed. Daniel received only 17 percent of the vote, the lowest percentage of any incumbent governor in Texas history. In the runoff, Connally beat Yarborough by only 26,250 votes, 2 percent of the total.

My support for Connally put me in fairly select company in Houston. Yarborough led the Harris County ticket in both the first primary and the runoff. Connally received only 21 percent of the first primary vote—he was in third place behind Daniel—and only 45 percent in the runoff. Harris County held 11 percent of the statewide vote, making it crucial to Connally's political future.

One of Connally's key players in Houston, former congressman Lloyd Bentsen, took note of my support. In 1963, he asked me to manage Connally's campaign in Harris County the following year and to help organize and promote a dinner honoring President Kennedy during his ill-fated trip to Texas in November 1963. The assassination attempt on Connally that fateful day made him a shoo-in in 1964. Nonetheless, I was proud to help him dramatically reverse his fortunes in Harris County with his race in 1964, when he swamped Don Yarborough by capturing 62 percent of the vote.

In recognition of my campaign help in Houston, and I believe also because he respected my potential as a statewide candidate and was eager to encourage my political career, Connally dramatically escalated my political fortunes and ambitions by appointing me secretary of state during 1966–1967. The two of us clicked because we shared a common approach to Democratic Party politics and state government.

Connally and I attempted to elevate the level of political discussion above the prevailing mix of personalities and name calling. We broadened the conservative agenda beyond the narrow, dour view of the rural-dominated legislature. We were open-minded problem solvers, not tunnel-vision ideologues. We believed Texans deserved political leadership that reflected their can-do spirit.

As secretary of state, I considered one of my most enjoyable duties to be standing in for Connally at speaking engagements he could not attend. These events gave me a forum in which to demonstrate my enthusiastic support of his aggressive higher education and economic development initiatives. My ornate, high-ceilinged office on the first floor of the nineteenth-century pink granite capitol in Austin was steeped in history, with pictures on the wall of such previous holders of that office as the first Texas colonist in the early 1800s, Stephen F. Austin. My office, which looked out on the south lawn where statues celebrating Texas' rich history were shaded by towering pecan and oak trees, was located adjacent to the governor's suite of offices. I enjoyed a rare insider's view of the levers of governmental power. If Connally intended to stoke the fires of my statewide political ambition, he was spectacularly successful.

The opportunity for a race for governor came sooner than I, or most of Connally's team, expected. He decided in late 1967 not to seek an unprecedented fourth term in 1968. He had attempted to groom a number of potential successors, but none was ready to run. His organization splintered, leaving a power vacuum quickly filled by the lieutenant governor, Preston Smith.

A Connally antagonist aligned with the rural status-quo legislators, Smith was a Lubbock businessman and a capitol fixture with eighteen years of office-holding experience. Connally's stalwarts scurried to find a home among the candidates who ran to succeed him. I jumped into that race, along with Smith and eight other candidates. But I was unprepared for the financial and organizational demands of such a campaign and achieved no traction. I finished in sixth place.

I returned to Houston to renew my law practice and keep my eye on future political opportunities. The election in 1970 offered no viable options, so I set my sights on 1972. The race for governor was shaping up as a showdown between two rival factions in the Democratic Party. One was led by Smith, who claimed the support of the conservative business community. The other was led by Lt. Gov. Ben Barnes of DeLeon, a protégé of Connally and Johnson. The leading candidate to succeed Barnes was Connally's brother Wayne, who was a state senator from Floresville. He was being challenged by two other well-respected senators, Ralph Hall of Rockwall and Joe Christie of El Paso.

All of these candidates were hopelessly out of touch with political reality. They were beat when they paid their filing fee. News media coverage of the Sharpstown scandal had been at saturation levels for a year. During the sixteen months between the filing of the SEC lawsuit and the Democratic primary, the *Dallas Morning News* published 455 articles on various aspects of the scandal—an average of one article every day. Newspapers in Houston and other urban areas, as well as most Texas television news programs, followed the same pattern.[8]

The Sharpstown scandal fatally tainted all of these candidates—particularly Smith, a beneficiary of one of Sharp's arranged stock purchase-and-sale deals, and Barnes, who failed to stop the Sharp bills in his role as the Senate's presiding officer.[9] Their obvious vulnerability attracted two outsiders to the governor's race: Uvalde banker and rancher Dolph Briscoe Jr., and state representative Frances Farenthold of Corpus Christi, a leader of the "Dirty Thirty" House dissidents who had harassed the Speaker over the Sharpstown affair. The lieutenant governor's race also attracted an outsider: *Houston Post* editor William P. Hobby Jr., son of a former governor.

I sized up my options and quickly decided against a race for governor. That prize still tugged at my heart, and I knew the scandal would give outsiders like me an unusual opportunity to overcome the traditional advantages of established politicians. But my sixth-place finish in the ten-candidate race in 1968 had me convinced that I needed to lower my sights.

I believed my standing among my colleagues in the legal profession was stout enough to create a solid base for a race for attorney general. My belief was confirmed in discussions with one of my most valued political advisors, Leon Jaworski. He was a legend among Texas lawyers and even nationally; later, as the celebrated Watergate special prosecutor, his unflinching leadership played a big role in President Nixon's decision to resign rather than face certain impeachment. He encouraged my interest in public service and backed my decision to run for attorney general.

The incumbent, Crawford Martin, owed his job to Connally and enjoyed strong support from the Connally wing of the Democratic Party. Martin was a Hillsboro lawyer who had been part of the dominant rural faction in the state's Senate for fourteen years before Connally appointed him secretary of state in 1962 to help move Connally's legislative program through a recalcitrant Senate. Frustrated by differences with Atty. Gen. Waggoner Carr, Connally decided he wanted a supportive attorney general to succeed Carr when he left office in 1966 to run for the U.S. Senate. Connally guided Martin's election as Carr's successor. No attorney general had ever served more than six years, but Martin chose to buck that tradition. He filed early for reelection, discouraging candidates who might have filed for an open seat.

I decided to bide my time and wait until the filing deadline in hopes of obtaining the one-on-one race I believed was essential for me to compete effectively. My strategy worked—almost. When I filed in the late afternoon on the deadline day of February 7, 1972, I was the only other candidate. My joy was short-lived, though, because a mail-in filing was received several days later. While this third candidate would not mount a serious campaign, I knew he could throw the race into a runoff that would enhance Martin's financial advantage over me. My chances definitely were not helped by this third candidate.

Several days after I filed, Martin told a group of staff members in a briefing on his campaign plans, "I've heard you can go around the world in eighty days, but I don't believe anyone can start a statewide campaign from scratch in ninety days and win."[10] His assessment of the difficulties of mounting a campaign in a state with two dozen media markets and a geographic span of 800 miles east-west and 830 miles north-south was well founded. I didn't have a moment to waste.

To manage the campaign, I called on the Austin plaintiff attorney who had run my campaign in 1968, Charles "Lefty" Morris. I also contacted Joe K. Longley, another plaintiff attorney friend in Austin with experience in two governors' offices and as a legislative aide, and he agreed to travel with me. John Rogers, the longtime public relations director for the Texas AFL-CIO, agreed to handle my press relations. I hired a Houston friend in the advertising business, Jan Norris, to produce bumper stickers, buttons, and the few television ads I could afford.

We prepared a basic campaign platform focusing on the issues I wanted to raise: consumer protection, pollution control, law enforcement, and my professional credentials. Longley and I hit the campaign trial in my

Lincoln or a rented Cessna 210, driving or flying to any gathering Morris and Rogers could arrange, to persuade my lawyer friends and other potential supporters around the state to contribute and recruit friends to do likewise.

One of our first goals was to get labor's support when their political action committee met a month after the filing deadline. I needed the financial support an endorsement provided, as well as having my name on the several hundred thousand "slate cards" the Texas AFL-CIO would distribute to their members as election day reminders. Rogers worked his contacts to achieve that support, and on March 4 the Texas AFL-CIO endorsed my candidacy, giving me new credibility in the fund-raising game.[11]

Our next goal was to develop an issue that would generate news coverage, which would provide clippings that reassured my supporters they were backing an aggressive candidate. That goal was met for us by the sensational trial in Abilene of House Speaker Mutscher and two associates on charges of conspiracy to commit bribery in connection with the Frank Sharp banking legislation.[12]

I would have preferred that "top-notch lawyer" or "he'll try to do what's right" pop into voters' minds when they saw or heard the name "John Hill." A compressed, ninety-day campaign overshadowed by four-way battles for governor and lieutenant governor, however, left me with no choice but to settle for "outsider" and "he'll clean up the mess in Austin."

I wasn't really an "outsider"; I had been in the Connally administration in Austin just six years earlier. And I had not been a vocal critic of the capitol leaders as the Sharpstown revelations unfolded. But my supporters' reactions at campaign events had me convinced that such labels would be my salvation. My attempts to generate excitement for my push to enact stronger consumer and pollution laws drew only polite response. But when I reminded voters I was not part of the leadership in Austin that had created this mess, and I promised to clean up that mess, I could feel the excitement as they shouted their encouragement.[13]

The news coming out of Abilene every day was providing us outsider candidates an embarrassment of campaign rhetoric riches. Sharp's personal secretary testified that about a dozen calls were completed between Sharp and Martin during a six-month period in 1969. That was the hook I needed to tie Martin to Sharp.[14]

I immediately started holding news conferences to point out this connection and to ask why Martin had not taken a leadership role in investigating the scandal.[15] Sharp also testified during the trial, repeating his story of the Houston hotel meeting in 1969 in which he and the Speaker arranged the politicians' sweetheart stock deal and their support for Sharp's banking legislation.[16] Prosecutors were miffed that Sharp's promise to testify produced only a recollection of a vague exchange between him and the Speaker that ended not with a handshake sealing a deal or a verbal quid pro quo but with "a tacit understanding" and "he smiled and I smiled."[17]

Those concerns were erased when a clean-cut McMurry College student in jeans and boots rose in the jury box on March 15 and responded to the judge's question, "How does the jury find the defendants?" Speaking on behalf of the twelve jurors who obviously heeded the prosecutor's plea to "send a message to the politicians in Austin," he stared determinedly at the defendants and replied, "Guilty!"[18]

The resulting tidal wave of media coverage gave my news conferences on the Sharp-Martin connection new traction. Norris developed a series of ten-second television spots featuring a newspaper headline "Sharpstown Scandal Exposed" followed by a sketch of the capitol with a cartoonlike cloud moving across the horizon, leaving the capitol darkened. The announcer's voice-over, accompanied by a dramatic drum roll, said in ominous tones, "When the Sharpstown scandal broke, where was the attorney general of Texas?"[19]

When we launched those spots in late March, they gave the campaign a big boost. Martin started fighting back, releasing his financial statement March 22 and challenging me to do the same.[20] His strategy was undoubtedly designed to dampen my fund-raising efforts by demonstrating to potential contributors that they didn't need to waste their money because my personal wealth was sufficient to fund the campaign. I therefore stalled for two weeks to deny him that advantage. I released my financial statement on April 17, showing a net worth of $2.5 million.[21]

The campaign's hectic final weeks included publication of endorsements by newspapers, and as I expected, I failed to get the support of the *Dallas Morning News* or *Houston Chronicle,* whose editors were Connally partisans strongly backing Martin for attorney general and Barnes for governor.[22] Published polls gave little indication of the impending massive voter retaliation against the Austin insiders.

Voters flocked to the polls May 6, pushing the Democratic primary turnout to a record high of 2,192,903, which was 57 percent of the registered voters. That easily topped the most recent hotly contested primary, in 1968, when 43 percent of registered voters cast ballots. Preston Smith, who had won five consecutive statewide races in a twenty-two-year political career, received only 9 percent of the votes—replacing Daniel's loss in 1962 as the lowest percentage of any incumbent governor in Texas history. Barnes, whom Lyndon Johnson once proclaimed would one day be president of the United States, received only 18 percent. My vote total of 999,573 was 101,652 more than Martin's. As I feared, even though he did not campaign, the third candidate drew almost enough votes to cause a runoff. My total was only 2,548 votes more than the 50 percent I needed to win outright.

The defeat of Smith, Barnes, and Martin jettisoned a combined sixty-eight years' experience in capitol elective offices. Along with their institutional memories and political networks, their defeat also weakened the 1960s-era domination of state politics by a handful of large corporate interests—oil and gas, chemicals, and railroads. Also dismantled was a highly centralized governing system that concentrated power in the hands of a few top officeholders who shared those industries' agenda of using government to minimize competition, protect them from effective regulatory scrutiny, and dampen any efforts to impose obligations benefiting employees.

In their place arose a more independent and diverse source of political power and leaders. Briscoe, one of the state's largest landowners, and Hobby, heir to a multimillion-dollar media empire, both brought their own financial and political resources to their jobs. I entered the attorney general's job with a larger financial net worth, and fewer political obligations, than any of my recent predecessors. Except for Briscoe's three terms in the House in the 1950s, none of us had previously held elective office. While many of our predecessors' political views were imposed on them by the dominant lobbying forces of the day, we each brought our own self-developed perceptions. We were all, as a popular political catch-phrase of the era proclaimed, as independent as a hog on ice.

For most of my fifty-three predecessors, the attorney general's office marked the conclusion of, or a strategic stepping stone in, a political career that started in the legislature or a local district attorney's office. I was not only an exception to that rule but also the first attorney who specialized in personal injury cases to run for attorney general.

Plaintiff attorneys were a fairly new development in the Texas legal profession. Their increased presence resulted from two factors. First, the state's increasing urbanization had created a critical mass of injured persons—mostly laborers with on-the-job injuries or auto accident victims—sufficient to warrant an attorney specializing in this area of law. The second factor was the increasing prevalence of insurance purchased by employers and auto owners to fund court judgments against them if they were held liable in an accident.

When I began my practice fresh out of the University of Texas law school in 1947 making $275 a month, trial lawyers were the poor stepchildren of the legal profession. My father's chagrin at my career choice reflected the low opinion of plaintiff lawyers held by business owners. Lawyers representing businesses and professionals dominated the big law firms and the State Bar of Texas leadership. I could have opted for one of those firms, but I wanted to be a stand-up trial lawyer. I wanted to represent people who needed a good lawyer and were not able to find one easily. I was determined to bring to the practice of trial attorneys the same respect held by corporate lawyers.

Also, I was in a hurry. I did not want to wait for the older partners in a big law firm to retire before I could handle the biggest cases. I knew my skills were sharper than most new lawyers—I was blessed with such clear recall that one of my law professors accused me of reading from notes when I extemporaneously rattled off details of court cases he assigned us to read. The only way for me to create a quick reputation was to take the risk of jumping into the hurly-burly world of courthouse trials.

It was an arduous, hectic career path that required a new lawyer to try as many cases as he could handle—sometimes two in a week. Almost every day, I skipped up the broad staircase leading into the white limestone Harris County courthouse and strode down polished hallways to the courtroom where my case was being tried if it was a weekday or to docket call if it was Friday.

Judges were more lenient in those days about allowing lawyers to move around the courtroom to employ their dramatic and oratorical skills. I was on my feet, working the floor, multitasking. Probing for reactions from the jurors that would tell me if my strategies were successful in drawing them to my arguments. Testing the judge's willingness to let me stretch my right to introduce evidence I wasn't sure would pass muster. Juggling in my mind the facts of the case I was trying then and the facts of the case I would begin trying in a day or two. Trying to keep the jury focused on the theme I had introduced in the jury selection questioning and would reinforce in my closing argument. My evenings were spent at my law office, preparing for the next day in court and the next cases I would try.

My love for this physically arduous and mentally punishing lifestyle began in my youth. In my hometown of Kilgore I was a talker and a leader. I loved to argue with people, I loved to try to persuade people, and I loved to help people. I was small for my age but enjoyed good athletic skills that allowed me an out-front role in sports that I eagerly embraced. I'm not sure where these traits originated in our family; my parents were Depression-era survivors who had to drop out of high school to go to work. My father and one of his six brothers formed a company to provide services for oil production, which was the major business in East Texas. It was tough, gritty work, but they succeeded and eventually owned a small company that transported oil and oilfield products.

Our parents were very ambitious for their children to have the opportunities the Depression denied them. They kept me and my sister, who was a year older than I, focused on being successful at whatever we did—studies, sports, church activities. In a preview of my future career, I served as the city attorney in a high school program in which students were allowed to take over the city government offices for one day. I argued several cases in traffic court, prompting the local newspaper to remark, "We saw a budding lawyer yesterday, serving as city attorney for Kilgore." I thrived in our high school debate program and went to the state finals, as did my sister. After high school, I enrolled in our local junior college, where I and another student won a national debate championship.

By the time I filed for attorney general, my count of jury trials exceeded five hundred. I won the vast majority of them. I could usually count on the other side, generally a large corporation or well-established professional, being represented by some of the state's best law firms, most of which had top-notch connections. But I found that these firms generally saved their best trial attorneys for big-dollar cases, leaving me modest competition in the small-dollar cases I was handling when I started my practice. Nothing succeeds, as my father always reminded me, like success, and my reputation grew quickly.

As the lawyers I bested spread the word of this accomplished new plaintiff's attorney who was taking them to the woodshed, I found myself settling most cases because of the opposing counsel's reluctance to challenge my well-recognized courtroom skills. Other lawyers began referring more complicated cases to me—product liability cases, maritime cases, and aviation cases. I was elected president of the Texas Association of Plaintiff Attorneys in 1955. The State Bar of Texas recognized me four times for my participation in legal education programs directed at helping lawyers develop courtroom skills.

The case that pushed me to the top of my professional stature involved the first commercial airliner crash in Texas. On September 29, 1959, the evening sky over a large rural area halfway between Dallas and Houston was lit by a huge ball of fire fifteen thousand feet in the air. Debris rained for five minutes over a square mile of brushy pastureland near the small town of Buffalo. All thirty-four people aboard the Braniff Lockheed Electra turboprop four-engine plane died.[23] The plane was a new model only nine days in service. The families of several of the victims from Houston hired me to seek compensation for their loss. This case allowed me to stretch to new levels of sophistication my pioneer working exploration of blending law and science into the trial of lawsuits. My challenge was the then new field of demonstrative evidence, actually demonstrating how an accident occurred so the jurors could more easily understand the cause.

To accomplish that, I immersed myself in learning airplane engine and body design and assembly. I arranged for remains of the wreckage to be brought to a Houston courtroom next to the court where we tried the case, removing some of the elevator cars from the shafts to move the reassembled wing sections and engine into the courtroom. I pointed to specific parts of the wreckage to help jurors visualize how the vibrations caused by the engines could be suddenly compounded to such a violent level that they would shear the wings and cause the plane to disintegrate. Then I helped jurors assign fault among the airline and the companies that manufactured the airliner and the engines—Braniff, Lockheed, and General Motors. Those were three of the biggest names in American business.

The trial, in 1962, lasted two months. Because another Electra had crashed under similar circumstances in Indiana six months after the Buffalo crash, my trial became a precedent for lawsuits seeking $55 million on behalf of ninety-six crash victims.[24] The jury instructions I developed with the opposing attorneys included fifty issues for jurors to decide. I won a $250,000 verdict against Lockheed and General Motors.[25] At that time, it was one of the largest death awards in the nation. I settled the remaining cases for similar amounts, increasing the total awards into the millions of dollars.

Nine years later, another Braniff Electra crash again thrust me into the spotlight of a major lawsuit. On May 3, 1968, near Dawson, a Houston-to-Dallas flight broke apart at sixty-seven hundred feet and created a fireball that plunged to earth only about fifty miles northwest of the site of the Buffalo tragedy, killing all eighty-five aboard. This time, the factors explored in testimony included a thunderstorm with fifty-six-thousand-foot-high clouds, the pilot's decision not to follow air traffic controllers' instructions to divert the flight east of the storm, and questions about the structural integrity of the Electra's wings.[26] Again, I won large verdicts for families of the victims.

The demonstrated legal skills I brought to the attorney general's race were contrary to tradition, as was my limited political experience. Most attorneys general were politicians first and lawyers second. I was the reverse. I was a working lawyer, not just a talking lawyer. My legal career, if plotted on a graph, would have been a gently rising line spanning twenty-four years. The graphed line of my political career would have spanned only five or six years, and it would have pitched up and down.

I loved being a lawyer and was blessed by the Lord to have the skills required to be among the leaders in my profession. When it came to politics, He did not give me the patience and tolerance for political games possessed by those who made politics their first priority and were willing to spend decades paying their political dues. I was good at it, but others were better and more devoted to it. All of this suited Bitsy just fine, because she did not want to live her days as a politician's wife.

I considered my atypical background a necessary credential for me to achieve my first objective after my election. I was committed to developing the attorney general's office into the finest law office in the state, one that could hold its own against the best law firms in a courtroom face-off. Most of my recent predecessors often accepted the fact that their staffs were mediocre, for which they compensated by allowing their state agency clients to hire law firms to represent them in major cases. I let it be known those days were over.

On my watch the attorney general's office would match up toe to toe with the lawyers they were opposing in the courtroom. I sent out the word loud and clear among my colleagues in the legal profession that I was hungry for lawyers of the highest experience and quality. I was not looking for cosmetic changes. I wanted wholesale change, because most of the attorney general's staff had remained static since the 1950s. The need for newcomers' fresh ideas and enthusiasm was manifest.

I was swimming against the tide of tradition and the reality of low state salaries. My recruitment efforts needed the boost provided by the excitement of an election that redefined and brought a new vision to Texas government. I was asking promising young lawyers to give up or delay their drive to obtain a coveted partnership in a law firm.

In return, I offered them a chance to work for the first attorney general in anyone's memory who was a successful trial attorney in his own right, one from whom they could expect to learn by example. They could depend on high expectations and a mandate to take cases to court with an objective of winning instead of settling cases to avoid the labor involved in going to trial. They would have a role in carrying out the voters' historic mandate to reshape government to make it more responsive to the needs of the average citizen.

(2)

Reforming Consumer Protections

Frank Sharp not only pushed me over the finish line in the attorney general's race. He also turned my otherwise "pumpkin" consumer protection proposals into one of the Cinderella's coaches of the legislative session of 1973.

Despite my oft-proven ability to coax jurors to "vote" for my client, I knew I would be shouting into the wind if I was forced to sell my consumer protection ideas to the legislature as it existed in 1971. Juries are supposed to be, and generally are, open to hearing both sides of an argument before they make a decision. Their job is to answer yes-or-no questions in a search for the truth. With legislators, the opposite is more often the case. They run for office based upon strongly held positions and spend their political capital advocating and defending those positions. The legislative process is no search for the truth. It is a Darwinesque survival of the fittest.

"My mind's made up—don't try to confuse me with the facts" is their traditional humorous description of the reality of legislative committee hearings and floor debate. Those made-up minds, more often than not, are greatly influenced by the sources of political power legislators rely upon to get elected. Those sources might be hometown business leaders, the local coffee shop crowd, Austin lobbyists, a local political clique, or a combination of those sources. It is seldom the average Joe or Jane that is uppermost in legislators' minds. And those were the folks whom I was trying to help in my consumer protection proposal.

In 1971, a consumer protection bill that was not as far-reaching as the one I proposed was treated like a mouse in a cat den—tossed around for amusement and then disposed of. It enjoyed a modicum of support among the Senate's urban members but found zero backing in the House and garnered no interest from the attorney general or governor. Consumer advocates were offered polite hearings and then ignored.[1]

Two years and a governmental scandal later, my views on consumer legislation jumped to the top of business lobbyists' list of potential problems. Consumer advocates who were smugly dismissed two years ago now found legislators and their staffs expressing serious interest in exploring the reformers' ideas. The ripples from Frank Sharp's splash were still rocking the governmental boat.

The voters' housecleaning to remove top officeholders in Austin was accompanied by a record turnover of state legislators. In a typical election, about one-third of the 150 House members and maybe 4 or 5 of the 31 senators are replaced. In 1972, the Sharpstown scandal helped remove 76 House members and 15 senators. Another change agent was that in 1971 a reapportionment replaced countywide elections for House members in the three largest counties with election by neighborhood-sized districts.[2] These new districts opened opportunities for minority and other liberal candidates whose election in 1972 contributed to the moderation of the usually conservative House.[3]

The House turnover also ensured the election of a progressive House Speaker, Price Daniel Jr. of Liberty. Daniel often played his politics close to his vest, just as his father had. But he owed his election to the "Dirty Thirty" coalition of reformers who braved the dictatorial reign of Speaker Mutscher to clamor for an investigation of the Sharpstown scandal. My consumer legislation was a top priority for the reformers, and Daniel was ready to give the bill his blessing.

The business lobby clearly faced some busy times when this new crew took office in January 1973. Election of a governor, attorney general, presiding officers of both houses, and half of the legislators having minimal influence from lobbyists was unprecedented in modern times. Business lobbyists' problem solving traditionally involved one telephone call to the lieutenant governor or the Speaker to rein in a troublesome legislator. Now they were forced to go hat-in-hand to individual legislators—many of whom they had opposed during the election—to protect their interests.

Because these lobbyists no longer claimed the ear of the presiding officers and because the presiding officers' leadership styles called for delegating much more power to the members, their opinions were no longer automatically treated as gospel by the new legislators. Facts and information gained new respect in the marketplace of decision making. Good-ol'-boy connections suffered a decline in influence.

This new openness was a key ingredient in my effort to recruit ambitious, aggressive young lawyers for my staff. My reputation as a lawyer's lawyer was important to this young talent, but they were smart enough to know that a recalcitrant legislature could easily undermine my best efforts to produce a first-class law office.

The legislature could ignore my budget increase requests or even cut my budget. They could pass laws to restrict my office's powers. They could ignore my staff's offers to help draft or advise on major legislation. I knew they could do these things because I saw it firsthand when I was secretary of state and Governor Connally was constantly battling legislative undermining of his initiatives. The perceived absence of this threat helped elevate my prospects for meaningful reform, at least in the minds of young attorneys seeking a role in modernizing our state government. The prospects for success rose from "possibility" status to the vision of a political movement with potential for lasting importance.

I wanted to start my hiring process with some winners whose presence would have others convinced that I was recruiting a strong team. My first hire was an easy choice. I needed a running start to pass my consumer protection legislation and I needed a trusted and politically savvy working partner. Joe K. Longley met both needs.

Longley had traveled with me during the campaign and doubled as my resource on consumer issues. I met him when he was a University of Texas law student working in the governor's mailroom and I was in and out of the governor's suite of offices while I was secretary of state. I drafted him to help me organize support among law students during my campaign for governor in 1968. After that, he worked for the attorney general's consumer protection office and then for the Corpus Christi plaintiff's law firm of Edwards and Deanda. He was back in Austin in 1972, struggling as a solo practitioner.

Always a wisecracker, Longley later named that period his "Crippled Bird Law Firm days." His photocopy machine was next door at a Circle K convenience store, and he spent much of his time as an unpaid lobbyist for the Texas Consumers Association (TCA), an advocacy group launched in 1970 by the Texas AFL-CIO. The TCA was headed by Lloyd Doggett, who graduated from the University of Texas law school in 1970. Doggett embraced the Ralph Nader exposé strategy, which he applied in coordinating a research project conducted by law students who in 1971 wrote a highly critical *Texas Law Review* article lambasting Texas' weak protections for small loan borrowers.[4] Doggett was known for his quick mind and sharp tongue. He had won election as student body president, graduated first in his class with a bachelor of business administration degree in 1967, and graduated with honors from law school.

Doggett was an example of a new breed of law student in the 1960s who dramatically changed the fundamental nature of law schools. This trend was a mixture of the new assertiveness of young people radicalized by the Viet Nam War, the media hype for public interest law created by Nader, and the general cultural upheaval of the 1960s that overwhelmed all institutions. Law school professors accustomed to students preparing for a career in a large law firm or corporation suddenly were confronted with students burning with desire to become environmental attorneys, consumer advocates, or other types of public interest lawyers. They wanted to use the law for progressive social change.

Because jobs for these graduates were scarce, TCA played a vital networking role in providing them a venue to share employment prospects and nurture their passion for reform. Along with Longley, Doggett recruited Jim Boyle, who graduated from the University of Texas law school in 1969, to work on consumer issues during the legislative session in 1971.

The fledgling group found a receptive forum for its viewpoints in the Senate, where the rural-dominated conservative culture was turned upside down by federal court rulings in 1965 that ended the limit of one senator per county. The single staunch conservative senator from Dallas now was joined by one Republican, one liberal Democrat, and two moderate Democrats. Similar changes rocked other big-city Senate delegations. The four largest cities' Senate representation went from four to twelve and included the Senate's first black woman, Barbara Jordan from Houston.

These new senators brought sufficient votes to nudge the Senate toward addressing concerns of urban voters long sidetracked by rural senators. They also brought a more activist approach to staffing their offices by expanding their payrolls and adding some of the new public interest law graduates just beginning to emerge from the University of Texas. Public policy agendas that previously depended on lobbyist resources were replaced with senators' personal agendas amplified and developed by eager young lawyers determined to reverse rural legislators' hesitant use of state regulatory powers.

Consumer protection was one of the hot-button issues of these urban senators and their staffs. In rural areas, door-to-door sales representatives such as the iconic Fuller Brush salesman were a necessity in the days before Wal-Mart. Rural legislators were reluctant to jeopardize this commercial resource by creating a regulatory system to deal with abuses. In urban areas, those who employed door-to-door sales were more likely to be scam artists preying on the elderly and racial minorities. Urban legislators were being pressured by constituents to regulate this type of business in a manner unthinkable to rural legislators.

The new urban senators' focus on stronger consumer protection laws reflected a growing awareness of consumerism nationally. The publication of Nader's book *Unsafe at Any Speed* in 1965 rocked the automobile industry by exposing the dangers of General Motors' Corvair. He published a critique of the Federal Trade Commission in 1969, triggering major restructuring of the agency. His corps of young lawyers then prepared investigative reports on the federal Food and Drug Administration, on the Interstate Commerce Commission, and on nationwide pollution problems.

By 1969, this investigative force had become a news media sensation, and the *Washington Post* dubbed it "Nader's Raiders." President Nixon responded to the growing consumer movement by appointing a popular Pennsylvania political leader and consumer activist, Virginia Knauer, as his special assistant for consumer affairs in 1969; her role was elevated in 1971 by an executive order creating the Office of Consumer Affairs. Congress pressured states by passing a "truth in lending" law that took effect in 1969 in any state without its own similar law.[5]

Texas was slow to react to these trends. Laws regulating various industries, such as the Insurance Code, included consumer protections enforced by different state agencies through administrative actions. But those agencies were precluded from taking court action, which was reserved for district attorneys. General types of consumer abuses were subject only to district attorneys' prosecutions under fraud statutes.

The new urban legislators were able to pass a law in 1967 creating the office of consumer credit commissioner with power to refer to the attorney general cases justifying court action for violation of deceptive trade prohibitions. But this law used a "wait until the horse leaves the barn before closing the door" approach—violations could give rise only to an injunction to prohibit further violations.

The practical effects of this limited enforcement tool were to allow scam artists to continue operating while the attorney general's injunction petition worked its way through the courts. They could simply start a new scam after a court entered an injunction. And they faced no risk of having to return scammed funds to consumers. In one case my staff cited during legislative hearings on our bill, Texas victims in a nationwide chain referral scheme lost $12 million while the attorney general struggled to obtain a court injunction.[6]

The consumer credit commissioner law also created for the first time a comprehensive set of prohibited deceptive trade practices. But the prohibitions' effect was limited to transactions not already governed by some other state law. The law was revised in 1969 to give the attorney general concurrent jurisdiction with the commissioner in deceptive trade practices cases. And a new enforcement tool was borrowed from the Federal Trade Commission—an "assurance of voluntary compliance." It minimized the time lag involved in obtaining an injunction by allowing the attorney general to demand that the violator sign the voluntary compliance order or face an injunction lawsuit with penalties of up to ten thousand dollars per violation.[7]

But neither the 1967 nor the 1969 law allowed the attorney general, or any other state agency, to obtain restitution for a cheated consumer. A consumer's only recourse was to hire a lawyer and file a fraud lawsuit under common law. For the vast majority of consumer abuses, the amount of money at stake was too small to justify an attorney's involvement. Common law fraud cases were difficult to win, leaving few lawyers financially able to take these cases. The U.S. Congress had considered creating a private cause of action in consumer cases, but the legislation failed. After that, states began passing laws to give consumers easier access to the courthouse to sue vendors who used deceptive advertising or sold faulty products.[8]

The urban senators pressing for new consumer protections were able, in the 1969 session, to create a study committee to research options for stronger consumer laws and report their findings in the 1971 session. One of those senators, Ralph Hall of Rockwall (he also represented part of Dallas County), chaired the committee, which held hearings in urban areas to gather evidence of consumer abuses and to solicit ideas for laws to address these problems. The committee was staffed with an extremely able counsel, Liz Levatino, another recent University of Texas law graduate. Levatino, whose married name is Liz Lacy, was later elected to the Virginia Supreme Court.

Doggett worked with Levatino to patch together a bill based on Federal Trade Commission powers and on a model act drafted by a commission on uniform state laws. The bill focused mostly on credit abuses and door-to-door sales issues. It provided two important enhancements of deceptive trade practices enforcement. It ended the concurrent attorney general–consumer credit commissioner enforcement, allowing the attorney general to take action independently—but only on the very limited number of issues where no other state agency enforcement powers were applicable. It addressed the restitution issue by empowering consumers to collect three times their actual loss from the violator. But the scope of the treble-damage provision was severely restricted with a two-thousand-dollar maximum recovery for the consumer.[9]

The bill was introduced in the legislative session of 1971. Despite the efforts of Longley and his TCA cohorts to focus sufficient attention on consumer issues to move the bill, opposition from credit bureaus and door-to-door sales firms delayed Senate passage of the bill until mid-May. This left too little time to mount an effort to obtain passage in the House, which was in a shambles because of the Sharpstown scandal's impact on the House Speaker and his leadership team. The end of the session was a mere two weeks away.[10]

The message from that legislative session's tepid response to the consumer protection initiative that the Hall interim study committee had attempted to create was not positive for any significant expansion of state enforcement powers. Ralph Nader and Virginia Knauer may have enjoyed receptive audiences in Washington, but consumerism counted few high-profile supporters in Texas. Despite the fact that many of the state's business leaders owed their wealth to the lucky happenstance of oil residing under their family's farm or ranch land, most Texans still embraced the frontier ethos that grit and determination account for business success.

The Texas business community was dominated by Texas-owned and Texas-operated businesses. Owners and managers of banks, brewers, manufacturers, insurance companies, retailers, real estate developers, auto dealers, and oil and gas companies were invested in their community, the Texas economy, and the Texas political leadership. A decade later, we saw industry consolidations wipe out this local business leadership, leaving a void filled with professional managers whose loyalties were to a home office in another state or another country. But that dismantling of our traditional business-political culture was yet to come in 1973.

The leaders of these business groups, and the legislators who depended on them for campaign support, agreed on a key public policy principle: the people who ran these businesses did not need government to tell them how to operate. And they sure didn't need the government, much less a group of trial lawyers, harassing them with lawsuits that would merely drive up the prices paid by consumers just so some lawyer could make a fee. Government's role, they believed, was to protect Texas businesses from out-of-state competitors seeking to enter the growing Texas market.

Because I made my living bringing lawsuits against these business leaders, I was only too aware of the strength of their grip on the political process. I knew that my effort to push for stronger consumer protection laws in my campaign for attorney general was not a strategy with a high probability of helping me get the votes I needed to win. The people most likely to support me on this issue, average consumers, were least likely to hear my pitch because I could not afford the extensive television advertising required to make certain the message had sunk in. The people most likely to be alarmed by this message, and to respond by increasing their support for my opponent—the Texas business community—were certain to receive the message because their lobbyists would send them copies of every newspaper item I could generate on the subject.

Nonetheless, my courtroom experience and sense of fairness led me to strongly believe this was an idea whose time had come. I had been willing to take the electoral risk by gambling that the Sharpstown issue would drag down my opponent so much that I could afford to use the consumer protection issue to excite my core supporters. Now that I had won my race, my support for stronger consumer protection laws gave the issue a huge boost in visibility and credibility. I was determined to capitalize on that new advantage. But I knew it would be a mistake to consider my narrow election a mandate that would guarantee success. I would need to mollify the opposition.

Soon after I defeated the incumbent, the business community lobbyists who had opposed my election started their post-election "late train calls" and visits to offer belated campaign contributions. The term "late train calls" referred to the lobbyists' need to be "on the train" with the winning candidates when they took office. Because my opponent had branded me a wild-eyed liberal, I used these meetings to reassure them that Longley and I were not reckless Naderites out to destroy Texas business. I pointed to passage of similar laws in other states and told them Texas could not ignore the nationwide consumer movement. I pledged to be firm but fair and urged them to help us pass a balanced bill.

Longley started drafting a bill, calling again on Doggett, a future Texas senator, state Supreme Court justice, and U.S. congressman, and Boyle to cobble together the best of provisions from other states and from federal law. Their favorite meeting place was Jaime's Spanish Village, a university students' and business leaders' lunch spot near downtown Austin. They chose that site for a marathon get-it-done drafting session in November. Because computers were not yet available, they were putting together the working copy of their bill by crossing out revised sections, scribbling new wording on legal pads, and numbering their insertions or changes for later compilation on an electric typewriter. They wiped off the chile con queso and salsa picante stains as they worked through the bill and their margaritas.

These three young activists were fueled by more than their margaritas. They knew the Sharpstown scandal had changed all the rules. They knew that the condescending brush-offs they had received from conservative senators during the 1971 session would be replaced in the 1973 session with serious consideration of them and their ideas. They knew this was a once-in-a-lifetime opportunity to strike while the business lobby was in retreat, because the pendulum would begin to reverse with the next election. They believed this bill needed to be packed with every conceivable feature to ensure the survival of the core provisions when dismantling efforts would begin in this and future legislative sessions. They were not interested in fairness—that would be achieved in the legislative give-and-take. They were going for overkill.

They quickly agreed that the pivotal issue would be whether the multi-billion-dollar insurance industry was included in the bill. Their experience included encounters with insurance industry intransigence, and they knew the new law would lose much of its potency if the attorney general was not empowered to haul insurers into court to achieve needed reforms.

Just as the Texas oil and gas industry converted state regulation into a protective cartel that the Middle Eastern nations copied when they established OPEC, Texas insurance companies used state government during the 1930s, 1940s, and 1950s to minimize competition from insurers operating nationwide. The Texas insurance regulatory agency actually set the price of homeowners and auto insurance, a rarity among state regulatory schemes, to inhibit competitive forces that could drive rates down. Their argument for this approach was that it protected consumers from price-cutting that endangered solvency. Consumer advocates believed otherwise.

Texas-based insurers historically were very active politically to ensure that governors appointed regulators sympathetic to their interests. Their lobbyists were partners in major law firms in Austin and Dallas, and they projected competence and confidence. One of the industry's own, life insurance company owner Lloyd Bentsen of Houston, was elected to the U.S. Senate from Texas in 1970.

Among their key lobbyists was Will D. Davis, who headed the insurance division of the attorney general's office in the 1950s and then was general counsel to the State Board of Insurance. Davis was a respected political leader. He was elected president of the student body when he was at Baylor University, he edited the *Baylor Law Review,* and he was chosen by Connally to chair the Texas Democratic Party from 1965 to 1968. He was not a backslapping booze-and-beefsteak lobbyist. He was a Baptist church leader who did his homework and played it straight. He and his colleagues working as lawyers for the insurance industry would put up a stiff fight to keep John Hill out of the courtroom—where I had victimized so many of the insurance industry's lawyers through the years—especially when armed with a new consumer protection law.

To include the insurance industry among the businesses to be subject to the legislation, Longley, Doggett, and Boyle provided a blanket repeal of any exemptions from the attorney general's enforcement powers established in laws governing various industries and professional and trade groups. Then they armed the attorney general with enforcement powers that included hefty financial penalties for violations of the deceptive trade practices listed. On top of that they added the threat of the attorney general representing class action lawsuit plaintiffs in lawsuits against violators of any of the listed practices. Then they layered a series of powers that the attorney general could use to expand the list of prohibited practices instead of limiting those practices to those on a legislatively created list. They could only guess at the heartburn they would create around the ornate conference tables in corporate law firms with their queso-stained regulatory declaration of independence from the insurance industry's shackles, drafted by three recent law school graduates in a Tex-Mex restaurant.

The second priority for Longley, Doggett, and Boyle was to provide to all Texas plaintiff attorneys the financial carrot needed to induce them to stop turning away consumers with small-dollar claims. They had taken a stab at that issue in the 1971 bill by allowing consumers to recover three times their financial loss, along with punitive damages, court costs, and attorneys' fees, in purchases tainted by deceptive trade practices. But political realities had required the two-thousand-dollar cap on a plaintiff's treble damages recovery in that initial bill.

Boyle advocated changing to penalties instead of treble damages. Doggett strongly insisted on removing the cap on treble damages and making them automatic; if a court found the consumer had suffered a three-hundred-dollar loss, the consumer would automatically obtain a nine-hundred-dollar award. Doggett prevailed. Now, insurance companies not only could be sued by the attorney general but they were also potentially facing a barrage of lawsuits from disgruntled consumers.[11]

When I reviewed their initial draft of the new bill, I felt like I was handling nitroglycerin. I knew this combination of public remedies enforced by the attorney general and private remedies available to consumers would be the strongest state consumer protection act in the nation if we could pass it. I also knew the business community would be scared witless by the image of hundreds of plaintiff attorneys swarming the courthouses with lawsuits by unhappy consumers of everything from automobiles to washing machines to homes.

The idea that one of the state's leading plaintiff attorneys would bring his feared courtroom presence to bear on behalf of consumers as the attorney general was very unsettling to the business community. I knew they would prove tough adversaries in the legislature if we didn't sell them on our concept. I asked Longley to set up meetings for me with Austin trade associations and to share the draft of our bill with business groups and seek their comments. He had worked with most of them on the earlier version of the bill in 1971, so he knew who would be most likely to help.

His first stop was the Texas Retail Federation, headed by Mickey Moore and represented by Jack Welch. Moore's members included a number of multistate companies such as Sears and Montgomery Ward, which meant that his association was familiar with laws being considered in other states. They knew that some other states' laws armed the attorney general with more weapons than what we proposed. Welch was a former legislator from a small town, and he advised the Texas Retail Federation that constructive criticism and cooperation were always more productive legislative strategies than stonewalling and sabotage. They decided to be a part of the solution instead of part of the problem, in hopes their participation would lessen the chance the bill could veer off track in the legislature. Moore and Welch worked with Longley to make revisions needed to achieve the association's support of the bill.[12]

That was the break we needed to meet legislative leaders' bedrock criterion for such a potentially controversial piece of legislation—that it be a "consensus" bill supported by both sides of the issue. Instead of being on the defensive from business groups' attacks, we could be more aggressive in resisting the inevitable weakening amendments. We could be sure we would get most of the loaf, not the half loaf that usually survives the give-and-take of legislative compromise.

The last piece of the consumer protection puzzle was lobbying and drafting help for Longley. He urged me to hire Liz Levatino, the Senate committee counsel who had spent the previous two years familiarizing herself with consumer protection laws around the country to help Senator Hall prepare his bill. I called her at the Legislative Council, where she was one of the primary bill drafters, and asked her to join our staff.

She brought not only superb drafting and research skills but also the respect of the new House Speaker, Price Daniel Jr., and key legislative leaders. Her first task was to convert the queso-stained bill Longley and his colleagues had drafted into precise legislative language. She was ready to introduce it by the end of January. Longley and Doggett set up a news conference on February 7, 1973, three weeks into the legislative session, to announce the bill's introduction. Welch agreed to join them and the bill's sponsors. Never at a loss for confidence, Doggett used the occasion to warn against any efforts to chip away at the bill's repeal of industry group exemptions—a veiled but pointed challenge to the insurance industry.[13]

Two of the new urban senators, Oscar Mauzy of Dallas and Bob Gammage of Houston, sponsored the bill, Senate Bill 75. Lt. Gov. Bill Hobby sent it to the consumer affairs subcommittee, a friendly venue. I was the lead-off witness at the committee hearing on the bill the next day. I knew the most difficult concept for legislators to embrace would be the private cause of action provision—allowing consumers to seek trebling of actual damages, along with attorneys' fees, court costs, and punitive damages from a seller of a defective or misrepresented product.

To address those concerns, I focused my testimony on our justification for those new and aggressive powers. I explained the simple economic barrier that stood between a consumer and a legal challenge to an unfair merchant. I told the committee that those of us who have practiced law know by our failures how futile it is under present law to represent a private citizen who has been defrauded: "The worst problem a consumer has for obtaining any real relief from the damage that was done is that he goes to a lawyer—and I have seen this so much, and one of the reasons that I am strongly backing this bill comes from my own experience as a public lawyer in this state for 23 years of seeing people come to your office who have suffered harm—and sometimes the cost is more for an hour's consultation with a lawyer than maybe the entire amount of the recovery that he would expect to get from going to court."[14]

Addressing the business community's concerns, I thanked the Texas Retail Federation for their support and told the committee several times that the bill was not antibusiness. Instead, I repeated, it was antifraud and antideception. No reputable, respectable honest business operator had anything to fear by passage of this law.

To give credence to this argument, we added to the bill a protection against frivolous lawsuits. The bill provided that, on a finding by the court that a consumer's lawsuit was groundless and brought in bad faith for the purpose of harassment, the court could award reasonable attorney's fees to the business operator. This was the first time frivolous lawsuits had been included in a Texas statute. Another safeguard we added to protect innocent businesses was to require a thirty-day notice before a consumer filed a lawsuit, with a provision that the seller could avoid penalties if reimbursement was offered.

After introductory remarks, I deferred to Longley, Doggett, and Levatino to answer subcommittee members' questions. As if to confirm Doggett's warning, one of the first questions, from a Fort Worth Republican, was about the inclusion of the insurance industry in the bill. Industry lobbyists, knowing this hearing was perfunctory, held their fire until the hearing before the full Human Resources Committee. The bill was quickly approved for the full committee's consideration.[15]

The next week gave us an even darker premonition of what was to come. I again led off the testimony and then turned it over to Longley and Levatino to explain the details to the Human Resources Committee. Our testimony was followed by a long, detailed, and carefully crafted critique from Will Davis.

Committee members' questions indicated that the insurance industry had successfully cultivated concerns about submitting the industry to two concurrent regulatory schemes—the decades-old, court-decision massaged scheme utilized by the State Insurance Department with heavy input from the insurance industry and the brand-new and untested deceptive trade practices scheme of a new attorney general.

One of the new urban senators we had hoped would support us, A. R. Schwartz, represented Galveston, the home of two large insurance companies. He announced his sympathy with Davis's position. The committee hearing became a jumble of confusion as senators and witnesses grappled with the huge changes being proposed and the warnings of overreaching made by insurance and auto dealer lobbyists. It dragged on for five hours.

An amendment was offered to bar the attorney general from defining and enforcing deceptive trade practices for industries already subject to such regulation by another state agency—an escape clause for the insurance industry. Mauzy and Gammage decided not to oppose it because they knew the insurance industry controlled enough votes to guarantee its adoption. Gammage warned that he would oppose the second step in the insurance industry's strategy, which was to bar the attorney general from representing private citizens in class action lawsuits for damages suffered because of deceptive trade practices.

Davis pointed to a conflict of interest if the attorney general represented private citizens in a lawsuit against an insurance company that claimed to be in compliance with a State Board of Insurance regulation. He also predicted a court challenge would void the bill's authority for the attorney general to add to the list of deceptive trade practices; that challenge would arise because of an unconstitutional delegation of legislative authority to the executive branch of government.[16]

The Human Resources Committee approved S.B. 75 on a 10-to-1 vote, making it eligible for floor debate. But the Senate required a two-thirds vote to bring a bill to the floor for debate, and the committee approval belied opponents' continued resolve to block the bill. February turned into March, April approached, and the bill remained stuck on the Senate calendar.

On March 28, I received a call from Lieutenant Governor Hobby inviting me to his office for a meeting to discuss the bill. As I walked past the huge framed composite photographs of senators from the 1880s and 1890s that lined the ornate corridor behind the Senate leading to Hobby's office, I steeled myself for what I feared would be a move to kill the bill. In the meeting were Hobby, Mauzy, and Sen. Charles Herring of Austin.

Hobby presided. He told me he wanted the Senate to pass a strong consumer protection bill. But he said he could count no more than fourteen votes for it, far short of the twenty-one needed to bring it up for debate. To secure passage, he said, the bill would need to be stripped of the item giving the attorney general the power to add to the list of deceptive trade practices. Businesses would need greater protections from frivolous lawsuits. Insurance regulation and enforcement would have to stay with the State Insurance Department. Punitive damages for consumers would have to be deleted. And the attorney general's authority to represent plaintiffs in class action lawsuits would need to be removed.

These revisions were too complicated to accomplish with floor amendments, Hobby said, so he was proposing that the bill be re-referred to committee. And, he wanted it sent to Herring's Jurisprudence Committee, not the Human Resources Committee that originally approved it. Mauzy agreed with Hobby that he didn't have the votes to pass the bill, but he said he could not vote for the re-referral motion.

I was agitated, unhappy, and frustrated. I complained that Herring was just carrying water for the insurance industry. Herring made it clear he was not interested in my opinion, at least not at this meeting. That made me even more agitated. I gave both him and Hobby a good tongue-lashing and warned that I would call a press conference to make certain their acquiescence to the insurance industry was clear to everyone. I also promised to include Hobby in the accusation if he refused to stand up to Herring. The lieutenant governor hurriedly adjourned the meeting.[17]

I returned to my office and told Longley and Levatino of our setback. We began sorting through our options. Reviewing the points of contention raised by Hobby, we concluded we could live with most of them.

Even though we would lose our power to represent consumers in class action lawsuits, a new statutory right of class action suits—a first in Texas—would be a major victory. I confessed to Longley and Levatino that I was relieved Hobby wanted to remove our power to add to the list of deceptive trade practices. I knew that was an important concept to Longley and Doggett, but to me it represented a needless distraction from our focus of attacking marketplace abuses. Our limited staff resources should be devoted to responding to the flood of complaints we were already receiving, not to responding to an endless quest for perfection from activists consumed with an agenda of ever-expanding prohibited practices. I also was not worried about Hobby's efforts to increase business owners' protections against abusive consumers. When we weighed the consequences of the Senate's planned reworking of our bill, we believed we were still hitting a home run.[18]

The Senate voted 21 to 9 the next day to recommit the bill to Herring's committee. Hobby arranged for the bill to be sent to a subcommittee that included Herring and Mauzy, and he gave the subcommittee ten days to revise the bill to remove the objectionable provisions.[19]

Longley and Levatino met with Davis and other insurance lobbyists to craft a compromise addressing their concerns over dual regulation by both the attorney general and the State Insurance Department. They offered to place in the Insurance Code wording similar to all of the provisions we were placing in the Business and Commerce Code, including the definitions of deceptive trade practices, the private cause of action with mandatory treble damages, and the class action provision.

Because of our concern that the Insurance Code's definition of who could bring a lawsuit for violation of the code might not extend to all consumers, the insurance lobbyists also agreed to place in the Business and Commerce Code a private cause of action for any violations of the Insurance Code's deceptive practices prohibitions. In return, we agreed to limit the attorney general's enforcement of insurance laws to cases referred to us by the State Insurance Department.

The insurance industry representatives got what they wanted—freedom from the threat of a crusading attorney general harassing them with endless judicial probing and maintaining their regulation by specialists with whom they had close contacts and good working relationships. But because they were so focused on the threat to that status quo, they paid a price that in later years proved to be extremely costly. They agreed to dramatically lower the bar for lawsuits against insurance companies and agents and to further encourage those lawsuits with automatic trebling of damages for individuals or actual damages through a class action lawsuit. Instead of meeting the usually impossible burdens involved in complex and costly lawsuits alleging fraud or some other common law abuse, consumers now had swift and sure recourse in even the smallest of cases involving disputes over insurance policy coverage explanations and claims handling.[20]

True to his word, Hobby held the subcommittee to his timetable, and Herring's committee approved the revised version of the bill on April 10.[21] It included all of the changes that Hobby had mentioned and we accepted. Mauzy brought it up for debate three days later, and it was passed to the House on April 17.[22] The House approved its bill at about the same time. The Senate's changes were incorporated into the House bill, which was passed May 7 and sent to the governor for his signature.[23]

On May 21, I joined Hobby, Daniel, Mauzy, Gammage, and two House sponsors, Carl Parker of Port Arthur and Arthur Temple of Diboll, at a signing ceremony in Governor Briscoe's office. The bill took effect immediately because its approval votes exceeded two-thirds majorities in both houses.

The queso-stained plea for help for Texas' consumers, drafted by three recent law school graduates in a Tex-Mex restaurant, survived a punishing gauntlet of business lobbyist challenges. It empowered consumers with new courthouse access and gave the attorney general broad new enforcement powers. It was probably the most far-reaching law ever enacted by the Texas Legislature that did not originate in a major law firm representing business interests.

In the coming years, our staff used it to prosecute negligent nursing home owners, con artists selling phony oil and gas investments, and national retailers such as Montgomery Ward that were advertising everyday prices as "sale prices," among dozens of other scams.[24] We obtained a $950,000 judgment against the operator of a group of trade schools, forcing him to return unearned tuition fees to students.[25]

More significant was the growing flood of lawsuits by individual consumers taking advantage of their new access to the courthouse in order to recover funds lost to unscrupulous vendors. The law worked exactly as we intended. The availability of treble damages for defrauded consumers attracted the attention of attorneys who previously turned away these cases because fraud was too difficult to prove in court. As we expected, the targets of these consumer lawsuits mounted vigorous legislative initiatives to emasculate the law. Except for caps being placed on treble damages and the elimination of automatic trebling in 1979, it survived pretty much unscathed until the nationwide tort reform movement in the 1990s produced significant limitations.

At the time it was passed, the Deceptive Trade Practices Act was the most aggressive consumer protection law of any state. It immediately became a model used by other states seeking to enhance their consumer laws. It was a tribute to the new political paradigm created by the foibles of Frank Sharp. Where the Hall bill's docile consumer protections were held hostage in the Senate until late in the session of 1971 and then killed in the House, the 1973 version of the bill sailed through both the House and Senate with overwhelming majorities. Without my election and the leadership brought to this issue by me and my staff, and without the election of a half-new legislature anxious to enhance their reform credentials, these historic consumer protections could not have been achieved.

(3)

Cleaning Up the Houston Ship Channel

While my consumer protection proposals leaped from the starting blocks and quickly achieved a stunning victory, my environmental protection proposals enjoyed no such easy and overwhelming success. Like consumer protection laws, pollution controls were out of favor with the business leaders whose lock on political campaign funding sources ensured their control of the state's public policy agenda. These issues likewise were not high on the priority list of a rural-dominated legislature.

Our consumer law reform initiative enjoyed several circumstances that helped us overcome these adversities. We benefited from embryonic statutes, a passive bureaucracy, a lack of unanimity among the businesses affected, and from the "bad guy" image of the target of our reforms.

When we devised the Deceptive Trade Practices Act, we were overhauling a statutory Model T to make it a modern race car. Our proposals for consolidating enforcement of consumer laws under the attorney general met no resistance from state enforcement staff or local prosecutors, all of whom were happy to rid themselves of a job they were ill equipped to perform. Our ability to recruit the retailers as allies for our consumer reforms marginalized our natural opponents in the business community and helped remove potentially large obstacles. We focused our rhetoric on ridding the state of sleazy rip-off artists who were conning old folks and minorities.

We enjoyed no such benefits when we attempted to muscle our way into the pollution control game. The companies poisoning our air and water were not fly-by-night operators. They were the mainstay of their local areas' economies and a major factor in Texas' economic health. Almost all of the polluters were national or international corporations facing the risk of government antipollution restrictions in other states as well. Their rigid public policy strategy was based on their fear that any escalated enforcement in Texas would ripple out to other states and cause a quantum jump in their pollution abatement expenses. They were quick to warn of plant closings and layoffs whenever tougher pollution controls were advocated. Their warnings were embraced and amplified by the business community. "Pollution is ugly, but unemployment and deprivation are uglier" was the way the West Texas Chamber of Commerce summarized its opposition to air pollution standards proposed by the state in 1971.[1]

These industries maintained a close working relationship with the state agencies regulating their waste discharges. They reinforced that relationship with potent political support for key legislators and the governor, who appointed the agencies' governing boards. Two of the three most influential lobby groups in Austin were the oil and petrochemical industries.[2]

Enforcement responsibilities were primarily focused in two recently created agencies: the Texas Water Quality Board (TWQB) and the Texas Air Control Board (TACB). They both were directed by active governing boards, managed by strong staff leadership, and armed with ample statutory powers to pursue and stop polluters. Secondary pollution enforcement came from four other agencies with clear mandates in the statutes and well-established involvement in water quality issues: the Department of Health, the Water Development Board, the Railroad Commission, and the Parks and Wildlife Commission. These state pollution law enforcers were not paper-shuffling bureaucrats. The issues they confronted were not easily defined problems solved with off-the-shelf equipment. Measuring, quantifying, evaluating, and controlling hazardous wastes was an evolving science constantly being altered by new research and technology.

The judgment calls made by these highly technical specialists involved huge economic stakes. Millions of dollars in payrolls could be at risk if plants were ordered to curtail production to meet waste discharge or emission standards. Destruction of one of the nation's largest shellfish producing areas could result from inadequate controls on polluters. Designing and building plant-specific pollution abatement equipment often was a multimillion-dollar undertaking for a single plant. These enforcement staffs depended on the superior resources of the engineers, scientists, and lawyers employed by the corporations being regulated to help them coordinate the law's expectations and industry's capabilities.

This closed system of communication often generated among these staffs a very understandable perception that theirs was the final word in deciding an enforcement strategy. Their past attempts at venturing into the foreign arena of courtroom action, through development of lawsuits with the attorney general's office, were uniformly unsuccessful. When the Senate Finance Committee questioned the assistant attorney general responsible for pollution law enforcement in 1971, he expressed frustration over his inability to combine forces with state regulators to bring lawsuits against polluters. The files regulators provided his attorneys contained woefully inadequate evidence, he said, and all of the meetings and discussions had not succeeded in resolving the shortcomings. Tough enforcement was promised but never delivered.[3]

The opposite point of view was held by the regulatory agencies, which faulted the attorney general for incorrectly interpreting his power to enforce pollution control laws. The rift surfaced at a meeting of the TACB in 1970, when a board member from Houston berated the attorney general's assertion that his lack of court action against polluters stemmed from state law requirements that toxicity of industrial discharges must be proved to win cases against polluters. "Under his standards, you couldn't prove San Francisco was destroyed by fire," the board member complained. "We've got to collect all this dust, smoke and glue in the air and feed it to guinea pigs and prove it kills them before he'll act. If we must prove toxicity, we'd better get a new law."[4]

The image of aggressive enforcement portrayed in that exchange was undercut a year later when the Air Control Board's top enforcement officer resigned in protest over what he said was pressure from the powerful House Appropriations Committee chairman to be more accommodating to polluters.[5]

On top of these crosscurrents of conflict lay public ambivalence about pollution. While consumer protection laws were perceived by most Texans as being helpful to them personally, pollution laws enjoyed no such strong positive personal connection. Most Texans lived in areas with few pollution problems. In my adopted hometown of Houston, where smog rivaling that of Los Angeles was becoming more common, public concern over pollution was slow to develop.

This was due largely to the fact that Texas in the early 1970s was a boom state and Houston was the number one boom city. In a boom mentality, the future is unlimited and the discomforts created by fast growth are viewed with pride as a symbol of galloping prosperity. The traffic jams, foul air, and dirty water were tolerated as a confirmation of unprecedented growth and the wealth it produced. Gulf coast residents supported smog control, so long as it did not affect their personal auto use. They favored clamping down on industrial polluters, so long as no jobs were lost and continued economic growth was not threatened. They wanted their cities to quit dumping raw sewage into waterways, so long as it did not slow the housing boom that was a by-product of industrial expansion.

Despite these handicaps, I was determined to carry out my campaign pledge to rigorously enforce antipollution laws, starting with my home city. Before I was elected attorney general, a glance out my sixth-floor law office window in the Houston First Savings building displayed the ugly price we in Houston were paying for our growth-at-any-cost mentality. Sometimes the sky would disappear for several days, and nearby buildings would be shrouded in haze when the lack of wind allowed air pollutants to hover over our city.

Yet that same view took in the impressive skyline that was testimony to our city's success in attracting jobs. Houston was the fastest growing big city in the nation. Its population of 1.2 million in 1970 had increased 30 percent in ten years. It was the nation's sixth largest city and the largest in the southern states. More than 360 corporate headquarters were located in Houston. Could this success story continue its magical ascent despite our ever-increasing pollution? I believed we were courting disaster, both to the health of our citizens and to the health of our economy, if we failed to see that corporate leaders would eventually rebel against a location where their employees were subjected to dirty air, polluted waterways, and intolerable traffic congestion.

Twelve blocks from my former Houston law office ran the stream that was the primary cause of both Houston's growth and its pollution. Buffalo Bayou begins thirty miles west of Houston and wanders eastward, roughly paralleling Interstate 10, through some of the most exclusive neighborhoods in the city. It runs alongside the River Oaks Country Club, Houston Country Club, and Memorial Park before it snakes through the central business district en route to its abrupt transition from idle stream to bustling port four miles from downtown. That's where the turning basin for the Houston Ship Channel is located.

The bayou flows eastward another several miles to its confluence with the San Jacinto River, near the site of the battlefield where Texas forces defeated General Santa Anna to achieve independence from Mexico. The combined waters then flow southeast for about five miles to Galveston Bay. From the twenty-three miles between that point and the turning basin, the channel more than fulfilled the dreams of Houston's founders in the 1830s.

The first steamboat docked on Buffalo Bayou at Houston within a year after the city was established in 1836. That began a cotton shipping trade that depended on Galveston's wharves for access to foreign markets. To bypass Galveston's port and its high wharf fees, Houston merchants banded together in the 1870s to finance dredging of a twenty-five-mile channel across the western side of the very shallow Galveston Bay. But their vision was greater than their pocketbooks, and it took the resources of the federal government to perform such a massive engineering feat. The U.S. Army Corps of Engineers completed the dredging of a twenty-five-foot deep channel in 1914. An oceangoing vessel loaded the first cotton shipment bound for a foreign port in 1919, launching Houston's future as a major international seaport.

The discovery of massive oil reserves in a broad swath of Texas to the north and east of Houston in the early 1900s turned the ship channel's mission in an unforeseen direction. By 1927, 83 percent of the oceangoing tonnage from the port of Houston was in the form of oil and related chemicals. Nine oil refineries fueled this production by 1930. In the 1940s, wartime demand for rubber substitutes led to construction of two plants on the channel that manufactured synthetic rubber from petroleum by-products, foreshadowing the channel's development as a center for the nation's petrochemical industry.

By the early 1970s, the port of Houston was handling 60 million tons of freight each year, making it the nation's third largest port. The upper part of the channel was home to one hundred large industrial facilities, making it one of the world's largest chemical and petrochemical complexes. Channel traffic averaged one ship every two hours, every day. Ship channel employers and related businesses' payrolls topped $3 billion annually. The names and logos on the sides of gigantic storage tanks and huge smokestacks were from Fortune 500 companies: Diamond Shamrock, Ethyl Corporation, Humble Oil and Refining Company, Armco Steel Corporation, Olin Chemical Corporation, U.S. Plywood–Champion Papers, and Southland Paper Mills.[6]

The rapid growth of the ship channel complex and of nearby cities quickly overwhelmed the abilities of state and local governments grappling with the infrastructure problems related to this economic windfall. Pollution, the by-product of economic boom, landed Houston on the Federal Water Pollution Control Administration's list of the ten most polluted cities in the nation in 1969.[7]

This news came as no surprise to those of us living in Houston. Buffalo Bayou was not a pristine, idyllic waterway lined with shops and restaurants like the River Walk area of San Antonio nor was it a recreation magnet like the Colorado River in Austin. Its function had been a dirty commercial one since the day Houston was founded.

Few viewed it otherwise, and none ventured to view it up close. As early as 1893, Houston newspapers complained about fish dying in the bayou from creosote poisoning. The Houston Cotton Exchange complained in the same year that the bayou was "an immense cesspool, reeking with filth and emitting a stench of vilest character." In 1895, the Houston District Medical Association warned that the city's water supply from a reservoir built on Buffalo Bayou in downtown Houston was "a menace to the lives of the people in this community."[8]

Official reaction to these early complaints and to others for the next eighty years was slow and inadequate. The first major effort at improvement, in a precursor to Washington's pressure for state clean-up efforts in the 1970s, resulted from a federal government carrot-and-stick strategy. In the late 1890s, the city successfully pushed a $300,000 bond issue for sewer system improvements after the Army Corps of Engineers made them a condition for construction of the ship channel.

The city got the ship channel, but the feds didn't get much better wastewater. The improvements proved so ineffective that the mayor estimated in 1916 that only 20 to 30 percent of the city's sewage was being treated before it went into the bayou. By then, the city had replaced the bayou as a drinking water source with artesian wells, thereby removing the main impetus for cleaning up the bayou.

In the 1940s, an investigation showed that 80 percent of the bayou's flow was sewage. In the 1950s and 1960s, anywhere from half to all but two of the city sewage treatment plants operated at less than 90 percent efficiency. Offered a chance to remedy these problems, Houston voters in 1968 rejected two bond issues to fund sewage treatment improvements.

By 1970, thirty-five of Houston's forty-two sewage treatment plants were discharging into public waters dirtier effluent than their permits allowed. In 1970, a federal review of municipal plants' discharges into Galveston Bay and bayous flowing into the bay reported that half of the 215 million gallons per day of wastewater was "raw, inadequately treated, or unchlorinated." Houston's four largest sewage treatment plants had no chlorination capability. Galveston was dumping 1.5 million gallons of raw sewage daily into the bay. When state officials announced in 1970 they wanted to investigate Houston's ineffective sewage treatment program, the city's public works director pooh-poohed the action and said there was nothing the state could do except "raise a big stink."[9] He may not have been technically correct, but the state did not try to prove him wrong.

With local and state public officials unconcerned or unable to rally public opinion against the continued degradation of water and air quality in the Houston area, it fell to Washington to focus attention on these issues. In January 1970, the Interior Department held, in Houston, a two-day meeting of President Nixon's Water Pollution Control Advisory Board.

The meeting opened with a dramatic announcement by Asst. Sec. Carl Klein that the agency was barring the city of Galveston from receiving federal water pollution control grants until it took steps to stop dumping raw sewage into Galveston Bay. A physician from Baylor College of Medicine told the board that viruses causing such diseases as infantile paralysis (polio), meningitis, and encephalitis were found in a stream fed by Houston's sewage treatment plants. Dozens of Gulf coast residents gave graphic evidence of the area's pollution problems. State officials responded by accusing Klein of "witch-hunting" and of failing to give Texas credit for progress in controlling pollution.[10]

President Nixon increased pressure on states later that year by reaching back to the Refuse Act of 1899 to order all new discharges into public waters to be approved by the Army Corps of Engineers. Nixon also succeeded in obtaining congressional passage of his plan to consolidate pollution control under a new agency, the Environmental Protection Agency, and he appointed an aggressive administrator, William Ruckelshaus. One of his first actions was to invoke federal law to hold an "enforcement conference" in Houston to address Galveston Bay pollution's threat to the shellfish industry. Scheduled for three days in June 1971, it stretched into six.

Ruckelshaus reviewed a federal report detailing the large amount of pollutants approved by the TWQB for discharge into the ship channel and bay: 110 million gallons daily of inadequately treated sewage and 55,000 pounds daily of oil and grease from eighty-one sources. In addition, samples from polluters' discharges indicated quantities of other toxic substances dumped in the bay daily: 1,600 pounds of lead, 5,000 pounds of cadmium, 7,900 pounds of zinc, and 1,000 pounds of cyanide. Federal officials suggested that Galveston Bay, where oyster fishing already was limited to about half of the bay, might need to be entirely closed to shellfish harvesting because of health hazards. Once again, state officials branded the federal study misleading and said it failed to appreciate steps taken to improve ship channel water.[11]

Four weeks after the conference, more negative headlines dramatized Houston's pollution problems. Thirty-five longshoremen working on harbor piers were overcome by yellowish smog along the ship channel. The most likely suspected cause was a nearby sulfuric acid plant. Similar smog had made one hundred longshoremen ill in April and fifty more in June.[12] The next year, the Houston Health Department reported that ozone levels over the ship channel had reached a level thirteen times the amount considered safe. A three-day episode of smog in September 1972 forced airline pilots to make instrument landings because of poor visibility.[13]

The contrast between the escalating frequency and gravity of these news articles on one hand and the response of public officials on the other concerned me. Our state agencies charged with cleaning up pollution and our attorney general were either silent or defensive about these gloomy developments. Federal and local pollution law enforcers could manage only a handful of convictions with fines in the five thousand- to twenty-thousand-dollar range, a level of punishment almost laughable in comparison to the multimillion-dollar value of the enterprises involved.[14]

My review of the situation in the months leading up to my swearing in on January 1, 1973, convinced me that the defeatist attitude of my predecessor's staff and the absence of effective local prosecutors required that I start from scratch in building a strong enforcement team. Most of all, I knew my plans to initiate a series of regional offices across the state put a high priority on opening a Houston office capable of slugging it out with the strongest law firms in Houston, the ones that represented the national corporations polluting the ship channel.

Just such a slugger appeared on my doorstep in late 1972: Terence O'Rourke. It was his second visit to my office. He had also visited with me in January 1972 to urge me to run for attorney general. On that first visit, he was working in the gubernatorial campaign of reform candidate Frances Farenthold. He urged me to run for attorney general because he believed her effectiveness as governor would depend on having an attorney general willing to buck the status quo.

On this second visit, O'Rourke told me he wanted to work for me because he wanted to sue polluters. "Put the wood to them," as he said. He wanted to be on the front line. He had fire in his eyes. His body language was taut. I knew he had the mettle to do the job. O'Rourke's credentials, for a twenty-five-year-old less than two years out of law school, were strong: bachelor's degree in economics and master's degree in hydrology from Rice University and graduation from the University of Texas law school. While in law school, he worked for several members of the legislature, researching environmental issues for the Senate Interim Committee on Beaches and for a committee analyzing oil and gas pipeline hazards.

His most high-profile contribution was designing the parliamentary strategy and drafting the resolution that Farenthold used to overcome the House Speaker's opposition to a House vote in 1971 on investigation of the Sharpstown scandal, in which the Speaker was a central figure. The resolution was overwhelmingly defeated. But the thirty members who voted for it gained notoriety as the "Dirty Thirty" and ignited a reform movement that seized the public's imagination and swept me and an almost totally new slate of leaders into office in the housecleaning elections of 1972.

To complement O'Rourke's scalding negotiation skills and litigation tactics that would be used to take on the attorneys for ship channel polluters, I needed in Austin a team of lawyers focused on lighting a fire under the pollution control bureaucracy. To head my environmental protection division, I selected Mike Willatt, a former law firm colleague. I had originally hired Willatt out of the University of Houston law school to join my law practice in 1965. He was very bright—first in his class in law school, had made the highest score on the bar exam, studied graduate-level chemistry at Rice, worked as a research chemist, and earned a bachelor of science degree from the University of London.

I hired Phil Maxwell to be assistant chief of the environmental protection group in Austin. Maxwell, a 1969 UT law graduate, had been practicing in the same plaintiff law firm in Corpus Christi where Joe Longley had worked. Because they were friends, Longley got Maxwell involved in my campaign. I utilized Maxwell's law firm experience on environmental cases involving the petrochemical industry to write my campaign issue papers and speeches on pollution issues. To join O'Rourke on the environmental protection staff in Houston, I hired Rod Gorman, another spitfire who was completing an eighteen-month stint as the Harris County district attorney's chief prosecutor of pollution cases.

O'Rourke hit the ground running. To set up his and Gorman's office in Houston, he needed the files on pending cases. Because I had replaced all but a few of the lawyers in the environmental protection division and there was still a lot of uncertainty over who was doing what, O'Rourke's calls to Austin for help in getting those files for transfer to Houston did not produce the immediate assistance he expected. He jumped in his car, drove to Austin, and showed up at my office. He told me he was having problems getting his office organized because no one in the environmental division seemed ready to release the files to him. "Let's just go get those files," I told him. We went together to the division offices and quickly located them. We grabbed some boxes, and I helped him load them into the trunk of his red Toyota. "I want those cases set for trial. Do whatever it takes to move them along," I told him. "You don't need to be nasty to the polluters, you don't have to try them in the newspapers, but I want you to do what's necessary to make them understand that they're going to come to justice."

"Firm but fair" was my mantra not only to O'Rourke but to all of my staff. Calling up an image of the 1970s' most hard-nosed professional football team, I told him, "Let's use the Green Bay Packer approach. Tell them where you are going and what you are going to do, and then do it."

In my campaign speeches I attributed the lack of court action attacking Houston's pollution to the incumbent attorney general's favoritism toward industry. But when Willatt, Maxwell, and I started digging into this issue, we quickly realized that favoritism was only part of the problem. A major cause of inaction was the statute's requirement that we could not sue a polluter until the Water Quality Board or the Air Control Board referred us a case for filing a lawsuit. No referrals, no lawsuits. That created a crucial additional step in trying to haul polluters into court. When we inquired about referrals, we encountered a well-entrenched strategy by the agencies to forgo the lawsuit threat in favor of continued negotiation and extensions of deadlines—all carrot and no stick.

Pollution control at both the state and national levels was still in its infancy in the early 1970s. The state only began requiring permits for discharges into public waters in 1961. The TWQB was not given separate agency status and the power to set water quality standards across the state until the legislature in 1967 bowed to federal pressure applied through the federal Water Quality Act of 1965. The Air Control Board was created in 1965, also as a result of pressure from Congress, and in 1971 it was still struggling to develop air quality standards that met federal requirements.

Educating industry and municipalities on the need to obtain a permit before discharging waste into public air and waters was no overnight task. It took several years for business and local government officials to realize their responsibilities. When regulators several years later started checking discharges to confirm that they met terms of the permit, they spent another several years educating polluters about how the enforcement system worked. State regulators were attempting to strike a balance between the pressure they felt from the federal government to reduce pollution and the pressure they felt from state political leaders not to frighten off industry. These trade-offs produced the "let's try to work it out" strategy that industry easily manipulated to postpone hard decisions.

When we realized we faced many months of pushing and cajoling to achieve results using the state agency referrals approach, we turned for immediate opportunities to our only really aggressive ally, Walter Quebedeaux, Harris County's pollution control director. Despite minimal results and dozens of setbacks in his twenty years of identifying and decrying polluters, he remained as enthusiastic as the day he was hired to create the office. He fought a lonely battle. The City of Houston, which initially agreed to help fund Quebedeaux's office, soon dropped its support because its economic development strategies were incompatible with Quebedeaux's aggressive enforcement.

A frequent critic of the TWQB's deferential attitude toward polluters, Quebedeaux was seldom advised or consulted by the board about its activities involving Houston. He used powers granted to county and district attorneys under the Texas Water Quality Act of 1967 to persuade the county attorney in Houston to bring lawsuits against some of the ship channel's worst polluters. The law automatically made the state a party to these suits, but Quebedeaux was unsuccessful in recruiting the attorney general or the state pollution control agencies to help bring these cases to trial.[15]

Because the county attorney lacked the legal horsepower to go up against the city's biggest law firms, these cases were stacked up on pending dockets when O'Rourke and Gorman went to Quebedeaux to look for cases to take to trial. They found four good prospects: lawsuits against Tenn-Tex Alloy Corporation and Champion Paper Company and two against Armco Steel Corporation.

To implement my directive to bring these cases to trial as I promised in my campaign, my Houston team faced two hurdles: the cumbersome nuisance theory approach used by my predecessor and by the county attorney and the delaying tactics that the companies' attorneys repeatedly employed to postpone trial settings. When O'Rourke and Gorman reviewed the pleadings filed in these four cases, they saw immediately that the cases were needlessly complicated by arguments over the toxicity of the polluters' discharges. Quebedeaux had been running his own lab tests on fish to demonstrate toxicity, but that approach slowed the progress of the case because of technical questions about statistical validity.[16]

Willatt, Maxwell, and O'Rourke believed such technicalities were an unnecessary burden. We were not plaintiff attorneys seeking to prove someone was harmed; we were attorneys for the state alleging a violation of state law. To use a traffic law analogy, we were not obligated to prove that driving 50 mph in a 40 mph zone was dangerous, just that the driver exceeded the speed limit. My team believed our only burden was proving that the company violated the law by exceeding its permitted discharge of pollutants. Once that was proved, the judge's only decisions were determining the amount of a fine to assess and setting a deadline for the company to achieve compliance.

Together with Willatt and Maxwell, O'Rourke and Gorman revised the pleadings in all of these cases to allege the polluter broke the law by violating the terms of its state-issued discharge permit. Having broken the law, the polluter must be fined and ordered by the court to fix the pollution problem within a specified time or face an order to shut down. We also invoked the laws' authority to request a preferential trial setting.

Gone was the mushiness of the nuisance theory approach that attempted to balance equities, weigh differing methods of proving toxicity, and base any penalties on actual harm proved. Gone was the endless testimony by company-hired doctors and scientists challenging every state witness and every piece of the state's evidence. In its place was the certainty that if the government proved the company violated its air or water discharge permit, the judge must fine them up to one thousand dollars for each day of violation. The judge also must issue an injunction prohibiting further violations and subject the plant to closing if the terms of the injunction were violated.

Our new strategy dismayed the companies' attorneys. Each was represented by one of the largest law firms in Houston, and each firm assigned a top litigator to the cases. Armco and Tenn-Tex were represented by Fletcher H. Etheridge Jr., an antitrust specialist with Butler, Binion, Rice, Cook & Knapp. Champion Paper was represented by Dick Miller and Walter Conrad at Baker & Botts, which traced its beginning to 1840 and was one of the largest law firms in the nation. While these law firms contained skilled attorneys, a large part of their practice was what I would call "relational lawyering"—their tight relationships with the informal network of political and business leaders in Houston often translated into courthouse influence that could produce favorable rulings from the bench.

The first responsibility of these corporate defense attorneys was to delay the pollution cases as long as possible, a strategy they had perfected so adroitly that the cases we encountered were already several years old. Each case involved expenditure of large sums, usually millions, to modernize outdated production technology for plants that were forty to sixty years old. Delay equaled sustained profits; failure to delay hit the bottom line hard.

A lawsuit by the state could become a blessing in disguise for a polluter, because the state regulatory agency would suspend any action against the company until the lawsuit was resolved. These lawyers' second responsibility was thus to tie the state's case in knots with a barrage of motions, lengthy depositions, and other tactics demonstrating their clients' superior financial resources—and their tight political connections with the judges hearing the cases—all of which overwhelmed the outgunned government attorneys.

Our new approach removed those advantages and gave us the upper hand. They faced no choice but to settle with us because they could not risk a jury assessing a large fine or a court order closing a plant. O'Rourke described it as our "Godfather" strategy, named after the popular movie in which the Mafia don's son euphemistically describes a death threat: "My father made him an offer he couldn't refuse."

We pushed for a trial setting on Tenn-Tex first because it was closely aligned with Armco. Tenn-Tex's smelted manganese production was almost entirely purchased by Armco to use in manufacturing steel. In addition, Tenn-Tex was located across the street from Armco, both were represented by the same attorney, and both trials would involve similar technology. If we could win a case against Tenn-Tex, which was a small firm, we were almost guaranteed a victory over Armco, one of the ship channel giants.

Harris County had sued Tenn-Tex in 1970, alleging it had violated its Air Control Board permit eight hundred times since 1967 by discharging dust and manganese particles from three furnaces at its Greens Bayou plant. It had only 150 employees. The cost of equipment to bring the plant into compliance with its state permit was the relatively small amount of $250,000.

Trial was set for February 26, 1973. O'Rourke and Gorman opened by filing a motion to divide the trial into two parts: one to determine if TACB permit violations occured, and a second to determine penalties. They spent most of the morning arguing it before District Judge W. P. Cunningham, going back and forth with Etheridge, who knew he was fighting a crucial battle. If he lost, he could not appeal to attempt reversal, and he would be saddled with a precedent that would marginalize his claim to fame as a litigator who could bury a case in delay tactics. Our argument appealed to Cunningham on a practical level of docket management because our approach would compress lengthy trials into very brief ones.

Cunningham ruled in our favor. Etheridge left the courtroom and went to a nearby hallway phone booth to report the results to his client. Gorman could see him in the phone booth, banging the wall with his hand in frustration. He knew he would lose this case and the Armco case.

The next day, Tenn-Tex officials came to our Houston office to share already-developed plans for pollution reduction and to negotiate a settlement of our lawsuit. My instructions to the staff in settling these cases were that the penalty must be significant and reasonable and that the company must accept a permanent injunction requiring them to comply with the law by a deadline that was reasonable but not dilatory. Tenn-Tex agreed to pay fifty thousand dollars in fines and agreed to an injunction requiring them to install their abatement equipment by January 1, 1974. The fine was more than double the size of any fine that had been levied in any previous ship channel pollution case.[17] The judgment gave O'Rourke and Gorman the victory they needed to establish my environmental enforcement staff as a dramatic change from their predecessors.

Next up was Champion Paper, with fifteen hundred employees at a Pasadena plant east of Houston. It was another case that had been filed by Harris County in 1970. The stakes jumped by several zeros because the lawsuit alleged fifty-two hundred violations since 1967. At a thousand dollars a day, the potential fine was $5.2 million.

The violations involved odor. Their emissions included methyl mercaptan, which has a skunklike odor; hydrogen sulfide, which smells like rotten eggs; and dimethyl sulfide and dimethyl disulfide, which smell like rotten cabbage. There was no scientific test at the time for odor. O'Rourke looked in the Air Control Board files for evidence of violations, but there was none. To create our own evidence, O'Rourke placed ads in the Houston newspapers asking people to call our regional office if they experienced odor pollution by Champion.[18] He lacked staff to handle the calls, so he recruited volunteers from the League of Women Voters. The phones started ringing, and we signed up close to one hundred people willing to testify. Residents of Pasadena and Galena Park spilled out their tales of headaches, nausea, and loss of sleep and appetite. Champion's lawyers were furious. They knew their stalling tactics were finished.

O'Rourke obtained a trial setting for March 12. On March 9, the Friday before the trial, the phone rang in O'Rourke's scruffy office in the M&M building on Main Street, four and a half blocks from the courthouse on Fannin. It was Dick Miller calling. "We'll pay the penalty," he said. O'Rourke called me with the news, and I told him I would be in court Monday just in case an agreement didn't hold. He and Gorman spent Saturday and Sunday in Miller's offices working out the terms of the settlement, conferring with Quebedeaux by phone to incorporate his demands into the settlement and get his approval of the final wording.

Champion agreed to a $100,000 fine, the largest fine for any air pollution case in the nation. They accepted an injunction listing required pollution control equipment, estimated to cost about $15 million, to be installed by July 1, 1974. The agreement held, and I was in court Monday morning to accept from Miller the state's $50,000 share of the fine after the judge entered an order incorporating the settlement wording. I told the news reporters covering the trial that I much preferred to settle these cases than to ask a jury to shut down a plant. "If we can get a company to pay the necessary fine and agree to install necessary equipment by a certain date, we're happy," I said. "We're in the business of eliminating pollution. We're not out to get anyone or to make headlines or to prove a point. It's better to settle in good faith than to take a hard-headed, hard-line approach."[19]

Our next target was Armco, our biggest fish. One of the ship channel's largest employers, with a work force of forty-five hundred, the Ohio-based steel manufacturer also was one of its biggest industrial polluters. Armco's reputation as an aggressively obstinate polluter also placed it at the top of the target list of the Environmental Protection Agency staff in Washington, which instigated a Justice Department lawsuit against the Armco ship channel coke plant just a week after the EPA was formed in December 1970.[20] A trial resulted in a Houston judge finding the Armco plant "patently antiquated from the standpoint of pollution control." His order of September 17, 1971, had called for Armco to immediately stop discharging into the channel every day more than half a ton of toxic chemicals such as cyanides and phenols and between three and six tons of ammonia.[21] A top Justice Department lawyer hailed the ruling as a landmark victory in EPA's expanding initiative.[22]

Ten days later, Armco's president, C. William Verity, sent a complaint letter to the White House protesting that the court order was inconsistent with President Nixon's recent speeches vowing not to make industry the "whipping boy" of environmentalists.[23] Verity was politically well connected enough to enjoy frequent White House visits and would become chairman of the U.S. Chamber of Commerce in 1980 and President Ronald Reagan's secretary of commerce in 1987. Verity also told the White House the court order would force Armco to fire three hundred employees.

The White House, it was revealed a year later, had immediately summoned an EPA deputy to the West Wing and instructed him to have the court order revised to avoid a shutdown of the coke ovens.[24] Before the EPA could initiate discussions between the Justice Department and Armco, Verity repeated his complaints in a speech before the Houston Rotary Club and indicated that his White House contacts had accomplished his goal of achieving a review of the court order.[25]

Encouraged by the White House support, Armco held out for an unconditional sixty-day stay of the court order. But they abandoned that strategy when their power play hit the newspapers. The *Washington Star* linked the lawsuit challenge to Armco's political contributions to Nixon's campaign in 1968, and that report immediately triggered investigative hearings by a House government operations subcommittee.[26] Armco agreed to the EPA's demands that it treat and then burn its waste, instead of pumping it into injection wells as they had insisted, and a revised court order was entered in November 1971.[27]

The pending Harris County lawsuits against Armco that we inherited, one for water and one for air, involved millions of dollars in expenditures to bring up to modern standards these out-of-date plants using decades-old technology. O'Rourke and Gorman failed to force Armco's lawyer, Etheridge, to agree to a trial setting or to comply with requests for information. They decided to take their case to the Armco home office in Ohio. They set up a series of depositions with Armco officials.

Before they left on their trip, O'Rourke asked me to sign a Letter of Visitation. This was the nuclear weapon in our arsenal, to be used sparingly if at all. Because state law makes the attorney general the holder of all charters for corporations, that official is granted power to demand immediate access to the books and records of any corporation doing business in Texas. Refusal to provide the requested records can result in termination of a corporate charter. I agreed to sign the letter demanding access to the company's records, and O'Rourke took it with him.

When they began their meeting at Armco's offices, O'Rourke and Gorman requested corporate information they needed to conduct their depositions concerning the Houston plant. Etheridge again refused their request. "I've got a Visitation Letter in my briefcase. All I need to do before serving it on you is to call General Hill," O'Rourke told Etheridge.[28] When he dismissed the threat, O'Rourke rose from his seat and left the room, heading for a telephone. Etheridge capitulated. Within forty-five minutes, Armco clerks filled a conference table with dozens of documents we needed.

That episode, and the loss of the Tenn-Tex case, cost Etheridge his client. Armco replaced him with Russell Kendall from Vinson and Elkins, another powerhouse firm whose former partner, John Connally, was U.S. treasury secretary during 1971–1972. Kendall was more of a negotiator than a litigator, and the young lawyers helping him on these cases were generations removed from Etheridge's reliance on relationships and delay. They were more technologically savvy and comfortable negotiating with government officials. That difference in approach opened the way toward settlements.

The Armco water case, filed in 1971, charged Armco with discharging cyanide, phenol, ammonia, lead, cadmium, and other hazardous materials into the channel on more than two thousand occasions since 1967. Once again, the maximum fine of $1,000 per violation made this a multimillion-dollar case. When Kendall called Gorman to initiate discussions on an amount for a fine, he offered a figure of $10,000 to $25,000, a ridiculously low amount considering how we had raised the bar in the Tenn-Tex and Champion Paper cases. Gorman could not resist the temptation to scare him. He recalled to Kendall that Quebedeaux had performed twenty-five hundred tests showing Armco had violated its permit. Gorman countered with a suggestion of $1,000 per violation, producing a fine of $2.5 million based on those tests, with no penalties for other violations.

Kendall was on the phone to me early the next day, complaining about my young staff in Houston being totally unrealistic and failing to understand the ramifications of their actions. If he expected a sympathetic ear from me, he was disappointed. "They may understand the ramifications better than you realize," I told him. "I think you just better explain to your client that they are dealing with someone in me that wants to be fair, but I'm going to be firm. I'm not going to handle this in a way to where it's just regarded as a slap on the wrist.

"I'm serious about cleaning up the environment in Houston. I just want y'all to get your business straight with the state. We're going to get this job done and that's the message I want you to help carry to the other friends of mine that are in the legal defense community of Houston—that

I'm basically a middle-of-the-road type of fellow that likes to work things out, but that I'm not a patsy, I wasn't born yesterday.

"I've got my own engineers, my own technical people that are advising me, and I want to go by what they tell me and not by what your people say they can do. If they're unfair or if they can't prove their case, we'll come to the table and we'll talk about it. And if we're wrong, we'll admit it. But if we're not, then we're going to insist that that's what you do."

After that exchange, the Vinson and Elkins lawyers and Gorman worked out an agreed judgment that fulfilled our principal goal of replacing Armco's state waste discharge permit, which, because it predated the law creating the TWQB, allowed them almost total freedom to pollute. So weak was Armco's old permit that the new one they negotiated with the TWQB cut by 90 percent the amount of pollutants previously authorized by the agency, and in fact it reduced the amount of cadmium, lead, and zinc to less than the requirements of the state's Hazardous Metals Law. Gorman told me it was one of the tightest permits on the ship channel. Armco estimated it would spend $300,000 on new equipment needed to meet a deadline of January 1, 1975.

Armco also agreed to a fine of $125,000, another record high penalty for us. The court accepted the agreement on April 3, and Kendall handed Gorman a check for $62,500, the share of the fine designated for the State of Texas.[29]

The Armco air pollution lawsuit filed in January 1970 was a more difficult challenge. It was the biggest air pollution case in the United States. The smoke from Armco and its next-door neighbor Tenn-Tex created a plume that was visible all the way to Dallas on satellite photos we obtained as evidence in the case. The TACB, still in its initial organizational stage, lacked experienced staff and the generally accepted technology needed to bring polluters to the negotiating table. While Armco's lawyers had been ready to settle the water case, they didn't feel the same urgency in the air pollution case.

To get the case moving, O'Rourke went to court in February to utilize the state Air Pollution Control Act's requirement that judges grant preferential settings to cases filed under the act. He lost that argument, so the next week he went to court to contend that Armco's pollution should be stopped immediately rather than allowed to continue until resolution of the lawsuit. He lost that case too, but it helped Armco understand the priority we placed on the case. The trial then was set for April 9, but Armco's lawyers again blocked us by successfully arguing that other issues in this case were pending in a different court. O'Rourke then filed a motion with the Court of Appeals in Houston requesting it to order the trial judge to set the case. The court denied our request, but the decision gave us enough support that we were able to convince the Vinson and Elkins attorneys that they needed to negotiate. They finally agreed in May to settle.

Armco's fine was $250,000, the largest fine paid by any industry in a pollution case in the United States. Their abatement requirement set a series of deadlines for installing equipment, the last deadline being July 1976. Armco estimated it would spend $3.5 million on pollution controls and possibly another $50 million if its coke ovens were replaced. The agreement was entered in court on May 25. At the settlement hearing, I accepted a check from Kendall for the state's $125,000 share.[30]

With those four big cases demonstrating the new day in Texas pollution law enforcement, my staff found other polluters much more ready to meet our settlement demands. By the end of 1973, we had collected more than $1 million in fines and developed significant pollution clean-up schedules for about one hundred polluters.[31]

Our challenge to industrial polluters was having a significant impact. But progress on that front was not repeated when we sought similar results on the municipal sewage front. The City of Houston was the biggest polluter of the ship channel and had been for years. And there was nothing I or my staff could do about it, except to try to convince the TWQB to approve a lawsuit against Houston.

I chafed at the statutory limitations on the attorney general's authority to sue polluters or other law violators without approval from a state agency. I believed I was the only lawyer available to represent the interests of the people of Texas. If they were being exposed to health hazards by a polluter, why should I not be able to use common law powers to sue on their behalf? I struggled with that issue throughout my term as attorney general. But I wasn't ready to push the issue in the City of Houston case. I decided to push as hard as I could on the TWQB.

I fired my first shot in September 1973. My ammunition came from our only strong ally, Harris County's pollution control director. In 1955, Quebedeaux began compiling annual reports describing persistent problems in the city's sewage treatment plants. He sent copies to the mayor and other top officials, but there was never any response. In 1972, he increased the frequency to every two or three weeks, but there was still no reaction. In September 1973, he compiled all the reports for the previous eighteen months and expanded his mailing list to include me.

It was a damning summary of extensive violations of state waste disposal permits. I took the unusual step—a first for any Texas attorney general—of requesting a regulatory agency to authorize me to take legal action on its behalf. I sent a letter to the new chairman of the TWQB, fellow Houstonian J. Doug Toole, citing Quebedeaux's evidence and adding that it was confirmed by the city's self-reports to the board. I requested that this case be certified by the board for the filing of a lawsuit asking appropriate injunctive relief and penalties.

Houston newspapers reported on the letter and quoted O'Rourke as saying a lawsuit would "get the city under court order so we wouldn't continue getting the same story three or five years from now. Every year a new city the size of Austin is added to the Houston complex, and Houston just isn't dealing with the growth."[32]

Houston Post environmental writer Harold Scarlett weighed in on our side in his analysis of the issue, saying he saw nothing "dreadful" about filing suit to "seek a court order binding Houston and its elected officials to do certain things by certain times to end Buffalo Bayou's days as a diseased ditch. If the city's next mayor and next public works director knew they could be hauled off to jail for letting sewage treatment slide, Houston would be a much healthier place."[33]

Willatt renewed my request at a meeting of the TWQB two weeks later. He told the board only forty of the forty-four Houston waste treatment plants had made complete reports the previous month, and thirty-nine of them were in violation of water quality standards for chlorination, total suspended solids, and biochemical oxygen demand. A court order, Willatt said, would be stronger than an order by the board because of its time deadline. He characterized the board's orders as offering the city the opportunity to "buy time" for additional delays in solving problems. Board staff responded that Houston had begun programs to correct most of its sewage treatment problems. The board voted to postpone action on my request until October.

At the October board meeting, I made a surprise appearance to emphasize the importance I placed on the issue. But the board pushed a decision even further into the future, deciding to review monthly performance reports on Houston's progress for six months before revisiting the lawsuit issue.[34]

At the board's December meeting, the staff offered a proposed order requiring Houston to present by the following June a master plan for solving sewage treatment problems. It was criticized as "toothless" by the Texas Parks and Wildlife Department representative on the board. He offered a motion to authorize a lawsuit against Houston, saying that "there is no question in our minds that the attorney general's office is not satisfied with the situation; Harris County is not satisfied with the situation; the Parks and Wildlife Department is not satisfied. If I lived in Houston, I believe I would not be satisfied." His motion died for lack of a second.[35]

Frustrated by the double-talk we were receiving from the technical experts working for the board and the city, my staff decided to hire our own specialist. Maxwell hired John Malouf, an environmental engineer, to conduct on-the-ground investigations of Houston sewage treatment plants so we wouldn't have to rely on data telling only part of the story. Malouf compiled a strong report on his findings of continued problems, and we planned a one-two punch for the meeting of the TWQB in July 1974.

Malouf presented his findings to the board, sharply criticizing the operating procedures at the plants. I followed him to the podium with another strong plea for a lawsuit against Houston. My comments were interrupted by a request from the chairman to meet in the hallway with the city's public works assistant director, who earlier in the meeting had presented a review of the city's new $300 million sewage improvement plan. After briefly discussing the plan with him, I returned to the meeting and said I was impressed with the city's plans and would withhold further efforts to seek a lawsuit so long as Houston lived up to its promises.[36]

Malouf continued the drumbeat of startling reports about the inadequacy of Houston's sewage plants at regular appearances before the board. The board, however, continued moving deadlines forward whenever the city failed to comply with clean-up schedules.[37]

These frustrations led me to propose during the legislative session in 1975 that the attorney general be granted new powers to sue polluters without the necessity of a certification from the pollution control agencies. I enjoyed strong support in the House, where the Environmental Affairs Committee issued a report in January urging that my office be granted independent authority to sue polluters. The report noted that the TWQB's self-reporting system had revealed that thirty-eight industries admitted they were "substantially out of compliance" with their permits, yet the board requested prosecution by the attorney general in only one case and Harris County sued another seven.[38] I pressed my argument at a meeting in January 1975 of the Gulf Coast Council on Water Resources and specifically called Houston to task: "The City of Houston sits flagrantly in violation of our pollution laws every day, and I think it's wrong."[39]

We were doomed by our own success, however. Our dramatic court victories against ship channel polluters frightened the business community into scare-tactics opposition that prevented me from moving the bill out of committee in the Senate. I was just about ready to give serious consideration to a common law nuisance suit against Houston when a key to unlock the courthouse door was handed to us by an unexpected benefactor.

In industrial pollution cases, I could overcome the refusal by the TWQB to authorize our filing a lawsuit by depending on Harris County to file and automatically making us a party to the suit. But local politics removed that option when I was unable to obtain authority from TWQB to sue the City of Houston. The two groups worked together on too many projects, and their political alliances were too intertwined to accommodate such a family feud.

So we were stuck with the uncooperative TWQB's refusal—until we suddenly were provided an opportunity to attack the Houston problem by tagging onto a lawsuit filed by another governmental entity. In July 1976, Clear Creek Basin Authority filed a suit against Houston alleging pollution of Galveston Bay and Clear Lake, which is on the western side of Galveston Bay, from untreated sewage discharged by city plants. State law gave us the authority to join Clear Creek as a plaintiff. The TWQB was opposed to my entering the lawsuit, but I rejected their "neutral" stance. This was the opening we needed, and we took advantage of it.[40]

Houston hired David Beck, from Fulbright & Jaworski, as their special counsel in the case. Beck and my staff negotiated a settlement under which Houston agreed to double its sewage treatment capacity in four years. The agreement adopted the timetable the city set for improving twenty-one of its plants. I went to court in April 1978 to present the agreement to the judge, who approved it. I told the judge it should resolve "a very serious problem that has faced the city of Houston for many years." I reminded him we sought no civil penalties so that no money would be diverted from construction in a $500 million city sewage improvement program then under way. The principal benefit of the court order, I said, would be to put the city's performance "in the public domain," under the court's scrutiny and out of the hands of "Austin bureaucrats."[41]

The lawsuit by Clear Creek Basin Authority allowed me to avoid a courthouse confrontation with the TWQB, but it merely delayed the inevitable. Relations between my staff and the board continued to deteriorate as the board rejected our efforts to stiffen enforcement actions. A clean break occurred in 1977, when the board weakened protections for the Edwards Underground Reservoir. I agreed with the City of San Antonio, which used the reservoir as its sole source of drinking water, that the board's decision should be challenged because it threatened to contaminate the reservoir with septic tank waste.[42]

The board replaced a two-year-old order that set uniform water quality standards for all seven counties that overlay the reservoir. In its place the board issued a separate order for each county, with less stringent subdivision requirements for Uvalde and Kinney counties, where the governor who had appointed a majority of the board members had his home and large ranches.

I believed the board's action to be flawed because it provided no compelling reason for not regulating all counties in the same manner. Although state law charged my office with serving as the attorney representing the board in court, I felt the unusual step of suing my "client" was justified because my obligation to the public overrode my responsibility to serve as attorney for a state agency. The board went to the Texas Supreme Court to prevent me from filing the lawsuit, but the Supreme Court denied the request.[43] I filed my lawsuit to block implementation of the board's Edwards Aquifer orders.[44]

An Austin district judge dismissed my lawsuit in August 1977.[45] I appealed his decision to the Third Court of Civil Appeals. My suit had been consolidated with a second case in which another district judge rejected my challenge of a state agency's action, this time the Texas Water Rights Commission's approval of a contract allowing the South Texas Nuclear Project to pay the Lower Colorado River Authority $50 million for water I contended belonged to the state, not the river authority.

Reading from notes I scribbled on a brown envelope in my office before I took the elevator from my seventh-floor office down to the appeals courtroom in the adjoining building, I told the three judges that the attorney general "is not a mere lackey to defend a state agency whether the action they took is illegal or not." I was asking the court to rule that English common law adopted in 1840 in Texas gives attorneys general the unrestricted right to sue on behalf of the people. "They flat acted in an illegal manner," I told the court in reference to the Texas Water Rights Commission case. "As attorney general, do I have the doors to the courthouse closed to me if I think an action is illegal?" The attorney hired by the state agencies countered that the attorney general "does not represent the public interest. He is not the people's lawyer. The attorney general is the lawyer for the state in Texas. As the lawyer for the state, he is obligated to represent these agencies."[46]

The appeals court affirmed the decisions by the district judges, holding that the attorney general is bound by law to serve as exclusive attorney for state agencies. The ruling came in July 1978, only five months before my term would expire, leaving insufficient time for an appeal to the Supreme Court.[47]

I accepted the court's ruling and abandoned my conviction that the voters who elected me expected and deserved an attorney general whose first duty was to look out for their best interests, to be their advocate. I was disappointed that I had failed to convince the judges to adopt my position. But I was content with my judgment that the integrity of our state's legal system demanded this issue be raised. And I was satisfied that I presented to the courts two clear-cut cases that dramatized the public policy dilemma in such a way that there could be no doubt about the practical consequences of the final decision.

(4)

Beating the Southwestern Bell Goliath

The timidity of state and local governments' attempts to control polluters in Texas in the early 1970s was, by comparison with their control of the telephone company monopoly, fiercely aggressive. Texas was the only state without a public utility commission to regulate phone rates. That left regulation of local rates to cities. All but a few of the largest cities lacked the resources or political will to challenge the political and economic juggernaut that was "Ma Bell" or AT&T. It was then the largest corporation in the world and owned 82 percent of the nation's telephones. Rates for calls between cities in different states were regulated by the federal government. Rates for calls between cities in Texas were regulated by no one.

In such a lenient regulatory environment, the telephone monopoly prospered mightily. Texas' rate of return on investment exceeded the Bell company average for two decades. It was the most profitable state for AT&T in all but seven of the years between 1956 and 1973. It produced $1.4 billion in revenue in 1973 for the five-state Southwestern Bell Telephone Company subsidiary of AT&T. Southwestern Bell leased 6 million telephones to its Texas customers. They were served by thirty-eight thousand employees working across the state in operations centers valued at $3.5 billion.[1]

Southwestern Bell was more than a major employer and economic presence in Texas. It was an institution, like the postal service or the electric company, that was essential to everyday living. Most adult Texans were like my parents, who grew up in rural areas where the arrival of telephone service in the 1920s and 1930s was a source of great celebration and a sense of pride. The goodwill generated by this national treasure that gave America the world's best and most affordable telephone service continued to warm the hearts of most older generations.

AT&T's central role in our national identity had been cemented by its vast technological contributions, which included adding sound to silent movies and developing television, radio telephony, early digital computers, transistors, silicon chips, and lasers. The Bell system was such a vital resource that it was nationalized during World War I. Its manufacturing subsidiary was so accomplished at efficient management that the government selected it to run the Sandia Laboratory in New Mexico, which produced atomic bombs after World War II, and to produce Nike Ajax and Hercules missiles during the cold war era of the 1950s.[2]

Politically, Southwestern Bell was bulletproof. It built its political armor and profitable rate levels at the local level, methodically cultivating the city council members who had to approve rates. So complete was its domination of local government that Southwestern Bell could depend on the cities' lobbying arm, the Texas Municipal League, to protect it from repeated attempts to pass a bill creating a state agency to regulate telephone rates. To that legislative clout could be added the influence of its thousands of workers, many of whom were members of unions with a strong political presence. And, of course, Southwestern Bell deployed its own lobbying force and political contribution machinery to back up its front-line defenders.[3]

The telephone monopoly's invincibility, however, faltered in 1974. On March 6, Microwave Communications Incorporated (MCI) filed an antitrust lawsuit against AT&T in a dispute over access to AT&T's local exchanges for MCI's long-distance service.[4] On October 17, the suicide death of its vice president for Texas operations triggered several lawsuits deeply embarrassing to Southwestern Bell and AT&T.[5] On November 20, the U.S. Department of Justice of the pro-business Republican administration shocked the business world by filing an antitrust lawsuit against AT&T to break up the Bell system.[6] In December, Southwestern Bell triggered the first challenge by a Texas attorney general of an intrastate long-distance rate increase. Also in December, Lt. Gov. Bill Hobby authorized the Senate subcommittee on consumer affairs to expand its research on creating a public utility commission to include an investigation of the charges made by the deceased Bell manager.[7]

These events were a small part of a fundamental transition in the communications industry that, over the next thirty years, would totally change the way Americans communicated with each other and the rest of the world. The unique business-government partnership nurtured so successfully by AT&T and its predecessors through almost a century of often turbulent economic, technological, and governmental vicissitudes began faltering in the late 1960s. Two related developments posed challenges that exposed the venerable corporate giant's weakening hold on control of its own destiny.

One challenge was inflation, which doubled during a period of rapid growth for AT&T in the 1960s. Instead of passing along the costs in higher rates, the twenty-three Bell regional managers sacrificed needed capital improvements to protect profitability.[8] That strategy led to massive service problems in such areas as Houston, where development of the new space program's headquarters spurred a huge increase in population and business activity, and in Manhattan, where fast-growing corporate headquarters' telephone requirements were expanding. These problems raised new questions in the minds of the public and government regulators about the viability of the trade-off at the core of the Bell system's being: that the government would allow it to operate as a protected monopoly in return for its providing Americans universal telephone interconnectivity and high-quality service.[9]

AT&T had attained monopoly status through vicious competitive struggles in the decades after its birth. Its victories over competitors resulted in a vertically integrated company providing the telephones used to make calls, the lines over which the calls were transmitted, the switching systems used to route the calls, and the research needed to maintain technological superiority.

It expanded beyond being a provider of local telephone service to become a manufacturer of telephone equipment through acquisition of Western Electric Company beginning in 1881.[10] It became a provider of research through its Bell Telephone Laboratories, a joint venture between AT&T and Western Electric formed in 1925.

The federal government's first effort to regulate the telephone industry occurred in 1910, when Congress placed jurisdiction over the industry with the Interstate Commerce Commission. AT&T shielded its monopoly status from the Sherman Antitrust Act (1890) only by voluntarily disposing in 1913 of its newly acquired 30 percent ownership of Western Union Telegraph Company and by promising the U.S. attorney general that it would give competing local exchanges access to its lines. Regulation was intensified by FDR administration reforms that produced in 1934 the Federal Communications Commission (FCC) and a four-year investigation of AT&T, but the monopoly survived intact. Likewise, the Justice Department saw its 1949 antitrust lawsuit seeking to force AT&T to sell Western Electric slip into limbo.[11]

The second challenge to AT&T in the 1960s came from technology. The targets of this challenge were two essential ingredients in AT&T's monopoly—its control of telephones used by its customers and its control of long-distance lines. When telephone inventor Alexander Graham Bell formed Bell Telephone Company in 1877, his business-savvy father-in-law decided the company would rent telephone service instead of sell telephones. With AT&T's Western Electric manufacturing the telephones, regional Bell companies leasing them to users, and users being forced to agree to use no other equipment, would-be competitors for the sale of handset or office switching equipment were frozen out of the market.[12]

That long history ended in 1968, when the Federal Communications Commission approved an application by a Dallas firm, Carter Electronics Corporation, to connect private two-way radios with the telephone system via a base station. The FCC ruling opened the door to the attaching of any customer-owned equipment to the Bell system. Competitors immediately began taking market share from Western Electric. In 1969, the FCC granted an application to MCI to operate an intercity private line between Chicago and St. Louis, using a less expensive microwave technology to transmit calls. The FCC ruling, which also forced AT&T to allow MCI to connect its users with the local Bell exchanges, led to a furious competitive and legal battle for lucrative long-distance service that culminated in MCI winning a $1.8 billion antitrust lawsuit in 1980.[13]

Despite these regulatory dismantlings of the AT&T monopoly, the Justice Department remained concerned over the requirement that regional Bell companies use only Western Electric equipment. Their investigations indicated that AT&T technology was failing to keep pace with microwave and satellite communications advances.[14]

The cornerstone of the regulated monopoly concept in this case—that a single company would connect more Americans to telephone service faster and more efficiently than could be achieved by competing companies—was no longer a factor now that the nation was blanketed with telephone service. The corollary premise of the private-public partnership, that a monopoly enterprise would provide the highest quality service and products, was, the Justice Department attorneys worried, never going to flourish in a noncompetitive environment.

These concerns were enlarged and encouraged by MCI's complaints to the FCC and Congress over AT&T's recalcitrance in granting it access to local exchanges. They were distilled into a proposed antitrust lawsuit in 1973, but it was a casualty of government turmoil caused by the Watergate scandal. After Vice President Gerald Ford became president when Richard Nixon resigned on August 9, 1974, the lawsuit was approved by the new attorney general and filed November 20.[15]

One week earlier, AT&T and its Texas operating system suffered the opening shot in what they knew would be months—and probably years—of a politically damaging and publicly humiliating ordeal resulting from the suicide note left by their recently deceased Texas vice president, T. O. Gravitt of Dallas. Gravitt's family joined with a Gravitt friend and colleague whom Southwestern Bell had fired the day Gravitt died, San Antonio division manager James H. Ashley, to hire San Antonio's most flamboyant trial attorney to sue AT&T and Southwestern Bell.

The attorney, Pat Maloney, used the detailed eight-page handwritten tell-all suicide note with dozens of supporting documents attached as the basis for his lawsuit pleadings seeking $29 million in damages. He alleged Southwestern Bell slandered the two managers in retaliation for their opposition to the company's underhanded rate-setting practices and political influence buying. It took the wily Maloney less than two weeks after filing the lawsuit to get into print, in the *Dallas Times Herald,* the most sensational sentence in the still unpublicized suicide note: "Watergate is a gnat compared to the Bell system."[16]

The lawsuit and its inflammatory accusations sent shockwaves not only throughout Texas but also the rest of the nation. Dallas, Gravitt's hometown, and San Antonio, where Ashley lived, were both very competitive two-newspaper cities. All four newspapers aggressively pursued the story, and their articles were sent nationwide by the Associated Press.[17]

Gravitt's extensive suicide note included a list of about one hundred items and records to substantiate his claims of improper political activities, participation with law enforcement agencies in unauthorized telephone bugging, and other questionable management actions. With Ashley confirming Gravitt's from-the-grave charges, AT&T was denied the strategy of passing off the revelations as a mentally unbalanced man's desperate imaginings.

The Gravitt-Ashley tales of political slush funds financed by phony expense reimbursements or forced salary diversions produced several months of news articles naming politicians who had received Bell contributions. The former North Carolina vice president for Southern Bell verified that similar political funding tactics were used in his state. The Missouri Public Service Commission began an inquiry into illegal political contributions involving Bell. The Securities and Exchange Commission investigated charges that corporate funds were used for political contributions. Federal grand juries in San Antonio and Houston investigated the Gravitt-Ashley charges.[18]

In the midst of this uproar, I was visited by Newton Hoverstock, Southwestern Bell's vice president of public affairs for Texas. When he called for an appointment in December, I expected our discussion to concern the Gravitt-Ashley lawsuit revelations.

My public statements on the case had been circumspect because I was wary of the sources—Bell had successfully sullied the reputations of Ashley and Gravitt, and I knew Maloney well enough to take his offerings with a grain of salt.[19] My only action, in response to a request to investigate made by a consumer advocacy organization assisting legislators in drafting a utility regulation bill, was to assign a staff member to attend court hearings in a monitoring role. My staff briefed me on these issues before our meeting, but Hoverstock surprised me when we met. He told me his mission was to advise me of Bell's plans to implement on March 1, 1975, a $45 million increase in intrastate long-distance rates. "Why are you telling me about this?" I asked him. "Do you believe I have any authority in this matter?"

"No, General," he said. "This is not a matter you have jurisdiction over. We just wanted to advise you, as a courtesy."

"Well, if I just sit here and do nothing, does that mean I approve it?" I asked.

"Not at all," he said. "We just wanted to be sure you weren't caught by surprise. We believe the increase is justified by our higher costs due to inflation. It'll be used to pay for improvements in our system. We've grown so fast we haven't always been able to keep up with demand. We've got some catching up to do and it's going to cost a significant amount of money."

I certainly didn't want to give him the impression I was content to stand by and watch while Bell took such a bold step, so I decided to leave open the door for action by my office. "Well, I don't know, Newt—the amount of the increase sounds awfully high to me," I told him. "I don't know if there's anything I can do about it. Maybe there isn't, but I need to find that out.

"If I do have some responsibility in this area, you can rest assured I will use every inch of authority I have. I'll try to do what's right—what's fair to you and what's fair to your customers. I try to take a balanced approach to all of the issues that come before me. I'm not on a crusade, I'm not out to get anybody, I want to be reasonable and just do what's best for our state. But I definitely want to look into our authority to review these rates."

After he left, I gathered my first assistant, David Kendall, and several other staff members around my desk to tell them what had happened. "This is outrageous," I told them. "They're going to increase intrastate rates by $45 million, when everybody knows you can call Lake Charles from Houston for lots less than it costs to call Beaumont.

"These rates are already too high and they're going to raise them even higher! They're socking it to their intrastate callers because there's nobody to stop them, and they're concerned they aren't going to get the rate increases they need from the cities. Well, I've got a surprise for them—we're going to ask the courts to decide whether I have any power to stop them."

Then I called Mike Willatt and Phil Maxwell, whose roles as leaders of my environmental division led them on a search for authority to allow our office to take action against polluters without waiting for the state pollution control agencies to certify a case to us for a lawsuit. I had believed since the day I was elected that Texans needed and deserved an attorney general who possessed broad common law powers to go to court to protect their interests.

Our state constitution, however, did not contemplate an attorney general's role as broadly as I interpreted it. Because of the era in which it was written, during the backlash against the centralized power exerted by the Reconstruction state government federally installed in 1864, the state constitution created weak executive officers. Our research of the statutes, constitution, and case law found no magic words that would instill in my office the role of principal advocate for Texas citizens. I told Willatt and Maxwell of Hoverstock's visit and asked them to renew their quest and to focus on possible lawsuits against the telephone company on behalf of the public interest.

The next day, Willatt called back with some interesting news.

"How's this for a coincidence?" he asked me. "The Texas constitution allows you to take action against corporations when they collect any 'tolls' that are 'not authorized by law.' I looked up 'toll' in the dictionary, and the definition includes this entry: 'A charge for some service, as for a long distance telephone call.' This is pretty unambiguous delegation of the very authority you need to challenge the intrastate telephone rate increase."[20]

I wanted to see this good news for myself, so I searched my wall shelf of black-bound *Vernon's* Texas law books and pulled down the volume that contained the state constitution to read the section Willatt had found. There it was, in section 22 of Article IV, a thirteen-line paragraph full of awkward sentences that spoke to the clumsy patchwork and piecemeal approach used to construct our constitution. The word "tolls" leaped off the page when my eyes reached the eighth line. I reread the paragraph several times to convince myself I was not misinterpreting this gift from heaven that had dropped in my lap. It recalled for me the biblical admonition from the Sermon on the Mount in the Gospel of Matthew I had heard so often through the years—"seek and ye shall find, knock, and it shall be opened unto you."

We had uncovered a provision so obscure, our later research revealed, no attorney general had used it in the last thirty years. It gave us the opening I had sought in vain for two years to break out of the suffocating restrictions on my authority I believed were wasting the precious resource of top-quality legal talent I had so aggressively recruited to do battle for the people of Texas.

The wording Willatt had found was drafted in 1875. That was a year before Alexander Graham Bell patented his invention, so it clearly was not inserted to address telephone rates. It undoubtedly referred to tolls imposed by corporations that owned wharfs, ferries, bridges, or roadways. But even if the literal meanings from ninety-nine years ago were different today, I knew a court would overlook that issue to comply with the intent of the framers. And the framers had made it pretty clear they wanted the attorney general to keep a sharp eye out for corporations that might be gouging the public.

When the attorney general was made a constitutional office in the constitution adopted in 1845 when Texas joined the Union, the office's powers were listed in statutes. The constitution written in 1869 at the insistence of the federal government during Reconstruction added to those statutory powers a duty to "represent the interests of the State in all suits or pleas in the Supreme Court in which the State may be a party."[21]

In 1875, after Democrats reclaimed control of state government, they convened a constitutional convention to reverse some of the Reconstruction-era provisions. One of the delegates was a colorful lawyer from Galveston, George M. Flournoy, who had been Texas attorney general in 1860 and a leader in Texas' secession from the Union in 1861. He served as a colonel in Walker's Texas Division during the Civil War, and after Texas rejoined the Union he fled to Mexico to serve in the army of Emperor Maximilian, whom France had installed after its forces led an invasion of Mexico.[22]

With only a brief explanation to the constitutional convention, Flournoy successfully proposed a lengthy addition to the 1869 document's statement that the attorney general "shall especially inquire into the charter rights of all private corporations, and from time to time, in the name of the State, take such action in the courts as may be proper and necessary to prevent any private corporation from exercising any power or demanding or collecting any species of taxes, tolls, freight or wharfage not authorized by law." The provision was one of several in the new constitution aimed at tightening control on corporations in the very rural and conservative Texas of 1875 that was suspicious of big government, big business, and high taxes levied by either or both.[23]

I met with Kendall and several other assistants to discuss our options. "Mike found us an opening if we want to take it," I told them. "I think this is the perfect opportunity for us to show that the attorney general does more than give opinions interpreting the law for state agencies.

"We're not just a bunch of green-eyeshade lawyers with our noses stuck in dusty old law books. We've got the smarts and the get-up-and-go to duke it out with the big boys in the courthouse and pin their ears back if they're not treating the people right. We've got as much brainpower in our office as any of the big law firms, and this is our opportunity to demonstrate that in a very convincing way. We can make a real difference here.

"But this isn't a lay-down hand. Ma Bell is going to have some good lawyers, and they've got some friends on the bench. I'm not interested in doing this if we're going to fall on our face because we're on the wrong side of the law. We don't need to have a locked-in case—I'm willing to take a risk—but we need to have enough of a legal hook so a judge who wants to help us can hang his decision on it and have it stand up on appeal."

We talked about Bell's motive and their vulnerability in court. "I wondered why they called it a '$45 million rate increase,'" I said. "If they were going to raise rates based, as they say they are doing, on the increase in inflation, they would have said, 'Inflation has raised our costs x percent over the last two years, we expect it to be y percent this year, and so we're going to increase rates by x plus y percent to pass along these costs to our customers.' Instead, they said, in effect, 'We need to earn $45 million more every year, and there's nothing anybody can do to stop us.' So it's clear to me somebody in the home office in St. Louis, or maybe at AT&T in New York, just called up the Texas office in Dallas and told them they needed to come up with $45 million more in income to plug a hole in their budget.

"Then the guys in Dallas looked around and said, 'Well, this Gravitt -Ashley lawsuit is going to dry up the market for city council approval of local rate increases, the legislature is getting ready to pass a public utility commission law that could dry up our future rate increases, so our only hope is to hit our intrastate rates as hard as we can as quickly as we can—we need to get while the gettin's good!'

"That means they'll have to scramble if we take them to court and force them to justify this intrastate rate increase. If we start demanding their rate of return data on intrastate calls, I'll bet they don't even have any data—why would they? They can charge whatever they want and nobody can do a thing about it."[24]

While I believed Bell was clearly vulnerable on the issue of justifying their rate increase, we still needed to have enough law on our side to overcome the separation of powers issue. Not only did the constitution say the functions of the executive, legislative, and judicial branches must remain separate, it also attempts to cut off every possible means of circumventing that mandate. It makes clear that legislative acts requiring the exercise by the judiciary of legislative functions are unconstitutional. For good measure, it adds that a function of government that the legislature cannot delegate directly to the judiciary cannot be conferred indirectly. Setting a rate that a utility could charge was most definitely a legislative, and not a judicial, function. We knew that was Southwestern Bell's strongest argument. We wouldn't last two minutes in a courtroom unless we could make the judges feel comfortable in setting that issue aside.

I asked Willatt to chip away at that obstacle. He found enough cases involving utility rate challenges to support an argument that there was an important distinction between asking the court, on the one hand, to set the rate Southwestern Bell could charge and, on the other hand, asking the court to determine that Southwestern Bell's rate was unreasonable.

No, a court could not set a rate, we would argue, but yes, a court could determine if a rate was unfair—maybe so unfairly low as to jeopardize the utility financially or maybe so unfairly high as to force the customer to pay an excessive price. No, we were not asking the court to set an intrastate telephone rate, but yes, we were asking the court to find that the rate was higher than could be justified on the basis of what it cost Bell to provide the service. We believed these cases would keep Bell from knocking us out of court with the separation of powers issue.

The next hurdle to evaluate was our constitutional authority to sue a corporation that collected any toll "not authorized by law." Southwestern

Bell's intrastate tolls were not covered by any state or federal law. If there was no law governing these tolls, how could we allege that the toll was so high as to be "not authorized by law"?

That one was easy. There were plenty of cases holding that a utility that enjoyed a monopoly was obligated to charge rates that were nondiscriminatory and reasonable. Any toll that was unreasonable would fall under the definition of "not authorized by law."[25]

So far, so good. But that raised the question of how we would prove to the court that the rates were unreasonable. Because we lacked staff experience in telephone rate cases, our first step was to tap into the network of consulting firms hired by major cities in Texas to review rate requests from Southwestern Bell or other telephone companies. We checked with several cities for recommended consultants and settled on Pat Locanto at Touche Ross and Company in Dallas.

We knew our time frame was short because Southwestern Bell was almost ready to pull the trigger on its rate increase when I met with Hoverstock in December. Over the year-end holidays and into January, my staff pushed hard to prepare a lawsuit once the rate increase was announced.

Meanwhile, the negative news reports generated by the Gravitt -Ashley lawsuit's allegations of political slush funds for local and state politicians continued to pile up. Southwestern Bell's president, Zane Barnes, flew from St. Louis to San Antonio on an image-repairing effort in late December. "It seems like we're operating under a cloud," Barnes lamented. "Almost every day, new accusations of wrongdoing have come to the fore against the company."[26]

In Austin, a city council member resigned in January after testimony in the lawsuit revealed his public relations firm had accepted, in violation of the city charter, printing business from Southwestern Bell. Austin's mayor declared Bell's proposed rate increase for its Austin area a "dead issue" until Bell "cleaned up its dirty laundry." The mayor was particularly peeved that the Ashley-Gravitt lawsuit's evidence included an inner-office Bell memo on Austin political figures that claimed the mayor had asked Bell to increase the size of its Austin rate increase so the city council could grant the amount originally sought by Bell while claiming credit for reducing Bell's request.[27]

At mid-morning, January 30, 1975, we received a call from a news reporter in Dallas asking if we would have any comment on an announcement scheduled that afternoon by Southwestern Bell regarding an intrastate rate increase. I called Kendall and Willatt, and we quickly decided to hold a news conference at the state capitol after the Bell announcement.

At their news conference, Bell officials said the rate increase reflected a 20 percent increase in the cost of Texas operations since the last intrastate rate increase, which had been expected to generate $23 million a year beginning in September 1973. They projected a bottom line increase in operating revenues of 2.8 percent from the higher intrastate tolls.

All of their references to costs the rate increase was designed to offset confirmed our perception that they never viewed the increase as a means of offsetting solely the expenses in providing intrastate long-distance service. Instead, they were combining all of their costs from local, intrastate, and interstate services and applying the income from all of these services to the combined cost without allocating expenses among the services.

Bell's representative told reporters, who asked what portion of the company's claimed $667 million in facilities expansions in 1974 was devoted to long-distance calls inside Texas, that Bell didn't keep those figures. And, the representative said, Bell did not know what rate of return it received on long-distance service in Texas. Their comments clearly confirmed our hunch that they were unprepared to isolate intrastate costs to justify the intrastate rate increase.

Two hours later, I told the capitol press corps I would take Bell to court to prevent implementation of the increase: "The time has come in Texas for the attorney general, pursuant to his constitutional, statutory, and common law powers, to challenge this monopoly in the area of unregulated rates, as to whether these rates are reasonable and lawful," I said. "It seems to me that at a time of mounting recession, this proposed action will have a very substantial adverse economic impact on our state and the consumers." I laid the predicate for our theme in attacking the rate increase by asserting that Bell's action "raised a very legitimate question of whether these rates are being raised in unregulated areas to make up for raises being held up in cities" that placed a moratorium on local rate increases "because of the washing of Southwestern Bell's dirty laundry in public." In response to Bell's announcement that the new rate structure "can result in considerable savings to many people," I told the Austin news conference, "That statement should be put to the test of its accuracy." The need for a court test of this rate increase's reasonableness, I added, was also demonstrated by the fact Bell had implemented a $23 million intrastate long-distance rate increase just sixteen months earlier. I said I would go to court in the next several days to seek an injunction against the proposed increase, and I added, "Irreparable injury will be suffered by the consumers of Texas unless the injunction or restraining order is granted."[28]

Southwestern Bell responded immediately to my news conference. By the time I returned to my office in the state's Supreme Court building a half block from the capitol after I concluded my news conference, a telephone message slip showed a call from Bell's new Texas vice president, Charles Marshall. I returned the call and listened as he proposed that I delay filing a lawsuit until I allowed his staff to share with me the financial data they had used to justify their proposal. I agreed to delay the lawsuit and to meet with his staff. We set the meeting for early the next morning, January 31. I gathered Kendall and several other staff members to discuss our strategy.

"The ball is in their court," I told them. "Clearly, they will try to talk me out of filing the lawsuit. I don't see how I could agree to that on the basis of a brief meeting. On the other hand, I want to be reasonable. We don't want to be seen as rushing to judgment.

"Let's say we agree to give them a chance to prove their case. If we do agree to review their data, I don't feel comfortable doing it behind closed doors. That's just no way to handle the public's business. What would you think if we proposed that I give them an opportunity to present their information to me in an open hearing, with the right to cross-examine witnesses? I doubt they'll want to accord me that much authority over these rates, so they will decline, and then we can proceed to court as we planned."

We discussed it and agreed to give Bell a week to decide whether to present their case to me in a public hearing. If they failed to respond or rejected the hearing idea, we would file our lawsuit on February 7.[29]

Marshall's representatives at the meeting the next morning were Hoverstock; his general solicitor in Dallas, Ford W. Hall; and Will Sears, a Houston attorney who, as special counsel, represented Bell in rate cases. The press was following every development in this case, so I told my public information assistant to advise them that they could gather in my office in advance of our meeting.

With news reporters and photographers present, I showed the three to chairs in front of my desk, smiled, and told them, "I felt our paths would eventually cross." I then asked the press to leave and closed the door for a private discussion. I listened as they reviewed with me their Texas operating results and their requests for local rate increases in ten cities amounting to $47 million. They elaborated on their need for income to bolster their earnings, since they would be paying additional costs for interest on funds borrowed to finance expansion. So far, so good—their comments confirmed our expectation that they were not equipped to justify their rate increase and believed they owed an explanation to no one.

Next, they vigorously challenged my legal authority to intervene in this rate increase, as I expected them to. I was listening for any new angles our research had failed to produce, but I heard none. I respectfully disagreed with their view of the law on this issue, but I decided leave it at that and not go beyond the basics.

Then I offered them the option of a public forum in which to justify their rate increase, and if they declined, I promised to file a lawsuit next Friday to block the rate increase. I told them I wanted an ironclad assurance they would not try to speed up the rate increase. They confirmed they would not implement it before the announced March 1 date. They promised to have a full written justification the next week, and we agreed to conclude the meeting after two hours.

I met with waiting news reporters and told them the Bell officials "presented a picture to me which indicated the increases they are seeking in intrastate long distance charges are reasonable and necessary. But I advised them we had other information which cast doubt on whether they are reasonable and necessary."[30]

I also said this case reinforced the need for a state public utility commission, which had been proposed in legislation introduced in the House the previous day with signatures of one-third of the 150 members. The number of cosigners indicated strong support, but the House Speaker opposed the bill and Governor Briscoe did not support it. Lieutenant Governor Hobby and I were the lone state officeholders strongly advocating a public utility commission.

The press coverage of the two days of news conferences on the Bell rate increase clearly helped the legislation's proponents. According to a United Press International article published on February 2, "Perhaps the biggest boost to the statewide commission idea yet came Thursday when Hill announced he would oppose Bell's plans to raise long-distance telephone rates within Texas to gain an additional $45 million in annual revenue."[31]

Southwestern Bell's next move was to send to me on the following Wednesday, with copies to the press, an eight-page memorandum with five pages of charts that their cover letter said "fully justifies the adjustments in our intrastate long distance and wide area telephone service rates scheduled to become effective on March 1, 1975."[32] To us, the memo again confirmed the validity of our core argument: that the intrastate long-distance rate increase failed to meet the constitutional and statutory test of reasonableness because it was based not on the need to offset costs of intrastate long-distance service but on the need to subsidize the cost of local service.

Bell's conundrum was demonstrated by the memorandum's contradictory assertions. On page 1, the memo stated, "We want to make clear at the outset that this increase in intrastate charges was *not* motivated by the absence of considerable rate activity involving local exchanges." Their evidence to support that claim was equivocal because they could only express their intentions to "resolve as soon as possible" three major rate cases pending in Dallas, Fort Worth, and Austin. But then, in the section labeled "Concluding Thoughts" on the next to last page of text, they admitted that the intrastate long-distance rate increase was indeed based on a need to subsidize local service costs:

> The fundamental concept of providing telephone service to all customers in Texas is based on the idea that local exchange telephone service should be available to everyone who needs it and wants it at reasonable cost. . . . It is apparent to us, and to Commissions in other states, that a principal foundation for this concept of the universality of service is to keep basic exchange local service at a reasonably low level, and provide at least some of the revenues to accomplish this from other revenue sources, which are discretionary. Long distance rates, whether they be interstate or intrastate, are discretionary.[33]

The memo also contradicted itself on the issue of justifying the intrastate long-distance rates by analyzing income and expense data. The second page of the Bell memo stated that "after considerable study dating back to early 1974, we determined we must seek revenues in the third area, intrastate long distance service." That "considerable study" statement proved to offer an opening for us to exploit when we questioned Bell executives in depositions after our lawsuit was filed. But on the last page of the memo, the company said that any effort to separate out specific rates of return on specific segments of their business "would take many months and cost a great deal of money." They also argued that such segmented rate of return data is not required by law in most states because regulators' principal concerns are low-cost basic service and sufficient overall Bell earnings to support that service, regardless of where in the Bell system those earnings are developed.[34]

I called Kendall and several other staff members into my office to review the memo. "If we can get a court to agree with us that they need to justify their rate increase on the basis of intrastate long-distance income and expenses, we will win this case. They don't have a leg to stand on," I told them. "Their entire case will have to be based on the separation of powers issue, to block us from ever getting a court to hear our arguments. If we can overcome the jurisdiction question, this rate increase won't survive to our challenge." I urged them to finalize our lawsuit pleadings and work with Locanto to prepare a list of documents to request and witnesses to depose.

Even as Bell was trying to make its case in the newspapers to support the rate increase, their public relations problems caused by the Gravitt -Ashley case continued to haunt them. The same day they publicized their memo to me, Bell suffered another bad headline from a report of a deposition Maloney took from a Bell official in St. Louis about a South Texas hunting lease used by Bell to entertain politicians. The deposition revealed that about $250,000 of corporate funds were used to pay for expenses involved in operating the hunting facilities at a location near Uvalde.[35]

On the deadline day for our lawsuit, February 7, I reviewed our pleadings with the staff as we awaited Bell's response to my offer to avoid an immediate filing of a lawsuit if they would agree to justify their rate increase at an informal hearing I would conduct. Hoverstock and Ford kept an appointment with me that morning to tell us Marshall would announce at an afternoon news conference in Dallas that Bell would not agree to a hearing. I told them we would file our lawsuit immediately after his news conference.

After we received a report on Marshall's news conference, I called Mary Jane Bode, my public information assistant, and told her to alert the press that we were on our way to the courthouse. I grabbed Kendall and several other staff members, and we jumped into the car to drive the six blocks to the Travis County courthouse.

Because we were filing a motion for a temporary restraining order that demanded immediate attention, our case was picked up by the first judge available. It was our good fortune that, at four o'clock on a Friday afternoon, the judge of the 167th District Court was still in his office. His name was Tom Blackwell, a stocky, bald man with a quick grin and a jaunty bearing whom I knew as a gutsy former district attorney and World War II paratrooper presiding over a mostly criminal docket.

"Your Honor, our office was provided only a very scanty bit of information to justify these increases," I said to Blackwell as he scanned our petition stating the basis for my authority to bring this lawsuit and our allegations that Bell's rate increase was excessive and unreasonable.[36]

I wasn't sure what to expect from him. The audacity of this case excited and energized me, but it left many of my staff pessimistic that we could prevail. The $45 million price tag on the Bell rate increase and the fact that we were taking on the largest corporation in the world pushed this gamble into a high-stakes poker game—and the cards we were holding were far from being sure winners.

Our fate hinged almost entirely on the attitude of the judges hearing and reviewing our case. If Blackwell granted our petition reluctantly, we would be hard-pressed to develop an overwhelming case in the short lead time we could expect for a hearing on a temporary injunction. If he denied our petition, we would never even get out of the starting gate. We needed more than a noncommittal approval of our application. We needed a strong push to get this shaky case airborne in a hurry.

As all these thoughts were rushing through my head in the silence of the almost-empty courtroom, Blackwell nodded, picked up his pen, and raised his eyebrows in anticipation as he signed the temporary restraining order. It prohibited Bell from raising its intrastate long-distance rates pending outcome of a hearing on a temporary injunction. The order, which we drafted, set a hearing for February 18 on a temporary injunction.

Then came the magic words we so terribly needed to hear: "I believe you have every right to file this motion," Blackwell said. "It's the job of the attorney general to protect the state against what he believes to be arbitrary and illegal acts. I certainly agree with you that the state is entitled to maintain the status quo until this matter can be adjudicated."[37]

Our anxiety evaporated. We knew instantly our gamble had succeeded. We would win this case at the trial court level. Blackwell was signaling that he would grant the injunction unless we failed to arm him with adequate evidence to support it.

I tried to keep my ear-to-ear grin and elation under control as I answered questions from news reporters who gathered around me after Blackwell left the bench. "They're saying virtually in effect that there's no power on earth that can come in and make them give us a rate breakdown. But the plain fact is that there is a power, and it has been used in other states," I told them.[38]

The lawsuit generated immediate and favorable reactions everywhere except Southwestern Bell headquarters. The House passed on a vote of 87 to 48 a resolution supporting the lawsuit, saying the legislature "does hereby approve, ratify and authorize the action of the attorney general." The resolution's sponsor, Rep. Jim Nugent of Kerrville, said, "This is an attempt to tell the attorney general to get after it and find out if he can get a fair hearing."[39] The *Corpus Christi Times* said in an editorial, "Atty. Gen. John Hill may find he has no standing in court to challenge a $45-million increase in long-distance telephone rates. But it is at least heartening to have an attorney general who does not perpetually claim he has no jurisdiction to take action. . . . Hill didn't just lie low when a public utility announced a substantial rate increase at a time when the economy is in a deepening crisis."[40]

The ten days Blackwell had given us to gather enough evidence to support a temporary injunction was an extremely tight timeline for such a complex case. It was, however, typical for temporary injunction cases, and we were prepared to hit the ground running. Locanto helped us assemble a list of thirty-five financial documents to request from Bell to assess the validity of their justifications for the rate increase. He also helped us select Bell executives from which to request depositions. Blackwell granted our motions on both items the following Monday.

But Bell was not about to submit willingly to having their unfettered right to intrastate rate freedom brought to heel by our lawsuit. The day after Blackwell granted our discovery motions, Bell filed a motion to dismiss the lawsuit. Blackwell set a hearing for three days later, on February 14. The focus of Bell's strategy was to convince Blackwell he was incorrect in assuming jurisdiction in this case. We knew that was their strongest argument, because their rate-making process was so casual it could not withstand close scrutiny. That fact made it essential that we prevail on this issue. Our strategy was to provide Blackwell enough prior court rulings and statutory law references to allow him to justify assuming jurisdiction, which we knew from his initial actions he was determined to do.

At the hearing on Bell's motion to dismiss, Will Sears's frustration at his disadvantage in trying to undo Blackwell's actions was compounded by his dismay over our having the upper hand in a lawsuit he believed completely without merit. A former city attorney in Houston with extensive experience in rate cases on both sides of the issues, Sears's expertise and the economic might of his client produced a haughty, bombastic style in his legal briefs and in his courtroom demeanor, reflecting the arrogance of Bell's imperious management.[41]

Sears opened the hearing by presenting Blackwell and me with copies of a list of twenty-four actions by Bell to revise intrastate long-distance rates since 1926. When he attempted to hand me my copy, I ignored his gesture and allowed the document to flutter to the floor as he told Blackwell,

"No attorney general, including the honorable John Hill, has ever claimed the power claimed in this lawsuit."[42]

Reciting his litany of reasons why our lawsuit failed to qualify for legal legitimacy, Sears's voice rose in volume as his indignation grew. Utility rates can only be set by legislative action, he said, and I was "attempting to smuggle legislative power through the back door of this court." Pointing at me, Sears almost shouted, "His entire argument is 'There ought to be a remedy, and, Judge Blackwell, fashion one and put it into the statute.' "[43]

I responded, my voice also rising in the heat of the argument, "If they're right, then we're in the preposterous position of admitting the public has a right to be charged a reasonable rate, but no one can enforce that right. . . . The real reason they don't want a hearing is that they can't justify these rates."[44]

At the conclusion of the hearing, Blackwell sucked all the air out of Bell's case by ruling from the bench that he was denying their motion to dismiss. In his ruling, he adopted our constitutional authority argument and our citation of a law passed in 1905, one that gave district courts authority to abolish "all extortionate and unreasonable rates charged by a public utility corporation." To make certain his intent was clear, he also commented that Bell frequently used the courts to challenge decisions of municipalities when they considered rates too low. By the same token, he said, the courts should be available to challenge rates set by the telephone company that are considered too high.[45]

Armed with Blackwell's nearly carte blanche support for our case, we contacted the Bell attorneys the next Monday, February 17, the day before our hearing on the temporary injunction, to implement our discovery. They were still in a state of disbelief over Blackwell's rulings. They firmly believed they were legally and politically beyond my reach. They fully expected my lawsuit to be laughed out of court. In the depositions, the Bell executives and their attorneys were incredulous of our snooping into their business. The idea that the inner workings of the telephone company could be subject to such detailed questioning, on such short notice, by the attorney general was clearly irritating to them.

When my assistants questioned them about the "considerable study dating back to 1974" that they claimed was performed to devise their revised intrastate rates, their responses clearly showed the words were hyperbole. All of our questions seeking justification for the rate increase were greeted with their amazement that we failed to understand that there was no statutory or business reason to calculate a rate of return on intrastate tolls.

The picture they painted was the one we had imagined: they needed to use their freedom available in unregulated intrastate rates to plug a hole in their budget that resulted from inadequate income from their other two sources that were both tightly regulated—local service rate increases and an interstate long-distance rate increase they had filed with the Federal Communications Commission in January.[46]

But the depositions also paid us an unexpected bonus. When we pressed one of the Dallas assistant vice presidents for an explanation of how they arrived at the amount of the intrastate rate increase, he handed us a smoking gun: the Dallas staff, he said, had proposed to the St. Louis home office a $30 million rate increase. The home office, however, sent back word that Texas should increase intrastate rates by $45 million.

"How did you finally come up with the $45 million figure for the proposed increase?" my assistant, Danny Goforth, asked the crusty Bell financial vice president, a company employee for more than forty years.

To Goforth's surprise, the Bell official replied, "That figure was developed by the rate group in St. Louis and was given to me." When Goforth pressed him as to what numbers he and the St. Louis staff discussed, he answered, "I told him we needed something in excess of 30 million."[47]

Thus, we had confirmation that the home office was the source of the rate increase, with the additional revelation that the home office pumped up the numbers even beyond what the Texas staff believed necessary.

There wasn't much time to celebrate this revelation's major boost to our case or to celebrate a Texas Supreme Court ruling handed down during our depositions: Sears's forty-two-page diatribe seeking dismissal of our lawsuit was rejected by the court less than an hour after it was filed in Austin.[48] Trial before Judge Blackwell was set for the next afternoon.

Introduction into the court record of the depositions and written evidence took all afternoon and the next morning, at which time I questioned our only witness, Locanto. His testimony was based on his review of all of the documents submitted by Bell and his attendance at all of the depositions. Even though this information had come piling in upon us in the preceding several days, he was comfortable expressing his opinions about the issues raised by the rate increase.

When I asked Locanto whether he had an opinion about whether the rates proposed by Bell were unreasonable, Sears sprang from his chair to protest: "I object to that, Your Honor, as calling for a conclusion of the witness upon insufficient data in this record. There has been nothing produced before Your Honor to show what the present rate is, what the future rate is, or anything by the State, who still has the burden of proof in this case, even on temporary injunction, to produce factual data before any expert can express an opinion on it. Whether Mr. Locanto is an expert or not, no expert can express an opinion upon data that's not in the record."[49]

Blackwell allowed me to pursue this line of questioning, with Sears raising objections eleven times in a twenty-five-minute span. I took Locanto through the steps in his review of the rate proposal. By using data from the recent Houston local exchange rate increase hearing, he calculated that Bell's intrastate rates would be producing a rate of return of about 20 percent. That was double the number Charles Marshall had used in his deposition when asked what percentage increase he would request if he were making his case to a regulatory commission. Then I referred Locanto to the Bell executive's deposition involving the Dallas office's $30 million increase, which was bumped up to $45 million by the St. Louis home office.

"You've been around a lot of rate cases and you've seen things happen in rate utility situations. Is that highly unusual without any additional back-up or explanation?" I asked Locanto. Sears objected, his vexation evident.

"It's nothing but a jury speech on the part of the Attorney General," he complained. But Blackwell overruled him, and Locanto answered, "The significance to me. . . was that the $30 million which was recommended in itself was not justified with any facts that the witness produced during his deposition. . . . In all of the rate cases I have been involved in, I have never seen a company request, or a commission grant, a rate of return to a utility anywhere in the vicinity of 20 percent."

I asked Locanto to expand on that point, and he added, "I see no way but to create an intrastate toll rate base, revenues, expenses, taxes, and a rate of return before anyone can determine that this increase is not unreasonable. . . . In other states, obviously, when they apply for an increase, . . . they will present a very detailed, direct case and justification for the requested increase." Despite the fact the state requested information on this point, he said that "to this date, the company has not furnished the information that would be required to calculate the numbers I feel that are required to justify such a rate increase."

What about, I asked him, the company's justification for the rate increase based on their plans for a $700 million construction program to improve their facilities? "Assuming that they are earning a fair rate of return, that fair rate of return will provide the earnings which will attract capital, and if the fair rate of return is achieved by existing rates, no increase would be required, and the existence of that construction budget would not impact the particular increase at this time," he said.

At last we reached the point in Locanto's testimony where we filled in the last blank space on our to-do list—his crystal-clear declaration that this rate increase was excessive. "Would you now state to the court," I said with a bit of added flourish, "your professional opinion as to whether the rate increase proposed by the Bell Telephone Company for $45 million for intrastate long distance telephone toll is probably unreasonable or not?"

Sears sat bolt upright and unleashed a full two minutes of objections: "We have nothing but this witness's speculation as to certain rates of return that he has made from his hasty examination of these depositions and from the document which we say is not even properly before him, the presentation to the Attorney General. . . . We don't think this question is a proper question nor is the witness qualified to answer it."

Blackwell overruled him, and Locanto gave us the words Blackwell needed to have in the record to justify his inevitable ruling in our favor: "In my opinion, based on the documents I have analyzed, the depositions which I have both heard and read, I believe that there is a strong probability that the rate increase is unreasonable."

That was the conclusion of our case. Sears offered no witnesses, telling Blackwell, "We submit, Your Honor, that the defendant in this case has no case to answer, that the plaintiff has wholly failed to make out the case that the law requires it to make out. . . . They have not carried out their burden of proof. And when the State enters the court, it has the same burden of proof as anybody else. We rest."

I closed our presentation by telling Blackwell, "Your Honor, I express my amazement at the defendant's resting without any evidence. . . . Our burden here was simply to show the Court probable right and probable injury. . . . Mr. Sears gave the case away, I think, . . . when he said to Mr. Locanto, 'Well, do you mean if we—let's assume we are charging 16 or 17 or maybe 20 percent in this $45 million to those people that are going to be using this service. Where else are we going to get it?'

"He gave the case away by apparently revealing the attitude of the company, which is, I think, the heart and root of this case, that they made the management decision as to the amount of gross dollars they wanted to come up with. And this was just a good place to—a little more fertile field."

I concluded by assuring Blackwell that "we have put before you the kind of solid information far beyond what one would normally expect on temporary injunction, and we respectfully request that it be granted."[50]

Sears's rebuttal was a five-minute tirade against the whole concept of the lawsuit. "The company has its obligation under its general undertaking to provide good service," Sears said. "It has its obligations to its stockholders. Low rates are not the be-all and end-all of regulation, and we don't concede that this Court is the place for regulation.

"Nor do we concede that the Attorney General has been appointed by the Constitution as a regulator. Now, we say, Your Honor, that there has not been one justiciable fact put into the record from that witness stand. The opinion of this last witness is just simply that. It is an opinion, a painting stuck out there to resemble facts so that there can be a pretense of facts presented to Your Honor to make a case. His opinion is not a fact. It can never be a fact. It is not based upon facts."

Sears told Blackwell our case was based on the impractical notion that Bell should seek higher local service rates rather than look to the intrastate rates to meet its financial needs. "The company cannot possibly go back and do the very thing that this witness by his backward calculation would have us do and, that is, institute rate proceedings from one end of this entire state to the other in every exchange to raise the exchange rates to every residential customer so as to lower what this man says is a rate upon the intrastate toll plant that is not reasonable," he said.

"You are being asked, Your Honor, to say upon the basis of assumption, hypothesis, surmise and conjecture that this company, in order to get the money that it needs to operate in a period of double-digit inflation, which nobody has troubled to deny, that we have got to go back and get the money from the residential customers. That's the Attorney General's case and that's all there is to it in this case," Sears concluded.[51]

Sears sat down and Blackwell leaned forward to address us from the bench. After complimenting both sides on overcoming the constraints of a short time period in which to prepare complex issues and present an understandable case, he began listing his concerns. "The first item I became concerned about developed from the evidence that I have heard is the failure of the State of Texas to have a Public Service Commission with the authority to regulate intrastate rates," he said. "And to me, this is a ridiculous situation when all the other states have it. . . . And with the Legislature in session, I hope they'll take note of the need of the State of Texas to have a Public Service Commission."

Blackwell's second concern was an issue we did not exploit. Referring to a list of interstate and intrastate tolls between various cities, he noted that a two-hundred-mile call from Austin to Houston was more expensive than a four-hundred-mile call from Austin to Lake Charles, Louisiana. "I certainly realize that Texas does not have anything to say about the rates imposed by the FCC, but the Court would have to take knowledge that the FCC has heard testimony and evidence and has authorized a fair return on their investment and in setting their rates that you'd have to assume that the FCC operated properly and that the rates set were reasonable, but, yet, the Texas rates, not being overlooked by any regulatory agency, are much higher for intrastate telephone calls," he said.

Blackwell's third and fourth points put the final nails in Bell's coffin. His third concern was the Bell executive's revelation that the Dallas office's recommendation for a $30 million intrastate toll increase came back from the St. Louis home office raised to $45 million with no rationale. "That method of procedure, which was not made open to the public or the State of Texas or to the citizens of the State of Texas and was made in the offices in St. Louis, seems to me to be unreasonable," he said. His fourth item was Locanto's testimony that the rate increase was unreasonable. He concluded by granting our request to enjoin Bell from "raising its intrastate long distance rates pending the final hearing in this lawsuit."[52]

The uplift our case received from Blackwell's ruling was enhanced the following day when the Texas Senate, with only three "nay" votes, adopted the House-passed resolution supporting our lawsuit.[53]

Blackwell's ruling was termed by the press as precedent setting. We considered that a positive accomplishment, but Bell's lawyers thought otherwise. In his appeal to the Third Court of Appeals, Sears derided our case and Blackwell's decision. "There is no jurisdiction in any court to fix a rate. This is an unheard-of proceeding," he told the court in arguments on April 2, adding, "There's never been a hearing like this in Texas in any court." He characterized our case as "virtually unintelligible from a legal standpoint" because it failed to define a rate level that was reasonable and therefore gave no basis for a finding that the proposed rate was unreasonable. Willatt argued our response to the appeals court, using an argument that was to later allow us to score a telling point with the state Supreme Court. Noting that Bell contended the state can challenge rates only where they are discriminatory, Willatt said that under that reasoning, "They could charge $300 a minute to call from Austin to Round Rock, so long as they charge everybody that rate."[54]

I knew from this court's prior decisions that it was less likely to look favorably on our case than the Supreme Court would, so I limited my comments at the hearing to a few summary points I hoped would shame them from what I perceived to be a strong predisposition to rule against us. "I'm sort of speechless. I've been practicing law 27 years and I've always looked for the perfect case, where you have all the law on your side and you have all the facts on your side," I told the three justices, adding that this case fit that definition.[55]

I also stressed that Bell had failed to present any evidence or witnesses during Blackwell's hearing: "If they can't, from their biased position think of anything to present in an evidentiary way, why would they suppose three distinguished jurists of this state not beholden to anybody will bail them out?"[56]

Our arguments failed to overcome the court's antipathy toward us. The appeals court on May 14 issued a ruling overturning Blackwell's decision and dissolving the temporary injunction.[57] Within hours of the decision, Bell announced it would begin collecting its increased intrastate rates the next day.[58]

I was outraged, and I expressed that feeling in a news conference. I angrily pledged to appeal the case to the Supreme Court. "If this ruling is correct, if the courts have no jurisdiction to end unreasonably high rates, then we're left in the ludicrous position that the telephone company can promulgate any rule, any rate of its own choosing without any basis other than a desire to make money. This is raw, monopolistic power. I do not believe that situation is the law," I told the news reporters. "This is still, in my opinion, a perfect case. We expect to win, and when we win, the people will win." Taking note of the legislature's adjournment date only two weeks away and its failure to pass a public utility commission bill, I called on Texans to contact their legislators. "I'm talking about right now. Tell them the people of this state are totally at the mercy of any corporation." The legislature needs to enact a "realistic, effective, public-interest utility regulation bill," I said. To do otherwise "would be unthinkable."[59]

My fulminations against the appeals court and Bell attracted plenty of attention. Lieutenant Governor Hobby joined my cause, telling reporters the appeals court ruling was "the strongest evidence yet of the need for a public utilities commission. I applaud Atty. Gen. Hill's effort to interpose the authority of the state to protect its citizens against the rate increase. It is more obvious than ever that the creation of a utilities commission is the best way to provide this protection."[60]

One of the capitol press corps's senior writers, Jon Ford of the Fentress Newspapers group, which owned newspapers in such places as Austin, Waco, and Port Arthur, advised readers of his popular Sunday column that

> Atty. Gen. John Hill is the only one of state government's Big 3 politicians who is coming through looking like much more than an amiable bumbler. Neither Governor Dolph Briscoe nor Lieutenant Governor Bill Hobby has been able to shine in the all-clown cast around the capitol these days. . . . While Briscoe and Hobby were having control of the school finance issue snatched from their hands by the teacher lobby and its legislative lieutenants last week, Hill actually was taking his lumps too. . . .
>
> But Hill, in defeat, managed to come on like Gang Busters and a Marine landing, denouncing "raw, monopolistic power," pledging to continue the legal fight and urging citizens, meanwhile, to lobby with their legislators for "realistic" utility regulation. He couldn't convince the court that he had "the perfect case," as he claimed. But those who watched his TV news clips following the judicial reverse saw a guy who seemed to be trying earnestly to exert some leadership and initiative in the public interest.

Comparing my high visibility in Austin with Comptroller Bob Bullock's, Ford said we both "seem to share the philosophy that the best way to look good to the voters is to do a good job. Hill is still ahead on points for finesse and hardnosed leadership quality, and he may be hard to catch."[61]

My push to pass a utility commission bill was definitely needed, with the two houses stalemated over the stronger House bill and the weaker Senate bill and no push from Governor Briscoe to pass a bill. Just hours before the session adjourned on June 2, a viable compromise bill was produced and passed into law.[62]

The new Public Utility Regulatory Act would in the future solve the problem of unregulated intrastate telephone rates. But creating the regulatory commission and equipping it to enforce the new law would take at least a year. During that time, Bell would still be able to raise intrastate rates at will unless we prevailed in the Supreme Court.

To secure our authority in these types of cases, our first task was to stop Bell from collecting the higher intrastate tolls it had implemented on May 15. We knew the state's Supreme Court would agree with us that the appeals court should not have dissolved the temporary injunction pending outcome of the appeals, but state law required us to exhaust our appeals to the appeals court before we could quality for Supreme Court action.

We jumped through those hoops as fast as the courts could respond, winning a Supreme Court order on June 4 to reinstate the temporary injunction. Our second job was to obtain a Supreme Court ruling affirming our authority to bring, and district courts' authority to decide, these types of cases. We won another Supreme Court order expediting the hearing on our appeal of the appeals court's reversal of Blackwell's order. Arguments were set for June 18, and I was anxious to go head-to-head with Sears before a tribunal that clearly displayed its distaste for Bell's overreaching on this rate case.

The hearing was even more enjoyable than I had hoped it would be. I opened the argument with a full-bore blast at Bell. I recalled the damaging evidence Goforth had elicited from Bell executive Sam Holcomb about their Dallas office's proposal for a $30 million increase in rates and the additional $15 million demanded by the St. Louis home office. "They just got greedy. These rates border on the extortionist side," I told the court. "They choose to reach out and say 'we're going to get more money because nobody can stop it.' It reminds you of the Arabs and foreign oil."

To dramatize the folly of Bell's contention that no court could interfere with their intrastate rates regardless of the amount of the rate, I repeated the example Willatt had cited to the appeals court, reducing his three hundred dollars per minute to a one-hundred-dollar per minute charge for a call between Austin and Round Rock, a town less than thirty miles from Austin.

Sears had barely launched his response argument when the justices started peppering him with questions. "Was there at least a prima facie case of unreasonableness?" asked Justice Zollie Steakley. "No sir, there was not," Sears replied.[63]

"Could you impose a rate increase of 1,000 percent?" Steakley asked.

When Sears did not directly answer the question, Chief Justice Joe Greenhill broke in: "A thousand dollars a minute from here to Temple, is that unreasonable?"

Sears was trapped and could only agree with that outlandish prospect by responding, "If the company is so foolish and didn't care about staying in business." Greenhill asked Sears about the $30 million increase being bumped up to $45 million, and Sears replied, "The man who testified to that was not even a department head. The attorney general has tried to make a big thing out of it."

Greenhill asked him, "You made no attempt to rebut his testimony?" Sears's lame response was, "We have nothing to rebut." Sears's comments were so damaging, I was impatient for him to finish so I could dismantle his case on rebuttal.

"Our attorneys took depositions from seven executives in the Dallas office of Southwestern Bell to determine the basis for this rate increase, and every one of them would defer to Mr. Holcomb. And then they make the ridiculous statement that he's 'just a department head,' " I said, drawing laughter from the completely filled courtroom.

Recalling Sears's response to Greenhill's question about the thousand-dollar per minute call from Austin to Temple, I told the court, "It's the first time that it has been made clear the telephone company feels it has unlimited power. They admit they cannot discriminate between customers, but they can charge what they want to otherwise. They're saying, 'We can pick everybody's pocket as long as we do it equally.' "

Press coverage of the hearings was devastating to Bell. The *Houston Post* headlined its story "SW Bell Accused of Greed." "Calls Actions Bordering on the Extortionist/Hill Hits Bell 'Rate Power Belief' " was the *Austin American-Statesman* headline. The *Corpus Christi Caller* headlined its story, "Lawyer Admits Bell Can Charge What It Likes."

The most damning article was Stuart Davis's column in the *Dallas Morning News,* whose editorial page was strongly pro-business. Under a headline of "Arrogance by SW Bell," Davis opened his commentary, "Southwestern Bell Telephone Co. this week displayed the kind of corporate arrogance that is causing it problems in the Legislature and the courts, while creating a jaundiced view in the public eye." He quoted several of Sears's insensitive comments and wrote that "the usually unflappable Supreme Court justices seemed literally startled to hear Sears argue that the company legally could charge $1,000 a minute for in-state long distance calls (if it thinks consumers would pay that much) without anyone being able to challenge such a charge. If Southwestern Bell's actions cannot be challenged in the courts, we have a corporate monster loose in our society, stronger than the sovereign state that allows it to do business." He concluded his commentary, which took up a whole column of type: "If Southwestern Bell has nothing to hide, it should quit acting like the only phone company in town, get off its high horse and explain specifically why it needs higher rates."[64]

Sears was so stung by my domination of the courtroom arguments that he used the final page in Bell's sixty-two-page post-submission brief to whine to the court,

> Throughout this case, the Attorney General has attempted to "bootstrap" the State's case by extravagant speeches to the effect that, if the injunction were not permitted, the Company would charge unheard-of tolls, using, at one point, the example of "$100.00 from Austin to Round Rock." This is just another example of the attempt (plainly stated in his Petition) to persuade the court to *legislate* on public policy. . . . During oral argument before this Honorable Court, the Company was subjected to a diatribe by the Attorney General in which the Company was accused of saying that it could "pick pockets" so long as it "picked pockets" equally; was charged with being "greedy" and was compared to the Arab nations charging for foreign oil. When questioned about the Company's motion to modify the injunction to allow the rates to be put in under bond, his only response was that he hoped that the Court would "stay with the people." As a result, the Company was subjected to widespread, unjust and lurid publicity to which it could not respond, in view of this lawsuit. It hardly needs to be said that calumny is not argument; and it needs even less to be said that the people can only be served when the courts *and* the Attorney General "stay with" THE LAW.[65]

The Supreme Court's opinion, handed down July 9, left nothing to chance. In affirming Blackwell's ruling, it supported and elaborated on all of our key arguments. There was not a crumb of support to be found for Bell's positions.

Willatt's discovery of the constitutional provision allowing me to sue a corporation to prevent collection of tolls "not authorized by law" was confirmed and set in stone:

> It is our further opinion that the Constitution of Texas confers on the Attorney General the authority to institute and maintain suit in the name of the State to restrain Bell from exacting unreasonably high charges for its intrastate telephone services in Texas, if such be the case. . . . It is self-evident, in our view, that the demand and collection by Bell of unreasonably high—and hence unlawful—charges for the use of its intrastate telephone service by the people of Texas would

> be an abuse of its corporate power as a public utility, the prevention of which would subserve the public interest. The Attorney General is authorized to take action in the courts to enjoin this being done.[66]

Despite this unequivocal rejection of Bell's case, Sears filed a condescending motion for rehearing that fully utilized his almost comically bombastic writing style to denote emphasis. Standard office word processing equipment in the 1970s was an IBM Selectric typewriter that offered different typefaces on interchangeable ball-shaped elements that had to be manually removed and replaced with each font change. His motion for rehearing opened with this windy statement:

> The real effect of this Court's holdings is this: Although this Company, in common with many others, has been lawfully empowered by the Legislature to fix its own rates, it must now do so under *the constant threat* that the Attorney General (1) will immediately file a petition (which can be, as here, almost completely devoid of facts); (2) will promptly secure a temporary restraining order; (3) will then proceed with the facade of a "hearing" (in which the Attorney General has no real burden of proof and need only produce an "expert" to recite that, in his opinion, there is a strong probability that the proposed rate is unreasonably high); and (4) will then succeed in enjoining the Company from obtaining the needed revenues; *all of this, without ANY regard to the irretrievable losses to the Company and to its ability to properly perform its public function, which damage could easily be prevented by the elementary and equitable remedy of the refunding bond or agreement!*[67]

While Sears was blowing off steam with meaningless motions before the Supreme Court, I contacted Marshall to initiate a compromise agreement on an intrastate rate increase. Marshall and I began our negotiations in my office on July 17. He reluctantly agreed to provide us the financial data they initially refused to give us.

Using that information, Locanto prepared a proposed intrastate rate increase of about $25 million. It also committed Bell to forgo any other intrastate rate increases until after the new public utilities commission was up and running in September 1976. We sent the proposal to Marshall, and he and Ford Hall met with me on August 8 to complete the negotiations process. We submitted the rate proposal to Judge Blackwell, and he approved the rate increase at a hearing on August 11.[68]

I was disappointed that Marshall and Hall continued to complain about their financial predicament. Hall told Blackwell bitterly that Bell was "deprived of its day in court" to fight our lawsuit in a permanent injunction hearing because the cost to Bell in lost revenue was too great. "The cold, hard mathematical facts are we are better off financially to accept lower rates now than to fight the case in court. We can now begin collecting about $100,000 a day," Hall said. He predicted the reduced rate increase would cause cutbacks in construction and staff. After Hall finished, I told Blackwell dismissively, "I think any man is entitled to make a $50 million propaganda speech, and I'm not going to reply to it."[69]

A year later, I used our experience in this case to intervene before the new Public Utility Commission in its consideration of a Bell request to increase by $298 million rates affecting all services except interstate long-distance calls. The commission approved a $58 million rate increase in December 1976, and I defended its decision in Bell's appeals all the way to the Texas Supreme Court.

But it was that first case in 1975 that gave me the greatest sense of accomplishment. We had bested one of the most powerful corporations in the United States by outsmarting and outworking them, just the way I used to win personal injury cases when I was just starting my law practice. This case had taken me back to my roots as a trial attorney and allowed me to live up to my campaign promise to the voters that I would be one hell of a tenacious advocate for them.

(5)

Corralling Maverick Child Care Home Operators

I focused on consumer and environmental protection during my first year as attorney general because the abuses in those areas cried out for attention but were ignored by our state's leaders in deference to business lobbyists. I quickly learned there were other abuses that also cried out for attention but simply were not heard because they could not compete against all the other issues that held our attention.

Such was the case of a stealth industry that had sprung up almost entirely unnoticed in the late 1960s and early 1970s to accommodate parents, social service agencies, and courts unprepared for the tidal wave of teenage runaways. I was caught unaware, as were most state government leaders, when this issue exploded in the summer of my first term.

Governmental regulation of these facilities for troubled youth was scant, allowing many of them to be owned and operated by untrained or unqualified amateurs unprepared for the level of physical and psychological challenges posed by the often turbulent personalities of these young people. Occasionally in self-defense or fear, often because they succumbed to frustration at their inability to cope, and perhaps because they were overcome by the temptation to punish a vulnerable younger person, the keepers of these facilities sometimes resorted to brutality.

Regrettably, the state's fledgling efforts to protect children in these privately managed facilities sometimes were compromised by a combination of factors. These included political interference, an ambiguous attitude in state government toward aggressive enforcement of regulatory laws, and parents so desperate to solve a problem with a child that they turned a blind eye to evidence of abuse or approved of its use as a deserved punishment for misbehavior.[1]

The increasing number of runaways was a by-product of the social upheaval of the 1960s, which unmoored many teenagers from the disciplined home life their parents had known. Use of marijuana, methamphetamines, LSD, and other mood-altering drugs by young people was popularized by countercultural entertainers, journalists, and political activists in the 1960s. Oral contraceptives became available in the early 1960s, freeing young people from most of society's inhibitions about premarital sexual relations.

New legal rights for women, along with growing employment opportunities, helped launch the women's liberation movement during this era. The divorce rate in Texas increased 28 percent from 1960 to 1970. Pushed by the passage in 1967 of a no-fault divorce law, the rate had jumped another 13 percent by 1972.[2] A *TIME* magazine cover story in 1970 chronicled the establishment of about three thousand "hippie" communes catering to alternative lifestyles.[3]

School dropouts resulting from by this turmoil quickly overwhelmed traditional social service and law enforcement facilities. Into this void stepped entrepreneurs such as Joseph D. Farrar of Houston. His unsuccessful career in college administration was followed by a job as a high school music teacher while he counseled students as a private sideline. He converted this off-hours job into a full-time business by advertising himself as a psychologist, in violation of a state law limiting that designation to holders of a PhD from an accredited university. As the business grew, he expanded the operation into a day school for students with learning and behavioral problems, a facility he never licensed with the state, and then a rural residential facility northeast of Houston, which he also declined to license with the state.[4]

Farrar's world had begun to unravel on Mother's Day, 1971. Charles "Sonny" Huey, a fifty-year-old deputy game warden responsible for patrolling an area in northeast Liberty County near the southern edge of the Big Thicket National Preserve, was driving near the tiny community of Rosemary when he received a mid-morning call on his car radio from a deputy sheriff in Cleveland, about ten miles away. He asked Huey to help find several runaways from a troubled teenagers' residential facility near Rayburn named Artesia Hall. This area of the state about forty-five miles northeast of Houston was densely wooded pine forests with small towns scattered along railroad lines and highways.

As Huey began his search along narrow roads crisscrossing the area, he spotted a girl running across a road and into the woods. He stopped his car, jumped out, started walking slowly, and began calling out to the girl, warning her of rattlesnakes and copperheads that could kill with one strike. He soon spotted a girl crouching in a briar patch about twenty-five yards away.

He reassured her that he was there to help, and he urged her to come to him. She started crying and begging him not to take her back to Artesia Hall—to take her to jail or someplace else where she could get help. He promised to take her to the jail in Liberty, where she could talk to the sheriff. She was quickly joined by two other girls hiding nearby, also both sobbing and pleading with him not to return them to Artesia Hall.[5]

Huey's innocently compassionate decision to take the girls about thirty-five miles south to Liberty, instead of back to Artesia Hall or seven miles west to Cleveland, where the Artesia Hall staff would have quickly retrieved them, set in motion a series of events that led to Farrar's downfall and a crisis in the state's regulation of privately owned facilities for juveniles.

Farrar had opened the facility seven months earlier so quietly that it was unknown in Liberty, the county seat located at the opposite end of the county from Artesia Hall. The culture of the "Piney Woods" areas of Texas in those days was small-town rural, uninfluenced by the urban malaise that locals believed made Houston an unsuitable place to rear a family or live a normal life. Cleveland and Liberty were towns of about fifty-five hundred. Everybody knew everybody else. The surprise appearance of a mysterious disciplinary home for wayward teenagers in their quiet communities was big, and unwelcome, news.

Farrar set up Artesia Hall in October 1970 on twenty-two acres of cleared forest land with one five-bedroom residence. He accepted two teenage girls as his first residents and hired a middle-aged farm couple to act as staff. He told parents who brought their children to him for help that there was no child so unruly as to be beyond his abilities to straighten him or her out. He wanted the worst of the worst because he was certain he could subdue them. As the number of enrollees grew, he added portable buildings and mobile homes.

Farrar built tall cyclone fences around several of the student dormitories and topped the fence with barbed wire. Anticipating that his eagerness to accept the most rebellious students would produce some kids requiring a humiliating isolation cell, Farrar ordered a five-by-five-foot concrete slab poured in the corner of one of the fences, and the other two sides were fenced to create a "cage" for detaining severely disruptive residents. His

East Texas neighbors would soon be referring to Artesia Hall disdainfully as a "concentration camp."

Farrar's plan was to keep these kids away from drugs, keep them busy with odd jobs and minimal classroom learning, impose a rigorous disciplinary regimen, and assume they would shed enough hostility to return to their families. For this therapy to be effective, he advised parents that they would have limited visiting times and that students' incoming and outgoing mail would be reviewed to screen out any information that would diminish his control over the environment. For a fee of at least four hundred dollars monthly and a minimum of a one-year contract, the parents could hand over to Farrar their vexing problem and buy some peace of mind.[6]

The harrowing tales of physical abuse at Artesia Hall the three hysterical runaways showered on Huey during his forty-five-minute drive to Liberty infuriated him. A father of children the same ages as these girls, he was outraged at the wanton cruelty they described. They told of girls being punished by being grabbed by the hair and shaken so violently that chunks of hair were torn from their scalps as they were slung against furniture with enough force to knock it over.

They said a common disciplinary action was hacking off a girl's hair with scissors applied unevenly to make clear it was not a professional haircut. They described "G.I. baths" in which a student would be immersed in unheated water in a large pail used to feed the livestock and scrubbed with a stiff brush or scouring pad wielded by other students. They described a climate of fear produced by the system of rewarding students who reported misbehavior by other students. And, even though they said they had seen no one locked in the "cage" in the corner of the fence, they described it to Huey and said it was cited by the staff as a punishment they could receive.

At the jail in Liberty, Farrar and one girl's parents arrived about the same time, Farrar barking to the county officials that the girls were liars and he needed to take them back to Artesia Hall. The deputy released the girl to her parents, who immediately turned her over to Farrar. The girl clutched her sister and sobbed that she did not want to go back to Artesia Hall. Farrar pulled a pair of handcuffs out of his pocket, put them on the girl, grabbed her by the hair and, with the father helping, forcefully began escorting her to his station wagon. Her legs gave way, so they dragged and carried her down the outside steps like a limp rag doll. Huey and a deputy sheriff were standing on the steps when they passed by.

"Wait a minute," the deputy said. "We don't treat dogs like that around here. You better straighten up because you might end up upstairs locked up yourself." Farrar and the father straightened the girl upright and continued toward Farrar's automobile.[7]

It was that image of Farrar dragging the girl to his car, and not the runaways' troubled personal histories, which was to dog Farrar when he sought acceptance among Liberty County citizens.

The three runaways included one who was seventeen when Farrar brought her in handcuffs to Artesia Hall from Houston just a few days earlier. Her life experiences were not those of a typical seventeen-year-old. Her parents placed her under a psychiatrist's care for three years, with treatment that included electroshock therapy. When she continued to rebel against them, they arranged through Farrar for her to be admitted to Mount St. Michael School in Dallas. She stayed there only two weeks before locking up some nuns in the fenced swimming pool area to facilitate her escape with two other girls. The three of them hung out with friends in Austin, then Houston, then on the beach in Galveston in some boys' mini-van, then Atlanta, Georgia, for a week to attend a rock music festival. They were using LSD provided by the boys. She ended up back in Dallas, where she was arrested for possessing methamphetamines and sent back to Houston for treatment in a drug rehabilitation program.

After several weeks in Houston, she ran away to join friends for a trip to Florida. After spending four days in jail there on drug charges, she met some new kids on the beach and camped out with them for several weeks, again using drugs. Then she went back to Houston and stayed with a boy she had met at a drug treatment program. When she contacted her mother, her mother arranged for Farrar to take her to Artesia Hall. At Artesia Hall, she quickly ran afoul of the rules and was told her discipline, to be administered the next day, would be to have her prized waist-length hair cut. To avoid that punishment, she joined four other girls the next morning to sneak out before breakfast.[8]

Their escape and capture soon became a source of deep concern to Clarence Cain, the county's sole district judge. Although he was only in his third year on the bench, the fifty-six-year-old Cain's service on the city council, as county attorney, and then as district attorney, along with two previous generations of his family who had been lawyers in the county, gave him high standing among his constituents.

He was unaware of Artesia Hall or the Mother's Day incident until the county attorney and the deputies told him of the girls' scandalous stories about the oppressive and abusive atmosphere at the school, Farrar's scurrilous disparagement of the girls at the jail, his handcuffing and dragging the girl to his vehicle, and his demands two days later for release of the third girl in order to collect a debt.[9] The stories, which he began hearing repeated back to him by others in the county, impelled him to take action.[10]

His opportunity came on June 15, when County Attorney Jack Hartel filed a lawsuit on behalf of the state's Department of Public Welfare (DPW) to close Artesia Hall because it was operating as a child care facility without a state license. Unfortunately for Judge Cain, Hartel's client became more and more ambivalent about the lawsuit. Politics intruded and slowly eroded the professional staff's strong opposition to Farrar. He stalled the process by hiring a Houston attorney named W. Kendall Baker, who just two months earlier had completed twelve years as an appointee of the governor on the three-member board charged with managing the DPW.

For his local counsel in Liberty, Baker hired Price Daniel Jr., a member of the Texas House of Representatives (who would be elected Speaker in eighteen months) and the son of the man who had originally appointed Baker to the DPW board. In actions that would later be investigated by the legislature, my office, and the state police (we all found no evidence of illegal acts but clear use of political power), Baker and Daniel succeeded in delaying Hartel's lawsuit long enough to give Baker time to maneuver around the professional staff's opposition and obtain a license for Farrar on the eve of a court hearing on the case.[11]

Judge Cain was stunned when he at last convened the hearing on November 22, 1971, five months after it was filed. Each delay fueled his growing concern over the DPW's refusal to prosecute this case. After the third trial date on July 26 produced another continuance, he requested that the local DPW staff member prepare a report on Artesia Hall. That report, delivered to Cain September 7, was highly critical of Farrar and Artesia Hall.[12]

At the hearing, Hartel and Daniel reported that a license had been granted to Farrar three days earlier. The Hartel suit was thus moot. Farrar was going to be out from under Judge Cain's jurisdiction. When Daniel put on the witness stand the DPW employee whom Baker had persuaded to issue the license, Judge Cain surprised Daniel by taking over the questioning himself. For several hours, he pressed the employee for details on Artesia Hall. When Daniel moved to dismiss the Hartel lawsuit, Judge Cain refused, instead taking it under advisement.[13]

On December 7, Judge Cain finally signed the order dismissing the Hartel lawsuit. But he was still not comfortable with that ruling. He took it upon himself to call the DPW headquarters in Austin in February 1972 to express his concerns. He started at the top, calling the board chairman, Will Bond of Hillsboro.[14] As a result, two Austin staff members were sent to Artesia Hall. Their reports in March concluded that, although Artesia Hall exuded a "stark, concentration-camp-like aura," they could find no evidence of child abuse.[15]

Despite that apparent exoneration of Artesia Hall, the issue's persistence in the community led to a review by a grand jury Judge Cain impaneled on October 2, 1972. The foreman, a politically active and assertive Dayton funeral home operator named Jim Sterling, sought investigative help from the state's top law enforcement officer, Col. Wilson Spier, in Austin on December 7.[16] When this investigation again produced no significant evidence of abuse, Sterling and Dist. Atty. W. G. "Dub" Woods Jr. began calling former students and staff members to testify about the "G.I. baths" and other stories making the rounds of the community. Almost immediately, they stumbled onto an angle they never expected.

"My ears went up," Woods recalled later of a puzzling reference made by a witness. One of the teenagers was being questioned about an incident at Artesia Hall. In an offhand manner, she placed the time of the incident as "right before that girl was poisoned." The grand jurors froze in surprise, then erupted in a flurry of questions. None of them, nor Woods himself, knew of a student at Artesia Hall taking poison or dying of any cause. Their inquiry into rumors of creepy goings-on at Artesia Hall suddenly became a murder investigation.[17]

The girl, they learned, was Danna Annette Hvolboll, an attractive blond and blue-eyed seventeen-year-old from Houston residing at Artesia Hall for more than a year. She died November 14, 1972. Like many of the stories involving Artesia Hall, the story of her death defied easy explanations.

According to the story that the grand jurors were able to reconstruct, the events leading to Hvolboll's death began when a student burst into an Artesia Hall staff meeting about seven in the evening on November 11 to report that Hvolboll was sick. Hvolboll told the student she had swallowed poison. Staff members gave her several concoctions that induced vomiting, but they doubted her story about taking poison.

When Farrar arrived from Houston several hours later, he accused Hvolboll of faking. He ordered the staff to walk her around the compound's sidewalks, which they did for several hours, Hvolboll stumbling as two people held her up. The next morning, she collapsed and began convulsing. She lost control of her bowels and bladder. She lost consciousness. Her body was sweaty and pale. The staff and students placed a spoon on her tongue and a hairbrush handle in her mouth to keep her from swallowing her tongue.

Farrar again said she was faking, and he called her parents to repeat that assessment. Later that morning, he came into her room, picked her up by her hair and arms, and dragged her limp body down the hallway to the living area. He sat her in a chair and attempted to keep her upright by using straps, but she kept falling out of the chair. He dragged her back to her bedroom. He returned later and used a cotton swab to place pepper sauce on her bleeding tongue to try to revive her. She made no response. He then ordered staff members and students to carry her to his station wagon. Accompanied by several students he brought along to help carry her, he drove her to the hospital in Cleveland.

The doctor on duty in the small facility gave her an antidote for the Ortho Sevin® insecticide she had ingested and then aspirated her lungs. He called an ambulance and arranged for her to be sent to Ben Taub General Hospital in Houston. By the time she arrived at midafternoon, her body color was blue. She was comatose and required breathing assistance. Several hours after she arrived, the hospital staff told her parents she had suffered a cardiac arrest that required resuscitation. She was placed on a respirator but never revived. She died shortly after midnight of November 14.[18]

As the grand jury was piecing this story together, they encountered more surprises. The boy Danna Hvolboll had been dating at Artesia Hall claimed Farrar had enticed him into a homosexual relationship.[19] Several current and former students said they were concerned over friends at the school who left without warning and were never heard from again.[20] The grand jurors requested, and Cain granted, a ninety-day extension when their term was set to expire on March 31.

When Sheriff C. L. "Buck" Eckols or his deputies began serving subpoenas on students and staff at Artesia Hall, Farrar realized he was under investigation. Sterling was surprised to receive a call from Farrar one evening while he was eating dinner at home. "He said 'some people had been telling lies on me, and they're not true, and I'd like for us to get together and talk about these things, for me to get to know you and you to get to know me. Maybe you and your wife could go with my wife and me to

New York and see a show and we could get to know each other better,'" Sterling later recalled. He declined Farrar's offer.[21]

By mid-May, Sterling and the grand jurors were so swamped that they requested, and Cain granted, authority to hire a special prosecutor, Bruce Stratton, to help Woods. A month later, Stratton and Woods prepared an indictment and the grand jurors voted to approve it. Farrar was accused of murder by willfully failing to provide proper medical treatment and timely hospitalization for Hvolboll. Stratton accompanied Texas Rangers Kelly Whitehead and Bob Elder when they arrested Farrar in Houston the next day, June 15.[22]

Houston news outlets exploded with coverage of the indictment and arrest. Television film crews and reporters descended on Artesia Hall and Farrar's home. By Sunday, June 17, both the *Chronicle* and the *Post* had filled their front pages with lurid details surrounding Hvolboll's death, Farrar's suspect credentials, and his alleged use of politically connected lawyers to overrun DPW field staff's opposition to granting him a license.[23]

The news reports touched a sensitive nerve with Steve Oaks, a Houston lawyer recruited by Lt. Gov. Bill Hobby to serve as his executive assistant. Oaks had been a student leader at William and Mary College in Virginia while Farrar was dean of men there in the mid-1950s. Oaks and his classmates, disgusted with Farrar's recruitment of student "snitches" to report campus rules infractions to him, had succeeded in convincing the William and Mary administrators to remove Farrar. Oaks still considered Farrar one of the most despicable people he had ever met.[24]

On June 19, Oaks contacted the DPW and demanded action to protect Farrar's students. The agency's top child care consultant, George Campbell, was sent to Artesia Hall the same day.[25]

Oaks's take-charge response, despite the fact the lieutenant governor's office lacked any legal or historical control over the DPW, enjoyed the full support of his boss. Hobby knew more about the DPW and its programs than all but a handful of people at the top levels of the agency. Immediately prior to his election in 1972, he had chaired a Senate special committee charged with responding to criticism of the state's welfare programs. He was a hands-on chairman who recruited a top administrator from the University of Houston, June Hyer, to serve as staff director. Their year-long research in 1970 left them skeptical of the DPW's leaders and the agency's ability to fully meet its responsibilities. Hobby summarized their findings by terming the department's administration "shockingly bad."[26]

On the morning of June 20, 1973, Hobby summoned DPW director Raymond Vowell to his office to discuss the Artesia Hall case. The combination of Vowell's dwindling political support—Vowell's champion, Gov. Preston Smith, had been defeated a year earlier along with many of Vowell's old-guard friends in the legislature—and Hobby's role as a well-informed critic of the DPW put Vowell on the defensive. At the meeting, Hobby and Vowell listened on a speakerphone to Campbell's report on his initial findings. Campbell reported that the atmosphere at Artesia Hall was one of suspicion and intimidation. The shakings and other punishments Farrar had promised to abandon once he was licensed were still being reported.[27]

Campbell's comments confirmed Hobby's concerns that the DPW was not doing its job. He told Vowell to involve my office and the Department of Public Safety in taking whatever steps were necessary to protect the students at Artesia Hall. He issued a news release saying he was "appalled and deeply distressed that this facility ever operated with the approval of the Department of Public Welfare in view of the serious charges that have been made about this operation over the last several years."[28] Vowell knew he was on the hot seat and could lose his job if he failed to act fast on Artesia Hall.

When Vowell contacted my office, I turned over this investigation to my first assistant, Larry York. He was a thirty-two-year-old Houston defense attorney I had opposed in court as recently as eighteen months earlier, when I was representing an injured railroad worker and he succeeded in deadlocking the jury. I was so impressed with his abilities, I recruited him to lead my staff. He and I met with Vowell the evening of June 20, after Vowell spent the afternoon scrambling to determine whether staff members at the state's mental hospitals were available to provide emergency supervision at Artesia Hall if we could remove Farrar from control.

York told us the court hearings to oust Farrar could drag on for weeks. Our best hope for immediate protection for the students was to seek a court order requiring Farrar to place administration of the school temporarily under the direction of state mental health hospital staff. York and I told Vowell we would start working on legal issues involved in implementing the plan.

On Thursday, June 21, York and two of my assistants, Tim James and Herb Hancock, flew to Liberty with several DPW staff, armed with authority to compel Farrar to open his books to us. Their missions were to use the authorization letter to obtain copies of business records we needed to confirm Artesia Hall's license was current and to match student records with teenagers at the facility, to allay concerns some students might be "missing."

When York and Randy Pendleton, a former West Texas legislator hired by Vowell as a troubleshooter, returned from their trip Thursday evening, they told me the Artesia Hall administrators cooperated with their requests for information. With a growing number of DPW staff members on the campus, they were satisfied the students were safe from any retribution resulting from Farrar's indictment and the continuing grand jury investigation.

Pendleton also instructed his Houston staff to start calling parents of Artesia Hall residents to alert them to Farrar's indictment, resulting in several students being removed that day. We left the office that night believing Artesia Hall was stabilized and that we were ready to implement Vowell's plan to bring in the Rusk State Hospital staff, which would allow us time to develop in the next week a legal challenge to Farrar's license to operate Artesia Hall.[29]

York was operating under that assumption the next morning when he received a surprising call from Vowell. "The governor wants a briefing on Artesia Hall this morning, and I'm on my way over to his office. Can you join me?" Vowell asked. York was surprised to hear the governor mentioned. His impression was that Hobby, not Governor Briscoe, was leading the state's push to take action. In all of our discussions with the DPW, there was no mention of the governor's office.

"No big deal?" he asked Vowell.

"Not too big a deal. He just wants to get a rundown on what's going to happen," Vowell replied.

"Sure. Come by on your way and we'll go together," York told him.[30]

What York and Vowell did not know was that Lieutenant Governor Hobby's already high level of concern about Artesia Hall had been elevated the prior evening to a crisis level. A speaking engagement had taken him to Anahuac, about sixty miles southeast of Artesia Hall, to report on the just-concluded legislative session at the Anahuac Promotional Association's annual awards banquet. As the event was concluding, Hobby was approached by Sterling, who introduced himself as the foreman of the Liberty County grand jury and asked him to get a message to Governor Briscoe.

Sterling, a Briscoe friend and local campaign coordinator, wanted the governor to know about the abuses at Artesia Hall that the grand jury had heard about. A stunned Hobby listened as Sterling told of the G.I. baths, shaking by the hair, students being dipped in septic tanks, and students unaccounted for.

"I'm an undertaker, so I'm accustomed to scraping bodies off the pavement. But that didn't prepare me for the testimony we have heard about Artesia Hall. It keeps me awake at night. We need the governor to help us close down this awful place," Sterling told Hobby.[31]

When York and Vowell were admitted to Governor Briscoe's high-ceilinged private office on the second floor of the capitol, what they found was, indeed, a big deal. Instead of being seated at his desk, Briscoe was standing behind the high-backed leather-covered desk chair embossed with the state seal. His face was flushed with emotion. The hushed room was packed with chairs occupied by Lieutenant Governor Hobby, Oaks, Rep. John Whitmire from Houston, the two top officers of the Department of Public Safety, Mrs. Briscoe, and several of Briscoe's staff members.

Just before York and Vowell joined the meeting, Hobby relayed to Briscoe the alarming comments from Sterling. Oaks then shared his deep concerns about Farrar and the urgency of preventing further abuse. Whitmire, who had toured Artesia Hall with York and Hobby aide Harry Ledbetter, argued that the school needed to be closed immediately. This cascade of crisis pressure left the normally placid and even-tempered Briscoe visibly angry.

Before York and Vowell could take their seats, Briscoe demanded in a loud voice, "Mr. Vowell, I want to know if that Artesia Hall school has been closed and had its license revoked, and if not, why not?" The stunned Vowell deferred to York, who described his trip of the day before and the legal issues involved in a takeover. He counseled the group to consider the difficulties of displacing the fifty to sixty students if the school was closed immediately. York responded, "We can close it down, but does it make sense to move the kids without any staff? The DPW said the kids are all on different medications. We can't separate the kids from their medicine and their records. It would be a nightmare to move them someplace else without the staff that is familiar with the medicines and treatment issues." The group worked through the issues and decided to follow York's advice. But they wanted court action immediately to remove Farrar from any involvement. Governor Briscoe wanted the state commissioner of mental health, Dr. David Wade, to go to Artesia Hall that afternoon with him and his wife to assess the situation and bring in staff from the nearby Rusk State Hospital to counsel the students. Lieutenant Governor Hobby said he would accompany them, as did the state police commanders and Vowell. York hurried back to his office to report to me.[32]

"This thing is moving fast," York told me as I was en route to a speaking engagement for the Texas Press Association in Houston. "We need to try to go to court today," he continued. "I'll start working on an application to the court for authority to transfer control to the mental health commissioner, and I'll join you in Liberty. I need for you to help us round up witnesses to give the judge the evidence he needs to grant us a temporary restraining order."

In my speech, I shared with the news organization the outline of our plan to have staff from the state hospital operate Artesia Hall "until our investigation is completed."[33] Then I drove to Liberty late that afternoon to prepare for the court hearing. As I was leaving Houston, I called District Attorney Woods to ask his assistance in providing witnesses for the hearing. Before I was attorney general, Woods and I had tried several lawsuits together when I retained him as local counsel in Liberty, so we enjoyed a good working relationship.

I arrived at the three-story white limestone courthouse at about five o'clock and angle-parked in front. Like most small-town courthouses located on a town square, it was the most imposing structure in the county. It was built in 1931 in the modernized classical style, its dark-framed windows recessed to provide a clean vertical break between two-story pilasters and to create the image of Roman columns. I walked up the massive stairway, entering through the heavy doors beneath images of large eagles. In his office, Woods introduced me to two prospective witnesses: DPW staff attorney Carolyn Busch and Joy Whitman, the latter a seventeen-year-old resident of Artesia Hall.

Busch told me she had found records showing that Farrar transferred assets of Artesia Hall eleven months earlier to a new corporation, which held no state license to operate the facility. Whitman told me how Farrar had shaken her by her hair so violently that her feet left the ground, her leg was slammed into a desk, and clumps of hair were torn from her scalp. Busch's evidence gave us a clear legal justification for removing Farrar from control of Artesia Hall.[34] Whitman's stories demonstrated the need to replace Farrar's staff with staff from the state mental hospital. Both said they believed the residents were in danger of physical and mental intimidation if Farrar remained in control.

Woods also provided more grand jury news that added even more urgency to our strategy. The grand jury that day handed down one new indictment against Farrar and two indictments against his son, who worked for him, both alleging they assaulted two Artesia Hall students. "The hold-over grand jury is still in session and may have more indictments," Woods told me.

I met with York to review his application for a temporary restraining order and make sure our witnesses' testimony would fully support the remedy we sought. With this unprecedented gathering of state officials in the courtroom audience expecting a quick state takeover, we wanted to make certain the judge would not balk at such unusually bold steps in a temporary restraining order. We decided to ask for removal of all of Farrar's staff, a prohibition against them interfering with Wade as he assumed the role of administrator, and the transfer of all fifty-two remaining Artesia Hall enrollees and their records to the state's control.

"These two witnesses will give the judge what he needs to grant our order. We don't need to try to parade a long list of witnesses through the courtroom. Let's use a rifle instead of a shotgun and keep this hearing short," I told York. He agreed and began previewing with each witness the points to cover in their testimony.

When Judge Cain arrived at the courthouse at about half past eight that evening, York and I explained our plan to be sure he wasn't surprised by any of our requests. I had tried several cases in his court while I was in private practice, so he and I knew and respected each other. He nodded in agreement as we reviewed the points of relief we were seeking.

"Judge, we know this is an unusual procedure, but we believe it's necessary, from what we have learned from the state officials who have visited Artesia Hall and from our witnesses, that we turn over operation of this school to the professionals from the state hospital who know how to deal with these types of children," I told him.

"I don't see any problems," he told us.

We left his chambers and walked down the hallway, which was noisy with animated conversations bouncing off the marble wainscoting and ceramic tile floor. Even though the rest of the courthouse was dark, the hallway around the courtroom was bustling with news reporters, television cameramen, state officials and their assistants, and various spectators eager to witness a once-in-a-lifetime gathering in this rural courthouse—or almost anywhere, for that matter—of the state's top elected officeholders and the directors of several major state agencies.

York and I took our seats at the large counsel table in the wood-paneled, elegantly formal courtroom. Seated behind us, inside the railing that separated spectators from the area where lawyers and the jury faced the judge's bench and adjoining witness stand, were Governor Briscoe and his wife, who was vigorously knitting; Hobby; Vowell; Wade; the director of the Texas Department of Public Safety; and Representative Whitmire. The courtroom's wooden benches were filled with the crowd that earlier was milling around in the hallway.

Judge Cain entered through a side door at about nine o'clock. By 10:00 P.M., we had presented our witnesses, obtained Cain's signature on the order, and scheduled a hearing for the next week on a temporary injunction. I closed the hearing by telling Cain, "I know I speak for the governor and lieutenant governor and Representative Whitmire and those who have sought out our suggestions of the possible court action to take that would be responsive to this situation and which would, first and foremost, consider the welfare of the children. Now, I think I can thank you publicly, and I know I speak for each of them, for taking your time here to hear us. But it was an urgent, important matter and I feel that the court has taken the kind of action that can only be in the best interest of the children, until we can take a further look at this thing next Thursday."[35]

The courtroom emptied, triggering a blaze of light from television cameras as news reporters swarmed around Governor Briscoe, Lieutenant Governor Hobby, and me, probing for details on how this drama was going to play out. Governor Briscoe announced he was ordering our office and the Department of Public Safety to "determine how an obvious failure in supervision of a state-licensed facility took place."[36]

The bright television camera lights followed the state officials and the sheriff and several deputies as they walked to their cars, which formed a caravan for the forty-minute drive to Artesia Hall to implement the judge's order. Their route took them by the jail where Farrar's son was being held on the charges brought that afternoon by the grand jury. Farrar was in Houston at a friend's house, trying to avoid news reporters gathered at his home and office.[37]

By the time the caravan arrived, most of the children had been removed by their parents. Those remaining were gone the next day. By the time Cain held the injunction hearing the following Thursday, June 28, Artesia Hall was a ghost town.[38]

Farrar wanted to fight our takeover. But his attorney, Richard "Racehorse" Haynes of Houston, one of the state's premier criminal defense attorneys, was warned by Woods that the grand jury, which Judge Cain agreed to hold over past its original expiration date, was still in session and considering further indictments. Haynes advised Farrar to agree to close Artesia Hall and his Houston school, Aston Hall, to avoid possible further grand jury indictments.[39] York met with Haynes's law partner, Mike Ramsey, and Cain in the judge's chambers before the hearing to review an agreed order for Cain to sign granting the state a temporary injunction prohibiting Farrar from operating Artesia Hall. Judge Cain agreed, and Farrar was out of business for good at the age of fifty-six.[40]

Pushed by relentless news coverage, the Artesia Hall case shot child care concerns to the top of state government leaders' agendas and heightened the awareness of local officials and parents across Texas to the dangers posed by unlicensed child care homes. News articles quickly began terming it the "Artesia Hall scandal."

I appointed John Odam, an attorney that York had recruited from his former law firm, to lead a new task force on child care issues. Governor Briscoe appointed an interagency youth task force, chaired by Vowell. The House Committee on Human Resources and its welfare subcommittee both held lengthy hearings and issued reports recommending reforms. Vowell assigned Pendleton the job of strengthening child care facility licensing standards, which had remained unchanged since 1951.

The issue was not limited to Texas, as we discovered when the Illinois attorney general contacted us about complaints of brutality suffered by some of the eight hundred Illinois children placed in Texas child care facilities because of a shortage of homes in Illinois.[41]

The scope of the Artesia Hall fallout expanded when Vowell revealed on June 29 that only 136 of Texas' 175 residential child care facilities were licensed. He issued a list of the 39 that had no license, prompting dozens of news reporters across the state to investigate homes on the list in searches for potential Artesia Halls. Odam and his staff began working through this list and the DPW files of brutality complaints to determine whether legal action was needed.[42]

Amid the flood of complaints was one from Corpus Christi that would keep my staff, and my successor's staff, in court for the next decade. And it would play a crucial role in my losing campaign for governor.

The county attorney in Corpus Christi, Franklin Smith, announced July 13, 1973, that he was going to ask my office to take action against Rebekah Home for Girls, a facility on the outskirts of Corpus Christi that housed 125 girls in a new two-story dormitory and that also had a two-story classroom building. It was one of the 39 unlicensed homes on Vowell's list. Smith was acting on statements taken by sheriff's deputies from sixteen people who were Rebekah students' parents or residents documenting beatings with fists, paddles, and straps, withholding of food, handcuffing, and solitary confinement as punishment. They retrieved from the home director a fifteen-inch braided leather strap said by many of the residents to be used in punishment. Smith sent that information to the DPW and announced the investigation to the local news media.[43]

The same week, local officials in Laredo called my office to report juvenile authorities were contacted by a sixteen-year-old runaway from Anchor Home, a boys' home in nearby Zapata. He showed them deep bruises on his buttocks caused by punishment.[44]

Both homes were operated by a Corpus Christi–based radio evangelist, Lester L. Roloff. When Smith's investigation was reported in the newspaper, Roloff was not the least bit chagrined. Most child care facilities generally lacked supporters beyond parents of residents, but Roloff's radio ministry generated hundreds of thousands of listeners he could recruit to help him challenge the government. He told reporters the allegations of abuse were untrue. "We have no one but the sweetest people in the world out there," he said of Rebekah's employees. "We don't know what the word 'abuse' is."[45]

In a strategy that foretold the challenge we faced in attempting to enforce the licensing law against him, Roloff used the next broadcast of his daily religious service to brand the charges an "untrue, un-Christian, and un-American attack." Two of the students who gave sworn statements to the sheriff's deputies confessed on the show that they had "lied." Broadcasting through one hundred stations across the country, he urged listeners to call or write my office, the county attorney, and the *Corpus Christi Caller* to vouch for the homes.

In the next several days, our office and the county attorney each received 200 letters; the newspaper received about 240. By the eighth day, the newspaper published a notice that it could no longer include any letters from Roloff supporters because it had received 400 in one day.[46]

I sent Odam and another young staff attorney, Lynn Taylor, to Corpus Christi to meet with Roloff to resolve this issue. They convinced Roloff's attorney they would present damaging evidence of physical abuse of children in Roloff's homes if the issue came to trial. His experience from the news reports of the county attorney's investigation must have helped convince him to avoid further bad press by agreeing to a court order requiring him to license all of his homes by October 1, 1973, and to stop mistreating the children.

But when Taylor, Odam, and Roloff's attorney, Harry Dobbs Jr., took the judgment draft they signed to Judge Walter Dunham, he looked it over and handed it back. Dunham was a savvy enough politician to know he did not want Roloff's followers blaming him for an action that Roloff could disavow because it was signed by his attorney.

"You need Brother Roloff's signature," Dunham told them. They went back down the hallway to the courthouse conference room where they had left Roloff. Odam persuaded him to sign it, arguing that the DPW case against him was so strong he would not only lose but also suffer more unfavorable publicity if the case was tried. The attorneys returned to Dunham's chambers with Roloff's signature, and Dunham entered the order on August 3, 1973.[47]

Roloff apparently never intended to honor his commitment.[48] The next day, he began a two-day "Rebekah Reunion" attended by former residents and religious leaders from across the nation. Among those attending was Jerry Falwell, a television evangelist who would later form the "Moral Majority" to mobilize conservative Christians into a potent force to support Republican Party candidates for public office across the nation.[49]

The theme of Roloff's two-day meeting was a refrain we would hear for the remainder of my term. It went something like this: "Why should we have to have a license to run a church home any more than we would have to have a license to run the church? It actually means that we take God's money and let the state, which is altogether unprepared to run a Christian home, run the home."

The next week, the House Committee on Human Resources, chaired by Rep. Carlos Truan of Corpus Christi, conducted three days of lengthy public hearings in his hometown, questioning DPW officials, Roloff, Smith, and others. Roloff parried the legislators' questions with relish. Referring to Roloff's professed concern for American society's increasing disrespect for laws, Rep. Tom Schieffer of Fort Worth asked, "How do you reconcile that you talk about disrespect for the law, but you disrespect the law by refusing to get a license?" As Roloff's two hundred supporters in the audience vigorously applauded, he replied, "If man's law conflicts with God's law, I'll have to stay with God's law." Holding in one hand the DPW's thirty-eight-page booklet listing requirements for child care facilities and his always present Bible in the other, Roloff lifted the booklet dramatically and said in a wavering, emotional voice, "There's no Jesus, no God, no Bible in this book. How are we going to get the girls straight if they don't get the word of God?" The DPW local staff member who had fruitlessly attempted to convince Roloff to license his homes detailed for the committee how Rebekah Home failed to meet the state's health, medical, dietary, and educational standards. The hearings concluded with Roloff unscathed and unbowed.[50]

I was personally given a dose of the Roloff charisma six weeks later. He decided to hire a lobbyist in Austin to give him access to state leaders whom he wanted to persuade to recant their accusations. He selected Eugene Palmer, a longtime Austin lobbyist, who contacted my office to arrange a meeting. I agreed. To prepare, I discussed with Taylor and Odam the evidence they had obtained. They related documentation confirming the frequent use of corporal punishment at his homes and showed me photos of the Anchor Home runaway whose buttocks were purple from a paddling he had received.

"I'd like to keep these for the meeting with Brother Roloff," I told them. "I want him to know we're not involved in this case just to get our pictures in the paper; we've got some serious abuses we're concerned about. I know he thinks he's going to come in here and charm us into backing off, and I want him to realize that's not going to happen."

Palmer arrived at the appointed time for our meeting. He, Odam, Taylor, and I went to the conference room that adjoined my office on the seventh floor of the Supreme Court building. We were sitting around the large conference table exchanging pleasantries while waiting for Roloff when we suddenly heard the sound of voices singing. Here came Roloff, Bible in hand, leading a procession of Rebekah Home girls singing a hymn. I was not amused. I turned to Palmer and said, "You set me up!" I could tell by the look of surprise on his face, however, that both of us were victimized by Roloff's relentless showmanship.

After everyone was introduced, Roloff suddenly dropped to one knee, held up his hand, closed his eyes, and began praying, asking God's help in resolving our dispute. He rose, turned toward the girls, and raised his arm in a cue to them. They immediately stood and began singing a hymn. He then excused the girls and began sermonizing to us about the need to follow the Constitution's separation of church and state, the unfairness of the DPW's requirements being applied to a facility that accepted no government funds, and the necessity that his work on behalf of the Lord continue unimpeded by any interference from what he termed "the Welfare." He cited as unnecessary the department's rules requiring that his homes' superintendents have a college education, claiming they had performed successfully for seven years.

"I can't give up my convictions and my conscience," he told us.

When I asked him if he was going to comply with Judge Dunham's order to obtain a license by October 1, which was only seven days away, Roloff asked if we would agree to a thirty-day extension.

"Only if the Welfare Department advises us they believe progress is being made toward getting the license," I responded. Then I raised the physical abuse issue, telling him I was concerned by his acquiescence in his schools' free use of force to punish these children.

"Better to have pink bottoms than black hearts," Roloff responded.

With that, I removed from an envelope the five-by-seven-inch Polaroid® color photos of the Anchor Home runaway, slid them over in front of Roloff, and said, "Brother Roloff, we're talking about black and blue bottoms."

His eyes widened in surprise, but he still refused to acknowledge the abuse his employees were committing. The meeting broke up with more pleasantries. We shook hands, and he walked away sadly.[51]

The October 1 deadline in Dunham's order posed a dilemma for us and the DPW. If Roloff failed to meet the deadline, we were obligated to ask Dunham to hold him in contempt and sentence him to jail. But we knew that would be handing him a tempting new opportunity to energize his supporters by playing the role of martyr. The religious angle, we agreed, was bogus because numerous religious child care facilities submitted to licensing by the DPW. Roloff himself had licensed with the DPW for twenty years a facility he owned personally, Park Avenue Day School in Corpus Christi.[52] Nothing in the DPW rules affected Roloff's ability to attempt to indoctrinate his students with his version of Christianity or to require, as he did, extended Bible study.

We guessed that although he might be exploiting the DPW confrontation because it was a boost for his radio ministry and its mailed-in donations, there were two issues at the heart of Roloff's stubborn resistance. First, he had painted himself into a corner before he signed the court order, railing against "the Welfare" on his radio shows and vowing not to back down. His followers responded to his exhortations by sending him money to keep the schools open. To renege on his commitment to fight would be to shatter the rock-solid image he had created. He would become one of those spineless denominational preachers he roundly scorned to his followers.

Second, his facilities were all managed and staffed by followers whose allegiance was to God first and Roloff second. Their loyalty, not their experience or training, was their sole qualification for their jobs. Using professional managers, educators, and counselors would not only drive up his costs but also rob him of the intense bond with extended family on which he depended to implement his ideas and beliefs with minimal justification or explanation. It would remove the spiritual spark that sustained him and his followers.

Correctly analyzing Roloff and using that analysis to craft a solution that included Roloff obeying the law were two different tasks we never were able to connect. I believed our only choice was to do our job and let Roloff choose whether to suffer the consequences.

On the October 1 deadline, Odam and Taylor, along with Vowell and Pendleton, met once again with Roloff, this time in Corpus Christi, to try to break the impasse. They agreed to give Roloff a fifteen-day extension, but the delay only gave Roloff more opportunities to escalate the rhetorical warfare. He began returning residents of Rebekah Home to their parents in anticipation of closing the school rather than licensing it. He announced he would file a federal court lawsuit against the DPW for violating the doctrine of separation of church and state. He held a special "last rites" service for one thousand at his People's Church in Corpus Christi to decry the impending closing of Rebekah Home.[53]

The day before the contempt hearing in Dunham's court, Roloff and his Rebekah Home student singers, the Honeybee Quartet, met with Governor Briscoe's chief of staff in the capitol to ask, to no avail, for the governor's help. That evening at the Austin Municipal Auditorium he conducted a rally attended by three thousand supporters bused in from around the country, many of them waving placards in the shape of a cross with red lettering that said, "ROLOFF TODAY YOUR CHURCH TOMORROW."

One of the warm-up speakers was Falwell, who told the crowd, "Christians are obligated to obey the law. The only ground for rebelling against civil authority is when devil authority violates divine authority." Tears rolled down Roloff's cheeks as he listened to a choir of forty Rebekah Home girls. "Every flag in Texas ought to be at half-mast," Roloff shouted. "Our three homes didn't die a natural death. They have been killed, and the killer's still at large." Roloff had invited me and Vowell to attend his rally, but we sent Taylor, Odam, and Pendleton instead. Odam, a strongly religious person, took his wife Peggy and carried his own Bible. At the end of the service, Roloff called them to the stage, introduced them, and then led a prayer asking God's guidance in their actions. He then invited his followers to come meet them. Dozens of people lined up to shake their hands and assure them they were in their prayers.[54]

The next day, Odam and Taylor filed a contempt affidavit in Dunham's court. He set a hearing for October 26 when he found Roloff Evangelist Enterprises in violation of his order of August 3 and issued a five-hundred-dollar fine. Taylor and Pendleton went back to court December 17 with another affidavit alleging Roloff was still disobeying the order of August 3, resulting in a show-cause hearing on February 1, 1974, to take testimony. Odam and Pendleton testified on Roloff's continued refusal to obey the ruling.

Roloff's attorney exploited uncertainty as to whether the law governing child care home licensing applied to homes with children under age eighteen, as my office contended, or only to children under age sixteen, as Roloff contended. His lawyer asked Dunham to sentence Roloff to jail to give them a vehicle for appealing to the Texas Supreme Court under a habeas corpus proceeding. Dunham reluctantly agreed.[55]

Amid the glare of television camera lights, Roloff reported to jail on the morning of February 12.[56] His attorneys and Odam argued the age issue that afternoon before the state's Supreme Court. The court sided with Roloff, freeing him late that night, and set arguments on the appeal for March 20.[57]

True to form, Roloff held a rally at Austin's Municipal Auditorium for eight hundred people the night before the hearing. Once again, tears streamed down his cheeks as held aloft a picture of George Washington kneeling in prayer beside his horse. He told the fervent crowd he wished the first president could be at his side in court the next day.[58]

In a ruling on May 29, 1974, the state's Supreme Court adopted Roloff's interpretation of the law's age requirement. It was the only court victory Roloff would enjoy in a decade of litigation. It forced us to restart our efforts to bring him into compliance with the law.

Our first job was to fix the inconsistency in the law, which we did by helping legislators draft a revision during the session of 1975. The bill passed despite a barrage of opposition calls and letters from Roloff supporters, but only after Lieutenant Governor Hobby kept it alive by breaking a 14-to-14 tie vote to defeat an amendment to exempt church-operated facilities. It took effect January 1, 1976.[59]

Once these statutory changes were enforceable, we resumed our effort to bring closure to the Roloff case. Taylor asked Judge Dunham in January 1976 to find Roloff in contempt of his 1973 order requiring Roloff to allow DPW access to his homes to investigate complaints. When he found Roloff in contempt on May 26 and sentenced him to jail, Roloff's attorneys brought another habeas corpus application to the state Supreme Court on June 21, 1976. The court held an informal hearing in its conference room. They questioned Roloff's attorney about why Roloff refused, after he signed the agreed judgment promising to allow inspections, to keep his promise. "It seems to me Brother Roloff is in the plight he's in because he agreed himself into it," Justice Jack Pope told Roloff's attorney. They also expressed their disagreement with Roloff's contention that his religious beliefs should provide him an exception to the new licensing law. "When we start making laws for people, we have to make them for all people," Pope said. They denied Roloff's appeal the same day it was heard.[60]

After that ruling, I decided to make one last effort to persuade Roloff to comply with the law. I was in Corpus Christi for a meeting and was accompanied by my wife. We made arrangements to visit Rebekah Home. Roloff introduced us to the residents and showed us around the campus. When he showed us a small implement shed, I said, "Brother Roloff, just get your license; you can tack it up out here on this little shack or storeroom, I just want you to get licensed. It's not any big deal, if everything is as you portrayed to me and Bitsy, it shouldn't be a problem in the world."

"Well, but it's the way they overregulate you, they're always in your hair, it's just the nuisance of it," he responded. "I think it's a matter of principle—people in God's work, we shouldn't have to be beholden in any respect to the state."

Bitsy, who is a very religious person, also tried to reason with him, telling him, "Brother Roloff, it says in the Bible, 'Render unto Caesar what is Caesar's, render unto the Lord that which is the Lord's.' John has his responsibilities he has to meet, just like you have yours; surely you can see this and both of you can work together for the benefit of the children."

"I'm not trying to be obstinate. We just have an honest disagreement," Roloff told her.

Roloff had still another trip to the state Supreme Court in the works. Taylor obtained a contempt ruling against Roloff in June 1976 by an Austin judge, Charles Mathews, who also ordered Roloff to comply with the state's new licensing law. Roloff appealed the Mathews ruling to the Court of Civil Appeals in Austin, which held in October 1977 that Roloff's contention that the law violated his free exercise of religion guaranteed by the First Amendment to the Constitution "is nothing more than a bald conclusion entirely unsupported by any factual evidence from which a jury could draw a differing conclusion." The court concluded, "It then becomes apparent that in applying the statute to the undisputed facts, its provisions do not in any way conflict with appellants' beliefs, nor do they restrict the exercise of those beliefs in any way."[61]

That decision became the final word on the subject when the Texas Supreme Court refused on February 8, 1978, to consider an appeal of the Third Court of Appeals ruling that affirmed Mathews's judgment and the Supreme Court of the United States declined to consider the case eight months later.[62]

Three weeks later, a segment of the CBS television network's Sunday evening news program *60 Minutes* was devoted to a profile of Roloff by their most aggressive interviewer, Mike Wallace. Taylor shared with Wallace the color photos of the bruised buttocks of the Anchor Home runaway. Wallace used them to confront Roloff. As the camera zoomed in on the photos he held in his hand for Roloff to see, Wallace said, "These are the buttocks of a young man who was here in your homes. Did you ever see any of these pictures before?"[63]

"Yes sir," Roloff replied. "I'd say this—even that is not beyond Bible discipline."

"Even this is not?" Wallace asked.

"No, not beyond Bible discipline. No sir. There is no lasting mark that's ever been on anybody except our workers. They've been bitten, they've been struck and hit with all sorts of things. The only people that have a lasting mark—and if you can find, Brother Mike—anybody in our home that's ever been with us that's got one lasting mark on them from a paddling or whipping, I'd like to see it. I don't think it's possible to find one."

When Wallace brought up the subject of beatings as he and Roloff stood before several rows of Rebekah Home girls dressed alike in red checked blouses and red skirts, several of the girls protested that the discipline at Rebekah was much less severe than at state juvenile homes. "You talk about lockups? You go to your state home. At least our lockup has a bathtub to take a bath in. Your lockup at your state homes don't have that. They put you in a four-wall cell so you can't see outside, you can't see nothing. With their lockup they've got white walls, our lockup has flowers on them. We can go to the bathroom. We don't have to bang on our wall to go to the bathroom," one girl told Wallace.

Wallace ended the segment with a quip from Roloff about the U.S. Supreme Court declining to hear his case: "The Supreme Court has shot the Holy Spirit out of the saddle."

Except for the *60 Minutes* segment, news coverage of the Roloff case had dwindled as our confrontations with him became numbingly familiar. The story disappeared from newspaper front pages, and the articles that did appear were brief.

But Roloff was still using the issue to vilify me, Taylor, and the DPW in his daily radio broadcasts, church sermons, and newsletters. "If America is right, then I'm right. If the flag is right, then I'm right. If our Puritan forefathers were right, then I'm right. If the Bible is right, then I'm right," he would chant to his supporters.[64] I was running for governor in 1978 and sensed that Roloff's attacks on me could easily spill over into my political race.

I considered my religious views a topic I would not discuss in my campaign or as an officeholder. I did not consider it appropriate to inject them into either forum. I came to terms with my spiritual beliefs when I was secretary of state and was privileged to join a golf game with Governor Connally and the Reverend Billy Graham, who visited with Connally frequently.

At that time, I was wrestling with my political career options, so I decided to share my concerns with Graham and seek his advice. I think he found my rambling discussion too self-centered, because he looked at me with those piercing eyes and said, "John, the first thing you better do is get yourself straight with the Lord." It stopped me cold. I took his advice to heart and began trying to give God top priority in my life and relegate my concerns to second place.

While I was comfortable that my religious beliefs and my devotion to the rule of law could and should, in a democracy, exist side by side, I saw no benefit in attempting to engage Roloff in a debate on the issue. If you do not have the rule of law in a free society, you have anarchy. It's the core value in a democracy. Of all the people that have got to honor that, it's people involved in upholding and enforcing the law. It's a big responsibility to be consistent in that way. I've never felt I was cute enough or smart enough to finesse that.

It frustrated me that Roloff was so adamant. The regulations he complained about dealt only with the safety of the children. They imposed no restraints on his religious teachings. Yet I was forced to absorb his incessant barbs and hope the voters would not accept his one-sided argument.

Roloff never used his pulpit or radio ministry to urge his followers to get involved in politics. Popular broadcast evangelists such as Billy James Hargis, whose *Christian Crusade* in the 1950s and 1960s was on 500 radio stations and 250 television stations, and Carl McIntire, whose *Twentieth Century Reformation Hour* was carried on 600 stations in the 1960s, combined religion and politics and gave birth to the "Christian Right" political movement. Hargis was a strong supporter of Senator Barry Goldwater's presidential campaign in 1964, and McIntire sponsored rallies in the early 1970s supporting the United States' military action in Viet Nam.[65]

Roloff followed their lead in condemning communism and in maintaining a fervent patriotism, but he avoided political personalities while focusing on personal salvation and spreading the Gospel as his primary messages. His followers were fundamentalist Christians with no history of coordinated political involvement. Political analysts thought their rigid views of cultural issues made them so disdainful of government and impatient with the equivocation of politicians that they would be unlikely to vote.

Roloff cast that history aside during my campaign for governor in 1978, when he seized the opportunity to politicize his predicament. After I defeated Governor Briscoe in the Democratic primary and was running in the general election against Bill Clements, Roloff telephoned me and I recall him saying, "I want to support you. I believe you are a good man. But I can't support you unless you'll agree to not require a license. Help me with the amendment I'm trying to get to the Child Care Licensing Act."

"Brother Roloff, I just can't do that, I'm sworn to uphold the law, and that's what the law requires," I told him. "I can't even say that if you can get the law changed I'll stand by and let you do it, because I don't think I would. I feel there's a need for reasonable regulations. I know the state can overdo regulation—I'm not much on government regulation, either—but in this area I really think we need these regulations. If I'm governor, I'd never have any hostile feelings toward you, I would treat you just like I would anybody else."

"I'm sorry to hear that," he said. "But I did want to have this conversation with you."

Three weeks before the election, Roloff sent a mailing to his supporters recommending Clements for governor. The Republican candidates, he said, are men "who have committed themselves to protect all churches and church related institutions." He urged his readers to "vote sensibly and wisely for the home, the church, the Christian school and Old Glory."

Clements later denied having made these promises, but Roloff continued to endorse him in paid political announcements immediately following his *Family Altar* broadcasts.[66]

The Sunday before the election on November 7, churchgoers at fundamentalist Christian churches across Texas found a leaflet under their windshield wipers. It was blasting me for persecuting Roloff and interfering with the separation of church and state, and it urged a vote for Clements to punish me for my efforts to license Roloff's homes.[67] I lost the election by 19,000 votes out of 2.4 million cast.

After the election, news reports revealed that Clements and Roloff had made a deal. Clements sponsored these propaganda drops on the Sunday before the election. This election marked the first time Republicans tapped into fundamentalist Christian groups to seize on their discontent with Democrats' association with liberal political and cultural issues. Roloff's ability to link patriotism and Christianity with his antigovernment tirades was a precursor to Falwell's Moral Majority, which was launched the next year and became an essential component of Republican presidential elections.[68]

PHOTO 1. *After he graduated from Kilgore High School in 1940, Hill spent his freshman year at Kilgore College, whene this photo was taken. He was a national collegiate debate champion at Kilgore. Photo courtesy Hill family*

PHOTO 2. *Hill married his University of Texas sweetheart, Elizabeth Ann "Bitsy" Graham, in her hometown of Olney, on April 4, 1946. He was married in his navy uniform, having served two years as a lieutenant commanding a flotilla of landing craft that ferried infantry ashore at Mindanao and Mindoro in the recapture of the Philippine Islands. Photo courtesy Hill family*

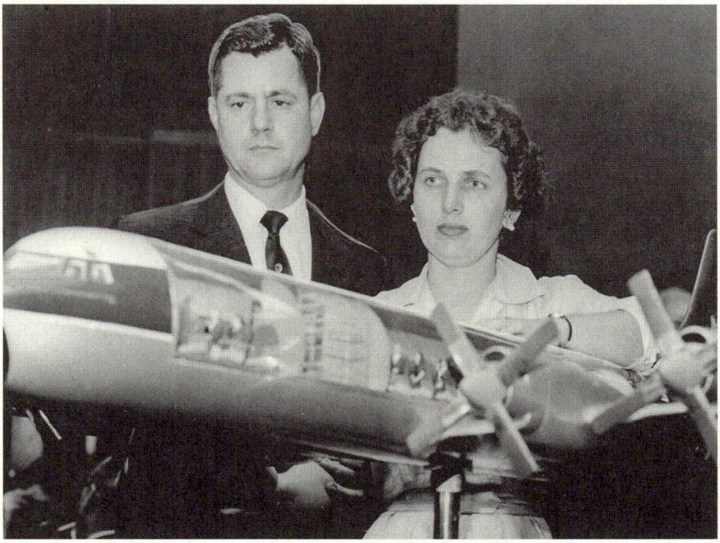

PHOTO 3. *In this "photo op" for the* Houston Press *in 1962, Hill and Suzanne Quick look at a model of the Lockheed Electra on which her husband was a passenger when it crashed near Buffalo, Texas. The model was part of Hill's extensive use of physical evidence, including an engine and wing segment retrieved from the wreckage, which helped him to win her a record-high $250,000 jury award in a lawsuit against some of America's largest corporations—Braniff, Lockheed, and General Motors. The victory prompted settlement of several dozen other lawsuits for awards in the millions of dollars and secured Hill's reputation as one of the state's most successful plaintiff attorneys. Photo courtesy Houston Metropolitan Research Center, Houston Public Library*

PHOTO 4. *Governor John Connally congratulates Hill on being sworn in as secretary of state in March 1966. House Speaker Ben Barnes hands Hill his certificate of office. PICA 71496, Austin History Center, Austin Public Library*

PHOTO 5. *Justice Joe Greenhill of the Texas Supreme Court swears in Hill as attorney general in January 1975. Hill had run unopposed for a four-year term. PICA AAS75-89207-7, Austin History Center, Austin Public Library*

PHOTO 6. *Hill's environmental protection division staff in May 1973. Bottom row (left to right): Lynn Taylor, First Assistant Larry York, Division Chief Mike Willatt, Hill, Division Assistant Chief Philip Maxwell, and Jack Traylor. Back row (left to right): Kenneth Norman, Don Allee, Skip Newsom, Rod Gorman, Troy Webb, and Terry O'Rourke. Allee, Gorman, and O'Rourke were key players in the Houston office's success in obtaining record fines and pollution abatement commitments from Houston Ship Channel polluters. Photo courtesy Phil Maxwell*

PHOTO 7. *Hill is shown congratulating his new First Assistant, Larry York of Houston, who took office in March 1973. To the right are two of Hill's division chiefs, Joe Dibrell of enforcement and Joe Longley (holding hat) of antitrust and consumer protection. Photo courtesy Larry York*

PHOTO 8. *Southwestern Bell officials confronted Hill on January 31, 1975, to persuade him not to block a planned $45 million increase in intrastate long-distance telephone rates. The Bell officials were (left to right) Ford Hall, general counsel in Dallas; Will Sears, Houston-based counsel; and Newton Hoverstock, Dallas, who was Bell's Texas vice president. Hill assured them he would challenge the rates in court if they did not agree to present their rationale for the rate increase to him in a public forum. They declined, he sued, and they eventually agreed to cut the rate increase by more than a third. Photo courtesy Hill family*

PHOTO 9. *At a capitol news conference on April 30, 1975, Hill protested a ruling by the Court of Civil Appeals in Austin overturning an injunction he had won against a Southwestern Bell intrastate rate increase. Even though Hill filed an appeal, Bell immediately implemented the rate increase, leading him to call the news conference to protest Bell's "raw, monopolistic power" and to rally citizens to push the legislature to enact a public utility commission law. A newspaper columnist described the news conference by saying Hill "managed to come on like Gang Busters and a Marine landing." Photo courtesy Hill family*

PHOTO 10. *Hill is shown entering the courtroom where he successfully argued before the Texas Supreme Court on June 18, 1975, that the state's constitution gave him authority to block Southwestern Bell's $45 million intrastate rate increase. Hill was the first Texas attorney general to assert authority over the telephone monopoly's intrastate rates. Photo courtesy Hill family*

ILLUSTRATION 1. Austin American-Statesman *editorial cartoonist Ben Sargent correctly summarized Southwestern Bell's Texas intrastate rate increase strategy in this 1975 drawing—Bell's inability to achieve rate increases on local and interstate service forced them to double up on in-state rates. Hill undermined the strategy by successfully attacking the economic justification for the $45 million intrastate rate increase, winning court rulings that led Bell to cut the increase by more than a third. Illustration courtesy Ben Sargent*

PHOTO 11. *On July 31, 1975, Hill traveled to San Diego, Texas, to confront a "do-nothing" grand jury. His on-the-ground leader for the Duval County cleanup was John Blanton, a former federal Drug Enforcement Agency attorney in San Antonio. Here, they are shown conferring outside the grand jury room. Photo courtesy Hill family*

PHOTO 12. *Hill and the Department of Public Safety created a task force that spent 1975–1977 gathering information for prosecution of criminal cases against more than two hundred Duval County officeholders, government employees, and businesses. They are shown in front of the building where they set up a temporary office in San Diego, Texas (left to right, assistant attorneys general hatless, Rangers in hats): Bert Pluymen, Ray Martinez, Gene Powell, Max Flusche, John Blanton, John Wood, John Odam, Rudy Rodriguez, and Jerry Carruth. Photo courtesy John Blanton*

PHOTO 13. *Hill went to San Diego, Texas, on April 8, 1975, for his first meeting with the grand jury and the judge regarding the invitation by District Attorney Arnulfo Guerra (right) to assist in the investigation of Duval County corruption. They are pictured in front of the Duval County courthouse. © 1975 Caller-Times Publishing Company. Reprinted with permission. All rights reserved.*

PHOTO 14. *On May 21, 1973, Governor Briscoe signed the Texas Deceptive Trade Practices–Consumer Protection Act, one of Hill's signature achievements in his first term. Shown (left to right) are Senate sponsors Bob Gammage of Houston and Ron Clower of Dallas, House Speaker Price Daniel Jr. of Liberty, House sponsors Arthur "Buddy" Temple of Diboll and Carl Parker of Port Arthur, Governor Briscoe, Lt. Gov. Bill Hobby, Hill, and Senate sponsor Oscar Mauzy of Dallas. Photo courtesy Joe K. Longley*

PHOTO 15. *In 1975, Governor Briscoe signed a bill pushed by Hill and Joe K. Longley, chief of the antitrust and consumer protection division, to expand regulation of mobile home dealers. Longley initiated the legislation in response to numerous complaints received by his division from buyers of defective mobile homes. Photo courtesy Joe K. Longley*

PHOTO 16. *Supporters of evangelist Lester Roloff were provided with hundreds of placards to publicize their plight at an Austin rally in 1976. The signs read "Keep Roloff Homes Open—they have no other place to go." PICA AS-76-93121-14, Austin History Center, Austin Public Library*

PHOTO 17. *Evangelist Lester Roloff of Corpus Christi held several rallies in Austin to protest Hill's efforts to force him to follow state licensing laws at his homes for troubled youth. Always holding a Bible, as seen in this photo, Roloff lost his court battles with Hill but used the confrontations to punish Hill politically by helping derail his campaign for governor in 1978. PICA AAS-76-93121-19A, Austin History Center, Austin Public Library*

PHOTO 18. *Hill was honored in February 1977 as "Mr. South Texas" as part of Laredo's annual Washington's Birthday Celebration. Riding with him and his wife Bitsy are their grandchildren, Elizabeth and Carter Perrin, whose father is in the front passenger seat. Photo courtesy Hill family*

L O G

continued/ Friday 30 June 1972	4:20 PM	Finished eating dessert. (one serving)
	4:45 "	Screening "SHANGHAI EXPRESS". Again!
	6:40 "	B/R.
	9:10 "	Chair
	11:00 "	Dessert
aturday uly 1, 1972	1:00 AM	Finished dessert
	1:10 "	Asleep in chair
	3:00 "	B/R.
	3:40 "	6 bbs.
	4:20 "	2 bbs. Bed.
	4:35 "	Asleep.
	1:30 PM	Awake, B/R.
	2:25 "	Chair, T.V.
	4:30 "	B/R.
	5:05 "	Chair, screening "CATTLE KING".
	7:35 "	Finished "CATTLE KING", OK to return.
	7:50 "	B/R.
	8:05 "	Chair
	9:50 "	B/R
	10:10 "	Chair
	11:45 "	B/R
Sunday July 2, 1972	12:15 AM	Chair
	1:55 "	B/R
	2:20 "	Chair
	3:15 "	8 E.
	3:40 "	Started eating (chicken). Screening DIAMONDS ARE FOREV
	5:15 "	Finished eating.
	6:30 "	B/R.
	7:00 "	Chair.
	7:50 "	Finished DIAMONDS ARE FOREVER.
	8:10 "	Started eating dessert.
	10:10 "	B/R.
	10:35 "	Chair, 5BB's.
	11:00 "	Screening "SEVEN WAYS FROM SUNDOWN". Reels 1 & part of 2.
	1:15 PM	B/R.
	2:40 "	Chair, working.
	6:25 "	B/R.
	10 "	Bed and asleep
Monday July 3, 1972	7:15 AM	B/R. Big E.
	9:45 "	Bed. 6 bbs. Asleep.
	3:40 PM	Awake & B/R.
	4:15 "	Chair, 2bb's.
	5:00 "	B/R.
	5:20 "	Chair.
	6:15 "	B/R & Big E.
	8:10 "	Bed & asleep
Tuesday July 4, 1972	12:50 AM	B/R
	1:25 "	Chair
	3:15 "	Started screening.
	4:30 "	Started eating chicken. Finished SEVEN WAYS FROM SUNDOWN--Can return it.
	5:45 "	B/R.
	6:10 "	Chair.
	8:10 "	Finished eating--2 desserts. Finished SHANGHAI EXPRESS
	8:15 "	B/R.
	8:50 "	Chair, screening "OCEANS II".
	10:50 "	B/R.
	11:15 "	Chair, resumed screening "OCEANS II".

ILLUSTRATION 2. *Hill's staff broke open their stalemated case against the Howard Hughes estate by persuading the U.S. Treasury Department to share copies of the highly secret log Hughes's staff had maintained during the final years of his reclusive life. The logs demonstrated Hughes's dependence on drugs and his inactivity, which his keepers assiduously kept from public view while maintaining that he was still actively managing his companies. The references to "BBS" in the early morning of July 1, the next evening, and the following morning refer to "blue bombers," which were ten-milligram Valium capsules Hughes took in double or triple the recommended dosage. Photo courtesy Rick Harrison*

ILLUSTRATION 3. *After Hill announced his candidacy for governor in September 1977, his subsequent actions as attorney general often were viewed by critics as politically motivated. This editorial cartoon pokes fun at Hill's denial that he was seeking high-profile cases to publicize himself and to further his political career. Illustration courtesy Ben Sargent*

ILLUSTRATION 4. *In 1977, Hill advocated the establishment of a statewide grand jury to allow his staff to enforce criminal laws without depending on an invitation from a local prosecutor. Despite support from John Clark, the U.S. attorney who obtained federal convictions of the Parrs and Carrillos in Duval County, opposition from district attorneys and Governor Briscoe killed the idea. Illustration courtesy Ben Sargent*

ILLUSTRATION 5. *Editorial cartoonist Ben Sargent took note of the business lobby's efforts in 1977 to challenge Hill on a consumer protection issue. When Congress passed a law in 1976 to allow state attorneys general to bring antitrust lawsuits on behalf of consumers, conservative House members in Austin sought to pass legislation allowing Texas to opt out of the new law. Hill mounted a strong counteroffensive, calling dozens of legislators himself, and successfully blocked the bill. Illustration courtesy Ben Sargent*

PHOTO 19. *Hill and Rick Harrison pose on the steps of the Supreme Court of the United States in May 1978 prior to Hill's argument in the Howard Hughes estate case. Hill was successful in preventing California from blocking Texas' claims to tax the Hughes estate. Photo courtesy Rick Harrison*

PHOTO 20. *Left to right: First Asst. Atty. Gen. Larry York, Executive Asst. Atty. Gen. Joe Bill Watkins, drummer Paul English, musician Willie Nelson, and Asst. Atty. Gen. Wardlow Lane. Unbeknownst to Hill, his staff filed a lawsuit in May 1974 at the request of state tax collectors demanding payment of delinquent entertainment taxes. At his next performance at the Austin Opry House off South Congress Avenue, Nelson displayed this homemade "Impeach Hill" banner in protest. Hill told his staff the following week, "I can't know everything 110 lawyers are doing, but I want to give you a guideline: if we sue Dolph Briscoe, Richard Nixon and Spiro Agnew, Darrell Royal, or Willie Nelson, I want to know about it." Subsequent attorneys general kept the guideline and termed it the "John Hill Rule." Photo courtesy Larry York*

PHOTO 21. *Hill could be counted on to recite Patrick Henry's "Give me liberty or give me death!" speech whenever a suitable occasion arose. Here, he donned an Uncle Sam suit to enliven a July 4 celebration where he gave the Henry speech. Photo courtesy Hill family*

PHOTO 22. *Hill purchased a ranch near Dripping Springs in the early 1970s to use as a getaway for him and Bitsy and their extended family. Pictured at the ranch in the mid-1970s are (left to right) Bitsy, the Hills' daughter Melinda, Hill holding granddaughter Elizabeth Perrin, their daughter Martha, and their son Graham Hill, holding John Graham Hill Jr. Photo courtesy Hill family*

PHOTO 23. *Pictured at the family's ranch near Dripping Springs in the mid-1970s are Bitsy on Old Sage, Martha standing beside her, Melinda on the right, and Graham petting Luke. Photo from a clipping, courtesy Hill family*

ILLUSTRATION 6. *The election of 1978, the first to be held after elected officials had served four-year terms, instead of the two-year terms that were previously the standard, generated high interest. Anticipation was building because Governor Briscoe was concluding his second term (a total of six years in office—a record at that time) and because Hill, Lt. Gov. Bill Hobby, and Comptroller Bob Bullock were considered potential candidates for governor. Illustration courtesy Ben Sargent*

ILLUSTRATIION 7. *The favorable newspaper coverage that blossomed for Hill as attorney general made him an easy target for gibes such as this one by Ben Sargent when Hill announced his campaign for governor in 1977. Illustration courtesy Ben Sargent*

ILLUSTRATION 8. *Because Bob Bullock, the irascible state comptroller, made it his business to trim the sails of any politician he considered too favorably treated by the press, he escalated his attacks on Hill as the election of 1978 approached and Bullock mulled a race for governor. In August 1977, Bullock attempted unsuccessfully to sue Hill for failure to collect delinquent sales taxes, along the way issuing many public statements criticizing Hill that, by inference, helped Governor Briscoe in his race against Hill. Illustration courtesy Ben Sargent*

PHOTO 24. *John and Bitsy Hill were jubilant after he defeated Governor Briscoe in the Democratic primary election of 1978. PICB19071, Austin History Center, Austin Public Library*

PHOTO 25. *Hill lugs a football as the ceremonial kickoff participant for an annual University of Texas–University of Oklahoma marathon held in October 1975 by two social groups working to raise funds for cancer research in connection with the schools' annual football rivalry. Photo from a clipping, courtesy Hill family*

PHOTO 26. *The Hill family gathered in Austin in May 1978 for the swearing-in ceremony of new lawyers, of whom Hill's daughter Martha was one. Pictured are (back row, left to right) Martha Hill, Melinda Perrin (Hill's eldest daughter, holding Hunter), Melinda's husband Mike Perrin, Bitsy Hill, John Hill, Jessie Hoover Hill and John Luke Hill Sr. (John's parents), John Graham Hill Jr. (held by his father), and John's son Graham Hill. Front row: Elizabeth Perrin, Carter Perrin, and Ruby Graham Pitcock (Bitsy's mother) of Olney. Photo courtesy Hill family*

PHOTO 27. *Two of Hill's top aides were recruited from the Houston law firm of Baker & Botts: John Odam (left), whose six years with Hill included prosecuting District Judge Oscar Carrillo in an impeachment proceeding before the Texas Senate, and Larry York (right), Hill's first assistant during 1973–1974. This photo was taken during Hill's final days in office. Photo courtesy John Odam*

PHOTO 28. *This was Hill's official photo when he became attorney general in 1973. Photo courtesy State Bar of Texas*

(6)

Attacking Corruption in Duval County

When I raised organized crime as an issue in my campaign for attorney general, I envisioned creating a task force to coordinate with state and local law enforcement agencies to investigate and prosecute sophisticated crime syndicates like the Mafia. To my surprise, the largest nexus of organized criminal activity to demand my office's resources was operated by small-town local government officials, not professional gangsters.

These crooks were not a handful of sinister underworld villains operating tightly disciplined gambling, prostitution, or drug operations. They were a loose confederation of elected or appointed public servants who had made a cottage industry of stealing from the public till. Their ill-gotten gains generally were readily evident in public documents and were common public knowledge.

Those conditions should have simplified our prosecution of their crimes. But that overly simple view addressed neither the convoluted paths these officials used to transfer money and thus cover their tracks nor the iron grip these outlaws held on local law enforcement and judicial systems. Bringing them to justice gave us every bit as much of a challenge as dislodging an entrenched Mafia operation.

The location of this enterprise was Duval County, situated halfway between Corpus Christi and Laredo. It was home to 12,700 residents, mostly gathered in three towns, and 74,000 head of cattle roaming mesquite-choked pastureland that overlay significant oil and gas deposits. It is situated in what was called the "Nueces Strip" in Texas' early days, a desolate and lawless no-man's-land between the Rio Grande and Nueces River.[1] The mouths of the two rivers are about 140 miles apart, and the Nueces Strip extends upriver on the Rio Grande about 300 miles, narrowing at some points to about 50 miles. It was a flat, forbidding scrub and brush landscape claimed by two governments. Mexico insisted the Nueces was its boundary with Texas, which claimed land all the way to the Rio Grande. The dispute precipitated the U.S.-Mexican War after Texas was granted statehood in 1845, and it cost Mexico the loss of 525,000 square miles of territory.

Too remote from either nation's major cities and military forces to warrant diligent law enforcement, these rural areas along the border saw frequent cross–Rio Grande raids by bandits, adventurers, and political schemers from both sides who were a menace to all but the most hardy settlers into the early part of the 1900s. Novelist Larry McMurtry immortalized the area in his best-selling book and television miniseries *Lonesome Dove* by selecting it as the site of the Hat Creek Cattle Company operated by the saga's two heroes, retired Texas Ranger captains Augustus "Gus" McCrae and Woodrow F. Call.

As the area's reputation for freewheeling social, business, and political cultures mellowed over the decades, the residue found its most fertile home in local politics. The *patrón* system of ranch management in northern Mexico, where large landowners enjoyed undisputed sway over a large underclass of manual laborers and their families, provided a cultural foundation easily exploited by political leaders intent on using their governmental powers to establish a fiefdom.

The corrupt local governments that ruled several of the Nueces Strip counties in the last decades of the 1800s and early twentieth century created a loose confederation of boss-ruled counties that slowly succumbed to reforms. Land developers took advantage of turn-of-the-century completion of railroad access and development of agricultural irrigation capabilities to attract hordes of opportunists, who replaced the feudal frontier society with a more democratic political system. While these developments and accompanying population growth brought modernity to counties along the lower Rio Grande, Duval County's remoteness and lack of significant irrigation water left it unaffected by the prosperity and political reforms one hundred miles to the south.[2]

Duval County's rough-and-tumble existence was tamed by men like Archie Parr, who parlayed his experience as a teenage trail boss for a cattle drive along the Chisholm Trail into a job in 1882 as manager of one of the county's large ranches. He later owned his own small ranch near Benavides in the center of the county. The county courthouse was located in San Diego, only fifteen miles to the northeast but a world away culturally. As both the political center and, because the railroad from Corpus Christi to Laredo went through it, the economic center of the county, San Diego was more anglicized and less Hispanic than the ramshackle outpost of Benavides.

Unlike many of the Anglo elite in San Diego who rejected the Hispanic culture and did not socialize with the county's predominantly Hispanic population, Parr's ability to befriend them and gain their respect as a benevolent patrón helped launch a political career that began with his election to the county commissioners' court in 1896. The wily Parr withstood several attempts by Duval County political rivals to end his one-man rule, which he had achieved by organizing a takeover of county government in 1907 and embellished by serving as a member of the Texas Senate for twenty years. In a precursor to many subsequent incidents in which evidence was destroyed in order to thwart investigations, the courthouse mysteriously burned to the ground in 1914 during one investigation of him and his machine.[3] In 1934, Parr passed his leadership role and his nickname, "the Duke of Duval," to his son George, who proved even more adept at consolidating power than his father had been.

George Parr's heavy-handed rule of Duval County continued despite his conviction for federal income tax evasion in 1934 and nine months in federal prison in 1936–1937. In 1948, it unintentionally thrust him onto a much larger stage.[4] By single-handedly clinching the election of Lyndon B. Johnson to the U.S. Senate, Parr accomplished two things: he gained a potent ally and protector who could shield him from federal investigations for the next two decades, and he made himself the target of life-long visceral enmity among conservative political leaders in both the Democratic and Republican Parties in Texas.

Parr's outrageous ballot-box stuffing for Johnson became such a powerful legend in Texas and American politics that a participant in the chicanery prompted researchers to delve into the LBJ Library archives. That revelation created a flurry of newspaper articles as far away as New York and Los Angeles when the election official told an interviewer almost three decades later that Johnson was present in Alice when the infamous "Box 13" revisions were made six days after the election.[5]

Johnson's victory over former governor Coke Stevenson by 87 votes out of the 988,295 votes cast earned him the nickname "Landslide Lyndon." That margin was secured by the addition of 200 Johnson votes to the initial total reported from Jim Wells County. Parr's political base in San Diego, on the eastern edge of Duval County where it adjoined Jim Wells County, extended into the neighboring county, where he owned the Texas State Bank in Alice.

The voter sign-in sheet, viewed briefly by Stevenson before it disappeared after he mounted a legal challenge to the election, contained a striking feature: the last 203 signatures were in identical handwriting, in a different ink than used on the rest of the voter sign-in sheet, and in alphabetical order. The additional votes gave Johnson 965 votes to Stevenson's 62.[6]

The deep resentment among Stevenson backers never abated. It surfaced four years later, when Gov. Allan Shivers and Atty. Gen. Price Daniel sent Texas Rangers and investigators to bolster efforts of reformers seeking to oust Parr's slate of candidates in local elections.[7] Several months after those elections, another event spurred Parr's opponents into more forceful action: the murder of Jake Floyd Jr. in Alice.

The murder-for-hire was a botched job. Floyd's father, an attorney and vocal critic of Parr's, was the intended target.[8] It sparked outrage in Austin, where Governor Shivers and the new attorney general, John Ben Shepperd, vowed to clean up Duval County.[9]

Parr's grip on the judicial system made those vows difficult to fulfill. Obtaining indictments was impossible without removing Parr's district judge and grand jurors. Parr's dominance over the residents who might serve on juries required moving the trials out of Duval County. Shepperd overcame those obstacles and obtained convictions against Parr and several of his lieutenants, only to have them all reversed on appeal.[10]

Shepperd's fate mirrored that of federal prosecutors whose extensive mail fraud prosecutions in Duval County in the 1950s fell to a U.S. Supreme Court reversal of George Parr's conviction by a Houston jury.[11] A maze of intertwined personal loyalties stymied all outsiders attempting to prove the massive embezzlement of government funds occurring in Duval County.[12] With each failed prosecution, Parr's invincibility grew and his detractors' enthusiasm for a rematch dimmed.

When I took office in 1973, my unease over this corrupt regime was tempered by the realities of my limited powers. In 1875, the framers of our state constitution had vented their frustrations with federal control during Reconstruction by limiting the powers of their state executive officeholders, including the attorney general's power to enforce criminal laws.

Grand jury composition is the exclusive province of local district judges. The attorney general or an assistant can prosecute a case only if they are appointed as a special prosecutor by the local prosecuting attorney. Local district attorneys were very protective of their authority to control the presentation of evidence, to recommend prosecution of an accused, and to present the case in court. Like my predecessors, my policy was to refuse risking a battle with a local prosecutor by inviting myself, or responding to an invitation from a grand jury, to present a case to a local grand jury.

These limitations demanded that I put aside my personal disgust at small-town corruption, which was based on a painful incident involving my father when I was in high school. A longtime city councilman, school board trustee, Rotarian, Mason, Baptist, and leader of all good causes, my father was asked by many people in 1939 to run against the county commissioner who was widely viewed as corrupt, as was most of the county government. He agreed and ran as a reform candidate.

The night of the election, I sat in our family Chevy outside the courthouse with my dad while the votes were being tallied. When it got close to midnight, I asked Dad why it was taking so long for them to come out and tell us who had won.

"Son, they're in there trying to make sure I don't win," he said.

"How can they do that?" I asked in my innocence.

"I don't know exactly. They do it a lot of ways, by putting votes of dead people in the ballot box for my opponent, by making up votes that were never cast. It's called stuffing the ballot box and it has been going on for a long time in the county. But I think I have so many votes, they may not be able to get away with it this time."

Well, they did get away with it. The election officials finally came out a little after midnight and declared the other man the winner by eighteen votes. That was my introduction to corrupt politics, and I have forever after had a special abhorrence for corruption in public affairs.

The practical constraints on my power to intervene in Duval County were almost as absolute as the legal ones. Even if I decided to target the Parr machine, its control of the prosecutorial, law enforcement, and judicial branches of government, as well as the local banks, posed a formidable challenge in gathering evidence, obtaining grand jury indictments, and achieving convictions in court.

Because it was such a closed society, Duval County offered scant opportunity for obtaining the insider information essential to framing and focusing such a broad-ranging investigation. Until that crucial element revealed itself, there was no place to begin.

Such an opportunity dropped into federal prosecutors' laps in January 1972. A routine Internal Revenue Service audit produced a startling admission by an Austin architect who operated a firm that designed and supervised construction of public school buildings. The unexplained checks to cash for which he claimed no tax deduction as a business expense, he told

IRS examiners, were for payoffs to public officials in Duval County who had hired him for a $2.2 million building program.

During the 1960s when Lyndon Johnson was in the White House, the Justice Department most likely would have looked the other way if presented this information. But the Democrats were out of power, leaving Parr vulnerable. Republican president Richard Nixon's Justice Department had control of the nation's prosecutorial force, which still chafed at what they viewed as Parr's ability to use his political contacts to win the Supreme Court reversal of his mail fraud conviction in federal court in Houston.[13]

The IRS investigation of the architect's mysterious $353,500 in checks made payable to "cash" produced an offer from the architect's attorneys. He would explain the transactions and name names if the IRS would provide immunity from prosecution. The IRS regional director in Austin called the U.S. attorney's office in San Antonio to request a conference.[14] Both being eager to capitalize on the stunning breakthrough this felicitous offer provided, the two agencies agreed to pursue the immunity request. It was approved by Washington several months later.

The task of converting the architect's explosive information into a prosecutable case that would lead to conviction fell to the new U.S. attorney in San Antonio, Bill Sessions, and his first assistant, John E. Clark. Both had recently left the Justice Department criminal division office in Washington headed by Will Wilson, a former Texas attorney general who had switched parties after losing a race for governor to John Connally in 1962. Sessions had been practicing law in Waco and Clark, in Austin, when Wilson recruited them to join the Nixon administration.

Sessions and Clark, along with IRS investigators, began searching for evidence to link the architect's reports of bribes to the recipients' failure to report the income on tax returns. The architect documented payments to Parr and the superintendents of the Freer and San Diego schools in response to their demands for kickbacks. Forty thousand dollars, in packets of hundred-dollar bills stuffed in a brown paper grocery sack, was delivered to Parr at night on a sidewalk outside the courthouse in San Diego. Despite the Parr machine's best efforts to sabotage the investigation through such tactics as the destruction of records, foot-dragging by Parr-controlled banks, and forgetful witnesses, the federal prosecutors completed the link.

The school superintendents' bank accounts revealed that most of their unreported income came from the Austin architect. But the investigators' review of Parr's records showed that the $40,000 from the architect was just a sample of the smorgasbord of government-related rip-offs he had masterminded. When the prosecutors totaled the trio's under-the-table income, it amounted to more than $386,000 over four years for Parr, more than $100,000 over three years for the San Diego superintendent, and more than $45,000 over three years for the Freer superintendent. They also caught in their net Parr's nephew, Duval County judge Archer Parr, who received an unaccounted-for $121,500, as well as the local district judge, O. P. Carrillo, who with his county commissioner brother was scamming about $80,000 a year in unreported income from several local government sources.

Fifteen months after that first meeting with the IRS and the architect's lawyers, Sessions and Clark obtained indictments against George Parr and the school superintendents. Judge Archer Parr was indicted seven months later, in November 1973. George Parr was convicted in a Corpus Christi trial in March 1974 and sentenced to five years in prison. His nephew was convicted two months later and sentenced to ten years in prison.[15]

The Parrs' convictions drained them of the political potency essential to maintaining control in the face of the increasingly restless Benavides-based Carrillo family that had shared power with the Parrs for several decades. George and Archer Parr were free on bond and the latter was still county judge. But George Parr was seventy-three, and his only heir apparent was his prison-bound nephew. The Carrillos made it known in Duval County that they were ready to take the leadership role after the Parrs were gone.

To this increasingly unstable political mixture was added a new, third political force: millionaire banker and rancher Clinton Manges of Freer. Unlike the Parrs and Carrillos, Manges's financial shenanigans were not government based. A prickly and secretive fifty-year-old deal-maker unhampered by his lack of a high school diploma, Manges burst on the South Texas business scene in 1971 by taking control of the 100,000-acre Duval County Ranch Company and the venerable Groos National Bank in San Antonio.[16]

Manges quickly became one of the state's most aggressive political players. One of his attorneys and close friends was Bob Bullock, the new state comptroller elected in 1974. His reputation as a big-time political donor was confirmed in 1974 when Governor Briscoe revealed that Manges had delivered a fifteen-thousand-dollar cash campaign donation to his Uvalde ranch during the campaign of 1972.[17]

Among the beneficiaries of Manges's political support was O. P. Carrillo, who held the district judgeship Parr had created to solve a perpetual problem with the judges of the four-county district who sometimes exercised independence.[18] Parr's plan to create a new, smaller district that included Starr, Jim Hogg, and Duval counties to provide a judicial seat for Carrillo was proposed in the legislature by O. P.'s brother Oscar, a member of the House, and passed in 1969.[19] Because judges controlled the makeup of grand juries, Carrillo's role assured Parr that he could prevent any would-be reformers from using subpoena powers to lift the lid on Duval County's pervasive corruption.

That strategy backfired, however, when Judge Carrillo decided not to impede a state grand jury investigation of the wrongdoing uncovered by the federal prosecutions of the Parrs and reported by the *Corpus Christi Caller.*[20]

The investigation resulted from the election of a new district attorney. The Parrs stalled any state investigation during most of 1974 by blocking appointment of a successor to Randall Nye, an ally, after he resigned in January 1974.[21] The office was filled by the election of Arnulfo Guerra, a soft-spoken forty-seven-year-old lawyer and weekly newspaper owner from Roma in Starr County, in November 1974.

Guerra's political history was scant and unimpressive—a losing race for county judge in 1968 and several unsuccessful races for the local school board that incurred the wrath of the longtime mayor of Roma, Joe Guerra.[22] Nor was his personal history completely tidy—he pleaded *nolo contendere* in 1970 to failure to pay income taxes in 1965 and was reprimanded by the State Bar of Texas.[23]

He owed his victory to the Parrs, who provided a margin of twenty-five hundred votes for him in Duval County to offset his loss of Jim Hogg County by fifteen hundred votes; he carried Starr County by four hundred votes. But he was such a stealth candidate—only spending several hundred dollars to buy a few bumper stickers for his campaign—that he took office in December as generally an unknown quantity. In a county where the Parrs made certain nothing in government happened by accident, the election of Guerra proved to be an unpleasant surprise to them.

Guerra's election was followed by Judge Carrillo's impaneling of a new grand jury on February 4. The next week, Guerra drafted several subpoenas demanding financial records from the Duval County public entities and had them served, requiring the records to be delivered to the grand jury meeting the next day.

Guerra's actions lacked even minimal prosecutorial acumen. He made no preliminary inquiries to any of the entities to evaluate the prospects of useful evidence. The grand jury was not apprised of his plans. He made no attempt to familiarize himself with investigations under way by my office, state police, or federal prosecutors. Because he was elected with Parr's support, and because the Parrs' affinity for destroying incriminating records was well known, all the governmental entities he targeted were reluctant to turn over their records to him for fear they would vanish. The pushback from the subpoenaed officials forced him to settle for only the Benavides school district records, and then only after assuring the board chairman that a district representative would not let them out of his sight while the grand jury inspected them.[24]

Guerra's clumsy launch of his investigation was puzzling to any who were attempting to discern the likelihood of a local investigation that would prosecute the violations of state law uncovered in the federal investigation. Guerra knew few people in Duval County and made no effort to meet any, driving from Roma to San Diego in time to attend the grand jury meeting and then leaving town immediately afterward. He claimed that all he knew about wrongdoing in the county was what he read in the *Corpus Christi Caller.* He professed no insights into the politics of the grand jury members and sought none. He clearly failed to perceive that he was creating a political tornado, one that would, in the next few weeks, suck all of the competing political leaders into a furious and destructive fight for dominance.

His attempt to digest the school district records quickly convinced him and the grand jury that he was outmanned. He and the grand jury foreman, who managed Manges's huge Duval County ranch, decided to ask Judge Carrillo for help. The foreman suggested one of Manges's attorneys, former state senator Jim Bates of Edinburg, as a special prosecutor. Carrillo appointed him on March 4.[25]

In his innocence, Guerra failed to anticipate the Parrs' reaction to being investigated by the employee of a man they suspected was encouraging the Carrillos to take over Duval County political leadership from the Parrs. Archer Parr retaliated by withholding approval for Bates's funding by the commissioners' court he chaired, stalling the grand jury investigation. George Parr retaliated by reneging on a promise not to challenge two Carrillo candidates in the Benavides school board election scheduled for April 5. [26]

Archer Parr's rebuff convinced Guerra to consider a removal petition to replace him. He also was receiving reports from two members of the Parr-dominated school board, who also were Carrillo family members, about missing district financial records needed for the investigation. He spent several days drafting removal petitions and arranged with Judge Carrillo to consider them the afternoon of March 19.[27]

Once again, Guerra's naiveté left him unprepared for the consequences of his actions. Word of his removal strategy preceded him by several hours to San Diego, where George Parr received the news with explosive anger. Manges telephoned Carrillo to warn him. They agreed to meet on the highway between Benavides and San Diego. Manges told Carrillo he saw Parr leave his house with a machine gun and was waiting at the courthouse to shoot him "the moment you walk in."[28] Carrillo went to his ranch and alerted the Texas Rangers, FBI, and the U.S. attorney's office in Corpus Christi.

When Guerra pulled into a curbside parking spot at the courthouse about four o'clock in the afternoon, his investigator, Robert Forche, was running toward his car. "Don't get out of your car. Stay there. There's trouble in the courthouse," Forche told Guerra, who asked what was going on. "George Parr is armed in there and he's going to kill Judge Carrillo. He's angry about something and he's been there since 2:30 and there's going to be some bloodshed here." Guerra got out of his car and stood on the sidewalk, surveying the scene of clumps of people standing around on the barren lawn of the courthouse. Archer Parr came up to him and heatedly told him, "This is what you caused by trying to remove people."[29]

Just then Manges drove up next to him and invited him to ride with him to Carrillo's ranch, where Carrillo went after learning of George Parr's threats. With Texas Ranger Gene Powell leading them, they sped to the ranch. They discussed the removal petitions and agreed they would be presented in open court the next day.[30] The next morning, Guerra arrived at the courthouse to see dozens of men with the vague outline of a pistol showing from beneath their guayabera shirts. Guerra himself was armed. Judge Carrillo was in his chambers with Ranger Powell.[31]

The petitions' complaints included expenditure of more than sixty thousand dollars by the Benavides school board for attorneys advising or representing George Parr and the school superintendents in their federal income tax evasion trial. Judge Carrillo signed the removal orders in his chambers, to avoid the necessity of running an armed gauntlet to walk up a flight of stairs to his courtroom, and appointed replacements for the ousted Parr supporters. His choice of a new school board chairman was a Manges ranch employee, which further angered the Parrs.[32]

The following week, Judge Carrillo stepped up the warfare to a new level. Responding again to a request by Guerra and the grand jury foreman, on Monday, March 24, he suspended Archer Parr from the county judge's seat he had held for sixteen years and replaced him with a Parr opponent. Archer Parr refused to acknowledge the order, resulting in two would-be county judges attempting to convene meetings of the commissioners' court.[33]

The same day, George Parr learned that his appeal of his federal court conviction was denied by the Fifth Circuit Court of Appeals. He also knew that federal agents were taking depositions from Duval County residents about his threats against Judge Carrillo and Manges, as well as about his aggressive displays of his pistol in the last week. His lawyer told him to expect the prosecutors to attempt to revoke his bail.

Cornered and desperate to survive, George Parr took the unprecedented step the next day of holding a forty-five-minute news conference to blame Manges for the Parr-Carrillo feud. Manges's motivation, he told news reporters in his folksy style, was revenge for Archer Parr refusing to fund the special prosecutor job for Bates. The new county judge, he said, was placed there by Manges because the man was financially indebted to Manges. The irony of Parr's criticism of Manges was noted in news articles—Manges had written checks totaling more than $260,000 for bonds guaranteeing the Parrs would appear in federal court.[34]

In Austin, the Parrs' advocate in the legislature, Rep. Terry Canales of Premont, sent to his Senate counterpart a bill he was asking him to sponsor. Its caption read, "Relating to the abolishment of the office of District Attorney, 229th Judicial District." Guerra was definitely in the crosshairs of the Parrs' political weapons.[35]

Two days later, Judge Carrillo upped the stakes in the hostilities, instructing Guerra to prepare a motion to hold Archer in contempt for defying Carrillo's order removing him as county judge.[36]

The next day, which was Friday and the last workday in one of the most traumatic weeks in Duval County history, it was the Carrillo family's turn to suffer a blow from the federal prosecutors. Judge Carrillo and his brother Ramiro Carrillo, a member of the Duval County commissioners' court, were indicted by a federal grand jury in Corpus Christi for filing false income tax returns.[37]

George Parr also got some bad news from the federal courts. Federal prosecutors filed a motion with Judge Owen Cox in Corpus Christi to revoke his bail and incarcerate him because of his volatile behavior.[38]

The following Monday, the Parrs suffered a defeat in the Texas Supreme Court, which rejected their efforts to void Judge Carrillo's orders removing Archer Parr from the bench and the Benavides school board members from their seats.[39] In Corpus Christi, Judge Cox set a hearing for four o'clock that afternoon on the government's revocation of bond motion, and he commanded George Parr to appear.

Also that day, Guerra took the final step that would bring down the entire Duval County political empire. He wrote me a letter explaining that his office lacked adequate staff to prosecute the "massive and overwhelming" corruption cases he had undertaken. He invited my office to provide resources to help him. "Except for the District Judge," Guerra's letter said, apparently attempting to maintain good relations with the just-indicted judge in whose court any prosecutions must proceed, "it appears that all other officials in Duval County are subject to the orders of those persons who are involved in the matter being investigated," thus prompting him to resort to outside help.[40]

Guerra delivered the letter personally the next day, Tuesday, April 1, so we could discuss the issue in my office. The tension provoked by the substance of the letter and the previous week's destructive political slugfest in Duval County was heightened by our knowledge that George Parr had failed to make his scheduled 4:00 P.M. federal court appearance in Corpus Christi the previous day, that he was armed with a .45-caliber pistol he had taken from his lawyer's office, and that federal, state, and local law enforcement officials were combing the county for him.

We learned during our meeting that George Parr's body was found on his ranch that morning in the driver's seat of his dark blue Chrysler, a bullet hole through his Stetson and his brain, the .45 in his lap. The second and last Duke of Duval was gone.

I knew that the cancer of corruption Parr had fostered remained for us to excise. But his family's hoary mystique that evoked *pistoleros* subjugating a cowering local populace and the smug flaunting of their absolute power in the faces of Texas Rangers, attorneys general, governors, and federal prosecutors had died with George Parr. While Duval County remained a daunting challenge for us, I was relieved it was one now shorn of its threat of imminent physical harm and legendary impenetrability.

I instructed my public information office to release a copy of Guerra's letter with a simple statement that my office would provide the assistance he sought. I knew my participation would become high profile soon enough. For now, I wanted to maintain Guerra's role as the out-front leader as long as possible to prevent any repeat of the hostility to meddling outsiders that tarred Shepperd's investigation in the 1950s.[41]

Guerra's letter was not entirely his idea, and my understated announcement of assistance belied the fact my assistants had been in and out of Duval County frequently over the previous twelve months. John Clark, the assistant U.S. attorney in San Antonio who had prosecuted the Parrs, kept me and my office generally informed of his progress during 1973 and 1974. Tim James, who headed my organized crime task force, sent several of his staff members to work with Texas Rangers investigating Duval County election fraud in a state legislative race in 1974. Two members of my staff spent seven months in 1974 investigating the Duval County water district's financial abuses; that investigation led to my requesting the Texas Water Rights Commission to place it in conservatorship in November 1974 at the suggestion of Archer Parr.[42]

Federal law prevented Clark from sharing his information on the Parrs and Carrillos with us until court approval was obtained, leaving me no choice but to wait out their prosecutions to obtain access to the rich trove of incriminating evidence they developed. We also were precluded from pursuing grand jury investigations because there was no district attorney in Duval County during most of 1974.[43]

From the moment Guerra was elected, the Parrs and Carrillos knew, and we knew, our involvement in any investigation Guerra might launch was the critical factor that would mean a death warrant for the politicians' thievery. Through my staff working on the Duval County water district issue and other back-door opportunities, we were planting the idea that he needed to invite my office to participate in his grand jury investigation of corruption.

The *Corpus Christi Caller*'s pressure for action also continued to escalate. In their editions on Sunday, March 23, 1975, the newspaper's lead editorial urged Judge Carrillo to "move promptly to bring greater credibility to the proceedings he has authorized concerning the Benavides school district. Much, if not most of the smell of politics which permeates the proceedings can be dispelled if Carrillo will ask Atty. Gen. John Hill for assistance. . . . Whatever the outcome of the present battle, however, the results will be more acceptable to the general public if an assistant attorney general has taken part in the investigations." Editor Edward H. Harte added in his column on the editorial pages, "The need for disinterested referees, armed with whatever power and prestige their state offices confer on them, is clear. What is not clear is why, if nobody in Duval will invite the attorney general to take a look, he cannot do something on his own initiative."[44] Guerra finally succumbed to the pressure and gave us the go-ahead in his letter of March 31.

A week after our meeting, I went to San Diego to join Guerra in advising Judge Carrillo of our participation and to introduce my assistants to the grand jury. It was a scene not many state attorneys general in 1975 would recognize.

With me were two armed Texas Rangers, Ray Martinez and John Wood. Rangers had already escorted Judge Carrillo into the three-story, sixty-year-old red brick courthouse framed by tall palm trees, the only building of any size in town. The windows were filled with curious faces of employees concerned how this drama would affect their lives, watching my armed assistants and the armed local sheriff's deputies who lent an Old West aura to the event. The previous week, Guerra had told a news reporter he had "very, very reliable information my life is in great danger."[45]

The previous weekend, the *Dallas Times Herald* had quoted a Duval County deputy sheriff as saying he talked Parr out of killing Judge Carrillo and Manges before he killed himself.[46]

Judge Carrillo, whose courtroom walls were lined with armed officers, was all smiles as I advised him that I had been invited by Guerra to participate in the investigation. "The Court welcomes you to Duval County. We are happy you are here," he told me. I met with the grand jury briefly to introduce John Blanton and Herb Hancock, the assistants who would be presenting cases to them. "We plan to conduct an exhaustive and fair investigation, regardless of the persons involved. We will let the chips fall where they may," I told the grand jurors.[47]

I assigned Blanton, a former federal Drug Enforcement Administration agent who began his career as a San Antonio police officer, to head our task force. It included Hancock, Jerry Carruth, and Ray Bravenec from my staff and Texas Rangers Ray Martinez and Rudy Rodriguez. Other Rangers, attorney general staff members, and investigators from the Department of Public Safety, Texas Banking Department, and Texas Education Agency also participated in the shared responsibilities during the next eighteen months. They set up shop in a newly remodeled two-story bank building owned by the county several blocks from the courthouse. It was space that had been intended for use by Archer Parr as county judge.

When I initially discussed this mission with my staff, I told them I believed that the groundwork laid by federal prosecutors and the investigative work we had done before joining with Guerra would allow us to complete the cleanup in several months. I realized how far I had missed the mark when I began receiving Blanton's weekly reports.

They were filled with every imaginable type of diversion of public funds and goods to private use. The cafeteria manager at the Benavides schools, who operated a catering business that often used the school cafeteria as the location of a catered event, was using cafeteria funds to buy rib-eye steaks, ham, and brisket that were never served to students. For the district tax collector, the school district purchased from the Sears store in Alice new kitchen appliances and carpeting for his house, and for a former school board member, a chain link fence around his property.

A car purchased by the district was traded for a new vehicle, which was titled in the name of an individual. A school van was taken to Brownsville and never seen again. A trailer home bought by the district was found on the property of a water district employee who was charging rent to the trailer's occupant. Not only were the Parrs and Carrillos stealing from the local governments, but they also refused to pay any of the property taxes assessed by their benefactors. A Massey Ferguson® tractor owned by the district was on Oscar Carrillo's ranch. Phony stores were created to allow payment for nonexistent purchases, the funds ending up in the pockets of a government official.[48]

These reports clearly demonstrated that the Parrs' total commitment to decriminalizing theft from the government spawned an aggressive virus that infected all but a handful of public officials and businesses. This illness was chronic and systemic, not an acute, localized affliction easily controlled by removing one or two scofflaw political leaders. Disassembling Duval County's labyrinth of convoluted self-dealing schemes was not going to be quick or easy.

The task force focused first on the Benavides school district, one of the Parrs' and Carrillos' favorite sources of illegal income for several decades, because they found it to be the most ready source of quick information. Credit card abuses by the district's tax assessor-collector were immediately apparent, so the task force chose him as their first prospect for an indictment.

Six weeks after it was created, the task force presented the case to the grand jury and won a vote to indict. The tax assessor-collector, Rudolfo Couling, who was ousted by Judge Carrillo in his purge of Parr supporters in district leadership roles, was charged with four counts of official misconduct and one of theft. The charges stemmed from use of a school district gasoline credit card for his family's six vehicles, in a single month charging the district for seven hundred gallons.[49]

The Couling indictments proved to be a turning point in our investigation on three levels. On the grand jury level, the ease with which we obtained the indictments was quickly revealed to be an anomaly instead of a predictor of what was to come. On the investigative level, they led to the most productive breakthrough we achieved in securing the assistance of an insider. On the prosecuting level, they gave us a witness who devastated the defendants in the courtroom.

Blanton's memos immediately began citing increasing balkiness by the grand jury. Any four members of the grand jury could block an indictment, which required nine votes. The twelve grand jurors were split almost evenly between Carrillo and Parr supporters. The foreman and another member were Manges employees, who were siding with the Carrillo partisans on any disputed votes. The Parr-Carrillo battles in the county continued to rage, with rival school boards both claiming the other was illegitimate and Archer Parr refusing to accept his removal as county judge.

"It is clear, from our four-hour session before the Grand Jury and conversation with Grand Jury members after the session, that it will be necessary to show a lot more than the usual legal probable cause to this Grand Jury," Blanton reported to me two days after the Couling indictments were returned. "Many persons in Duval County expressed shock and surprise that the Grand Jury indicted anyone, as apparently several members had been issued instructions by Archer Parr not to return indictments," Blanton added. "Several members of the Grand Jury are subject to [a] considerable amount of pressure concerning the return of indictments."[50]

The swirling uncertainty in the community caused by these Parr-Carrillo tensions and our investigation was exacerbated by an impeachment movement in Austin to remove Judge Carrillo, the family's most prominent officeholder and a key leader. Representative Canales called Carrillo on May 11 and warned him he would press for impeachment by the legislature if he did not step down or stop his judicial housecleaning of Parr officeholders. Four days later Canales introduced an impeachment resolution. That was followed in two days by the House's creation of a select committee on impeachment.[51] Carrillo was forced to spend most of June in Austin participating in hearings.

In his report of June 8, Blanton gave an example of his problems with the grand jury. At a meeting on June 5, with nine of the grand jurors present, he presented six proposed indictments against a grandson of Carrillo clan patriarch D. C. Chapa and the ousted vice president of the Benavides school board, who were billing the school district for several hundred dollars a month in gasoline purchases.

"The Grand Jury deliberated for a considerable period of time and I was notified they had failed to indict," Blanton wrote. "An argument ensued concerning the political aspects of their failure to indict, as Chapa's grandson was a favorite member of the Carrillo faction. After a short civics lesson, the Grand Jury requested the opportunity to vote again, and this time returned true bills on all six indictments." He continued: "Discussion was then had concerning the pressure that has been put on Grand Jury members not to indict by local political figures and other pressures, and it was requested that no attempts be made to obtain a judge for return of these indictments until the full complement of the Grand Jury could be available so that nine members voting for indictment could not be so easily identified."[52]

Blanton chafed under the political interference. In his report to me on June 28, he described how an airtight case against Cty. Comm. Ramiro Carrillo, a brother of Judge Carrillo, was sabotaged when the four Carrillo supporters on the grand jury killed the indictment with their "no" votes. Ramiro's personal business was paid nine thousand dollars for hauling harvested grain to an elevator in Alice using county-owned tractor-trailers. He also told of Texas Rangers taking a statement from a grand jury member who said he was questioned by Oscar Carrillo, another brother of Judge Carrillo, about the indictment of Chapa's grandson and that Oscar told him he also had questioned another grand juror about the indictment and promised that Judge Carrillo would stop the investigation when he returned from legislative impeachment hearings in Austin. "Texas Rangers are continuing to investigate other Grand Jury members to determine if any bribes or undue influence have been exerted on them," Blanton's report added.[53]

Newspaper reporter Joe Coudert was following the story closely enough—the courthouse walls were thin enough to allow hallway occupants to hear raised voices inside the grand jury room, and the pained look on the faces of those leaving the room signaled general discontent—to sense our problems. One of his colleagues, in an editorial section column on June 27, noted that "our Duval man, Coudert, reports that dissension is surfacing in the grand jury. . . . But something's happening inside that jury room, something that has angered some jury members and also members of the attorney general's staff. Perhaps it's time the attorney general, John Hill himself, comes down and takes over this investigation. . . . Mr. Hill, we need you."[54]

The next week, a planned meeting of the grand jury failed to produce a quorum of nine members after the foreman called several grand jurors and told them not to attend because he was out of town testifying in a court case—despite the foreman's promise to Blanton that his absence would not affect the grand jury meeting. That action pushed Blanton's patience beyond his limits. He and Hancock drafted a news statement and released it July 2 to Coudert, the Alice-based *Corpus Christi Caller* reporter who was dogging the Duval County story.

"We have good reason to believe that some public officials are tampering with the grand jury," their statement said. "It's become obvious that certain powers that be are impeding this investigation. Texas Rangers are now conducting an investigation of allegations concerning coercion and bribery of certain grand jury members and we anticipate we will release the names of persons under investigation in the near future."[55]

My public information assistant, Mary Jane Bode, brought me the clipping of Coudert's article when our office reopened July 5 after the Independence Day holiday. The Associated Press had picked up the story, and it was being published all over the state.[56] I was appalled.

"Get John Blanton on the phone!" I told my secretary. My rule regarding my assistants' comments to the news media was one I had announced to my eleven division chiefs and other top assistants at my first staff meeting and renewed often: "You are free to talk to the press, but I will hold you responsible for what they print, regardless of what you told them."

"John, I'm disappointed in you," I told Blanton. "We're in Duval County at the invitation of the local district attorney, and it's vitally important we present that picture to the public. That's why I went down to meet with Judge Carrillo and the grand jury, to assure everyone in Duval County, and to assure the news media, that we're not outsiders trying to take over the county. When you tell the press you believe the local grand jurors are being bribed, that's going to destroy your credibility, and mine. You and Herb need to calm down and do your job, and work your way through this instead of trying to bully the local people."[57]

The next grand jury meeting was the next Tuesday, so I flew to San Diego to make amends. I reassured the grand jury we were there to help them and were not trying to usurp their power. I encouraged them to be responsive to the evidence my staff was presenting, which I assured them was compelling. I urged them to reconsider the evidence against Ramiro Carrillo, but they again refused to indict him.[58]

Then I met with Blanton and his team to discuss the lack of indictments. Because Ramiro Carrillo's theft of county property crossed into Jim Wells County, where he was paid, Blanton obtained the cooperation of the district attorney for that county to take the evidence to his grand jury. I approved that strategy and urged them to consider any other counties that might have jurisdiction.[59]

Blanton's memos during July continued to paint a dismal picture of any meaningful indictments being returned. On July 17, the grand jury mustered only eight votes to indict Dan Tobin Jr., whom Judge Carrillo had appointed to replace Archer Parr as county attorney, despite clear evidence he was using county funds to pay a worker on his oil lease. When Blanton tried to present cases against Archer Parr and County Commissioner Carrillo, the grand jury, he reported, "indicated that they did not wish to hear any additional cases." On July 23, the grand jury refused to indict Commissioner Carrillo for using Duval County welfare funds to pay for his and Judge Carrillo's groceries. When Blanton presented evidence that Archer Parr had received a four-thousand-dollar credit toward purchase of a tractor in his name by trading in a county-owned tractor, "several members of the Grand Jury advised me that they felt that they could not vote to indict Parr since a few members of the Grand Jury had failed to return an indictment against Carrillo."[60]

I decided this impasse had lingered long enough, that I needed to address it in person. I talked to Blanton, and he convinced Guerra to send me a letter of invitation to the grand jury's last meeting on July 31. "Perhaps if you and I were both able to meet with the Grand Jury at this final session to discuss presentation of pending cases for their final consideration, it might be well received," his letter said, adding, "at that time, we could also thank them for their work during the last six months."[61]

Despite everything I read in Blanton's reports, I was not prepared for the reception I received when Blanton, Guerra, and I presented the grand jury with an open-and-shut case against the superintendent of a small county school in the tiny community of Ramirez. We offered confessions from the superintendent and his assistant documenting use of school funds to purchase television sets and kitchen appliances for their personal use as well as travel and lodging costs for several out-of-state vacation trips and to pay for nonexistent extra work so the checks could be converted to cash. We left the room, the grand jury voted, and we were told when we returned to the room that they would not approve the indictments.

I was livid. I asked Blanton and Guerra to leave, and I gave the grand jury the roughest tongue-lashing I could produce. "We're not going to give up. We'll stay here until hell freezes over," I shouted to them, muttering on the way out, "Thanks for the use of the hall!" Outside the grand jury room, Guerra and I told Coudert we were pleased with the work of the task force, but I criticized the grand jury. "I am extremely disappointed with the inaction of this grand jury, but we will plow ahead and find other means of obtaining indictments," I told him.[62]

The conclusion of this do-nothing grand jury's term worsened our case backlog because the pending cases would need to be resubmitted to a new grand jury being impaneled the next week by Judge Carrillo. As many as thirty investigators from different state agencies were in and out of Duval County, churning out dozens of investigative reports every week. We presented at least fifty cases that the grand jury had refused to consider.

Judge Carrillo's list of new grand jurors was a collection of his family's cronies and hangers-on, assuring no action would be taken on our cases.[63] Carrillo's impeachment case was moving through the legislature and before the Texas Judicial Qualifications Commission, where my staff would assist the commission in its fact-finding—putting us in the awkward position of working in Austin to assist in the removal of the judge in whose court in San Diego we were attempting to return indictments. We had no option but to look for other venues.

While the grand jury stalemate was clogging the presentation of cases, the investigation end of our project stumbled into a bonanza when we discovered Rudy Couling was more than a credit card abuser. We knew little about him when we made the case for his indictment. An unassuming man of modest stature in his fifties, he was pleasant and businesslike in his interviews with Bravenec, who questioned him about such obviously dubious expenditures as appliances the school district purchased for his home.

On August 13, Bravenec answered his room phone at the Rodeway Inn in Alice to hear Couling's voice. "I would like to meet with Mr. Blanton and Ranger Martinez," he told Bravenec, with no further explanation. "Can you arrange that?" Bravenec assured him he could. Couling described a spot along U.S. 281 about ten miles south of Alice where trucks pulled off on a wide shoulder, and he asked them to meet him there about nine o'clock that evening. Couling arrived at the meeting place with his son driving the family car because Couling's poor eyesight made night driving difficult. When the three members of our team arrived at the meeting place, Couling explained the purpose of his call. The Internal Revenue Service had advised him that their investigations of the Parrs and Carrillos indicated he owed about $300,000 in additional taxes on unreported income. The income, however, was not his—he was a conduit for laundering stolen county, school district, and water district funds destined for the Carrillos. He wanted to make a deal with the government to solve his IRS problem. Blanton and Bravenec told him they would discuss it with the federal attorney but that he needed to hire an attorney to negotiate that type of agreement.[64]

This short man with a receding hairline, mustache, thick glasses, and combustible insider information suddenly was the intense focus of our investigation. We worked with his attorney and federal prosecutors to develop an arrangement for him to evade prosecution in return for assisting the investigation. An agreement was completed on August 20, and his debriefing began immediately.

"Couling has told us his story of corruption almost beyond belief," the usually reserved Blanton reported to me excitedly on August 24. "During our investigation, we noticed a large amount of money being paid to Benavides Implement and Hardware Co. from the Benavides School District, Duval County, and from the Water District. We have learned from Couling that with very few exceptions, all of these checks are bogus and are issued to cover some schemes or theft by D. C. Chapa or his sons, O. P., Ramiro, and Oscar. Also included are Chapa's grandsons, D. H. Carrillo and Rogelio Guajardo. Most of the transactions are covered in checks issued by Couling to the various members of the Carrillo faction, causing his statements to be extremely well corroborated."[65]

In his second day of debriefing, Couling dropped the first of two evidentiary bombshells. He told us he was directed by Chapa, the school board president, to destroy the Benavides school district financial records in 1974 to evade the San Antonio federal grand jury investigation. Instead of destroying them, he had hidden them. They were still where he had secreted them, in the crawl space above his office. It was accessible by a trap door into the attic of a private bathroom connected to his office.

The minute he heard the story from Couling, Blanton called Rangers Wood and Rodriguez and sent them to the tax office, a small building next to the school classrooms. They climbed into the attic and recovered a huge cache of canceled checks and vouchers for the years 1968 through 1972, all arranged in clearly labeled expandable file folders.

It took them almost three hours to maneuver the folders down the attic ladder and onto the office floor. Loading the treasure into Wood's Dodge, the two men filled the trunk and the rear seat. The folders were stacked to within two feet of the car's ceiling, and their weight was enough to cause the rear bumper to scrape as the car entered a driveway. In another example of just how pervasive Duval County corruption was, one of the several retrieved checks for payment to school officials' relatives or friends who did no work was paid to a member of the grand jury.[66]

"Full contents of the hidden records will not be known for several days. But this may be the breakthrough the attorney general's task force has been looking for these past months," the *Caller* editorialized the next day. "The attorney general has pushed the inquiry with vigor and pledges to continue. He is to be commended for it."[67]

On a Sunday three days after his first revelation, Couling dropped his second bomb. He called Ranger Gene Powell at home in Bishop and told him he would direct us to a spot where he had buried more school district records.

They agreed to meet the next day on a highway east of Alice. Bravenec and Ranger Powell appeared at the designated time and place, and Couling led them several miles to an abandoned town, then on the Driscoll Ranch over several miles of unpaved roads, crossing through several cattle gates.

He and his son got out of their pickup truck and began digging with shovels in the brush country's sandy soil. Right beneath the surface they could see envelopes with bank statements and canceled checks poking up through the dirt, the edges of the documents slightly charred from a failed attempt to burn them. Couling and his son kneeled in the loose soil, began pulling the diesel fuel–soaked documents from the hole, and handed them up to Bravenec and Powell, who secured them in plastic garbage bags.[68]

Blanton notified federal prosecutors and IRS agents of our find and offered them access to enhance their evidence in the federal income tax evasion trials of Judge Carrillo and Ramiro Carrillo. They spent a week selecting the evidence they needed.

The volume of information was overwhelming. Couling also provided Blanton with original copies of checks he wrote on his Benavides Implement and Hardware Company account to the Chapas as part of a money-laundering scheme utilizing government funds. Blanton decided to utilize a court reporter to record Couling's explanation of each item. Because we were concerned about Couling's safety, Blanton arranged to take him to Austin along with Ranger Martinez. They used Bravenec's house in north Austin, gathering around his kitchen table every day for a week to sort out the damning evidence. The transcription of his comments filled 350 pages.[69]

Couling's debriefing tore the veil off of disguised payments from public bank accounts the corrupt politicians had refined during almost a decade of escalating thievery. As school district tax collector since 1962, Couling had occupied a ringside seat while the Parrs and Carrillos experimented with different techniques to line their pockets. He gave us a detailed road map of the interwoven transactions used to disguise the conversion of public money into payments to the politicians.

One approach they taught Couling was to issue a check to a nonexistent company, forge an endorsement, cash the check, and deliver the money to the politicians. Another was to use sham invoices from the small store he opened in 1971 in Benavides, the Benavides Implement and Hardware Company. Ramiro Carrillo, the county commissioner for Benavides, kept a supply of the store's blank invoices in his office. At least once a month, he would enter a fictitious purchase on an invoice, order a county check issued to the store, and have the check delivered by a county employee—to avoid exposing himself to federal mail fraud charges—to Couling. Then Couling would write a check in the same amount to Judge Carrillo.

The Carrillos and the Parrs used the sham invoice technique repeatedly, creating three phony stores to bounce checks to and from before the county, school district, or water district funds found their way to a Carrillo bank account. An audit of the school district showed more than $500,000 was embezzled during 1974–1975.[70]

Couling became our star witness. He testified over an eleven-day period during the legislature's impeachment trial of Judge Carrillo and helped federal prosecutors send Judge Carrillo to prison for five years and his brother Ramiro to prison for four years.[71] He also provided testimony to the Duval County grand jury that led to indictments of Judge Carrillo and several family members, and then he completed the cycle by providing essential testimony at their trials.[72] Judge Carrillo was sentenced to four years in prison on the state charges.[73]

While we were developing the Couling evidence in August, the Carrillo impeachment process provided us with an unexpected lift in the form of a new and stabilizing district judge. The Texas House voted 126 to 16 on August 5 to impeach Carrillo, resulting in his suspension.[74] He was temporarily replaced by a Brownsville judge, Darrell Hester, who moved our investigation into high gear.

A former district attorney, the fifty-year-old Hester had spent the previous four years on the bench, where he had earned a reputation as a "hanging judge" because he presided with a no-nonsense approach.[75] He was not able to help us turn around the obstructionist grand jury that Carrillo had appointed—over the strenuous objections my staff members Tim James and Bert Pluymen raised about every appointee—before being suspended. But Hester dramatically changed the courthouse atmosphere for the good by replacing Archer Parr's appointed successor as county judge in October with a Benavides pharmacist with no ties to the Parrs or Carrillos and by appointing a new grand jury in 1976 that was independent of the warring factions.[76]

With interference from the Carrillos and Parrs diminishing, our task force burrowed into the hundreds of cases of illegal activities with renewed commitment. A big factor in the grudging acceptance we earned among the county's residents was the nonthreatening personalities of the two Texas Rangers, Martinez and Rodriguez.

While Blanton, Bravenec, and my staff members were spending their evenings attempting to organize the daunting flow of interrogation reports and evidence analysis, Martinez and Rodriguez were socializing with the working folks in local hangouts. This was a decided reversal of Duval County citizens' previous Texas Ranger experiences, which featured George Parr and fabled Ranger captain Alfred Y. Allee engaging in several physical confrontations over the previous thirty years.

Martinez and Rodriguez, who roomed together for two years in the Alice Rodeway Inn while working on the Duval County cases, used their social skills to good effect by bringing in leads offered by local residents whose confidence they had gained. Partly because of their ready acceptance by the community, our task force gained a local nickname, "Los Hilitos." In South Texas, a Spanish term was used to designate the ranch owner for whom cowboys worked, usually by revising the surname to add "os" to the end, such as *kineños* for King Ranch cowboys. In my case, it translated as "Hill's men."[77]

While the field work in Duval County was under way, I also was called upon by the legislature and the state's Judicial Qualifications Commission to assist in the impeachment and removal actions against Judge Carrillo. I assigned John Odam to assist the commission, and he was joined by Liz Levatino in presenting the House's impeachment case before the Senate in a trial in January 1976. As he did in our criminal cases against him, Carrillo never once allowed the overwhelming evidence against him to prevent every possible challenge to our evidence and all possible court appeals before and after the impeachment. He lost every attempt.[78]

The investigation in Duval County stretched over two years. It also involved grand juries in Austin and Alice when we were unable to obtain indictments in San Diego, and it resulted in almost every public official in the county being indicted, along with several bankers and lawyers. We obtained more than one hundred indictments.

We brought civil lawsuits seeking $381,000 in damages against Archer Parr and six members of the Carrillo family and more than $2 million in damages against the president of Parr's San Diego bank, Archer Parr, and Oscar Carrillo. We recovered so many bulldozers and tractors purchased with school district, water district, or county funds and converted to use by the Parrs or Carrillos that they overflowed the county's equipment yard, where they had been gathered for auction.

We seized several county-purchased bulldozers with a combined value of $1 million from an export yard in Laredo, where one of the Duval County politicos had taken them in preparation for sale in Mexico. We tried dozens of criminal cases, winning convictions against Archer Parr, Judge Carrillo and his brothers, and all of the other major players. We lost only two.[79] It was the most extensive and successful state court prosecution of official corruption in Texas history.

(7)

Fighting California and Nevada for Howard Hughes's Estate Taxes

The Howard Hughes case provided a major test of my determination to replace the passive reputation of the attorney general's office with a dynamic culture that attracted talented lawyers capable of holding their own against the legal profession's best.

The Hughes empire had been represented by the powerhouse firm of Andrews, Kurth, Campbell, and Jones, then a seventy-five-year-old pioneer Houston law firm with impeccable credentials as a resource for corporate clients; Hughes's father had hired them when he formed Hughes Tool Company in 1909. In the 1960s, Hughes also hired a New York lawyer, Chester C. Davis, who became a member of Hughes's small inner circle through his membership on the board of directors of Summa Corporation, the Hughes holding company.[1]

These lawyers were tough and tenacious. All of those traits were essential to accommodating this client's enormous wealth, impetuous and aggressive management style, notoriety, and compulsive behavior that had generated dozens of punishing court battles over several decades—litigation that so bedeviled Hughes he left the United States in 1970 to avoid testifying.

Hughes did not return to America alive. His lifeless and gaunt seventy-year-old body arrived at the Houston airport on April 5, 1976, aboard a chartered jet from Acapulco and accompanied by three aides. It was claimed by a cousin he had not seen since 1938.[2]

So mysterious was his existence that the Internal Revenue Service, which circulated an internal memo as early as 1972 speculating that Hughes's insiders may have used a double to disguise the fact Hughes had been dead since 1970, ordered fingerprints lifted from the cadaver.[3] They were transmitted to Washington for comparison with those submitted in the 1930s with his airplane pilot's license application. The Federal Bureau of Investigation confirmed his identity six hours after his remains were buried in Houston on April 7 at a brief service attended by a handful of relatives.[4]

Barely eighteen when his father's death made him a multimillionaire, Hughes led a very public life in his flamboyant youth during the 1920s and 1930s. He blazed trails in aviation by setting speed and distance records as a pilot and by aircraft design innovations. He broke into Hollywood at the top by producing Oscar-winning movies and dating the most popular actresses of the era.

But as he charged headlong into often reckless multimillion-dollar business deals, such as the purchase of Trans World Airlines in 1940, his obsession with secrecy began expanding from his professional life to his personal life. It eventually consumed him, leading to his spending the last twenty years of his life more and more shut off from the world.

The lid Hughes firmly placed on public knowledge of his bizarre personal life was still intact even in death. His Los Angeles public relations staff continued until the end its mission of protecting Hughes's image, insisting he died of a stroke and that he had not been in poor health lately. That deception lasted only several hours, until doctors at Methodist Hospital noted in a preliminary examination that the body was "remarkably emaciated and dehydrated." Doctors who performed an autopsy the next day attributed the cause of death to chronic kidney disease, but they released only one fact indicating Hughes's debilitated condition—he weighed only ninety-three pounds. Unreported, until we wrested the full autopsy report from the Hughes estate five months later after a court fight, was a toxicological study showing astronomically high levels of codeine, x-rays showing fragments of hypodermic needles broken off in both arms, needle tracks along his arms and thighs, and bedsores on his back. An oral surgeon who participated in the autopsy revealed a year later he had never seen an example of tooth decay worse than that of Hughes.[5]

The information vacuum surrounding Hughes and his death was quickly filled with reports of confusion among his managers and lawyers, as well as a new national pastime of creating phony Howard Hughes wills. Within a week, news stories began reporting fruitless searches for a will by representatives of Hughes's business managers and his family.[6] The articles caught the eye of Karen Johnson, chief of the estate tax division for Bob Bullock, the state comptroller.

"I hate to be a vulture, but we should claim Howard Hughes a resident of Texas for estate tax purposes," Johnson wrote in a memo to Bullock. He agreed and sent Johnson and staff auditors to the Internal Revenue

Service to determine if Hughes had filed his income taxes in Texas. The answer came back "yes," so Bullock dispatched Johnson to request my taxation division chief, Rick Harrison, to initiate court action.[7] When Harrison briefed me on their findings, I approved an investigation. He learned that Hughes's lawyers, a week after the funeral, had filed simultaneously in Texas, Nevada, and California courts the documents necessary to establish family members as administrators of the estate.

"Let's get our name in the hat," I told Harrison. "It's clear the estate is moving quickly to exert some control and stop the confusion and speculation about a will. I'm sure they expect phony heirs to start coming out of the woodwork. Go down to Houston and file an appearance for Texas in the probate court so we will receive notices of any hearings and depositions."

Our filing was greeted by derision from the Hughes camp. While we were buoyed by Bullock's preliminary findings and the fact that Hughes was returned to Texas for burial, a quick review of Hughes's life showed he spent all his adult years outside Texas. He left Texas for California in 1925 and returned only for several brief visits to Houston. He left California in 1966 for Las Vegas, then began in 1970 a six-year international odyssey as an exile vagabond to avoid mounting legal and federal income tax problems.

At first, we could not understand why the Hughes estate was so hostile to our desire to have Texas declared the domiciliary state. Federal income tax laws provided for an offset of up to 16 percent, the amount of the Texas inheritance tax, for any state death taxes. That meant the total tax liability of the Hughes estate would be the same if he was declared a resident of Texas or of Nevada, which imposed no death tax.[8]

I asked Harrison to set up a meeting with Will Lummis, the Hughes cousin who had emerged as the family's spokesman and leader in the probate cases, as well as the choice of Hughes's managers to hold together the diverse components of the business empire. Lummis was an attorney at Andrews, Kurth. I knew him from my legal and social activities in Houston, but our casual friendship failed to dent the opposition of the Andrews, Kurth lawyers to our involvement. At our meeting, Lummis deferred to Jim Dilworth, the lead attorney for the Hughes businesses, who would entertain none of my entreaties.

"Why are you tilting toward Nevada—why do you care?" I asked them. "We think he was domiciled in Texas. Why doesn't the estate just stand neutral and we will proceed and establish Texas domicile?"

"John, we just don't want to deal with you or the state of Texas. We think this should be handled in Nevada, and we're going to go that way," Dilworth told me. We left the meeting with no resolution of our differences.

Later, we learned their reasoning. They had two concerns: controlling the list of heirs and multiple-state taxation.

Their strategy on heir determination was directed at the more compliant Nevada, where they could specify William Lummis's mother as sole heir and thereby maintain close control over Hughes's far-flung business ventures. Texas law posed significant complications by requiring that the estate be split equally between his mother's and father's families. The estate also viewed declaration of a Nevada domicile as a solution to the dangers posed by the flood of purported wills being filed in states across the nation. Each of the purported wills popping up across the country posed somewhat different challenges to the estate because states used varying processes for declaring a will valid.

The Andrews, Kurth firm's preferred tax strategy embraced Nevada partly because the absence of a state inheritance tax left the volatile issue of valuing the estate to the Internal Revenue Service. Hughes managers were intimately familiar with IRS operations and personnel because of frequent negotiations in the past.

They also saw Nevada as a means of preventing California from imposing its 24 percent inheritance tax. Tacked on top of whatever federal tax rate applied based on the size of the estate (probably about 77 percent), the California tax would push the total tax bite up to 85 percent after the 16 percent state credit was applied.

The estate viewed the Texas claim as weaker than either California's or Nevada's, but it posed the threat that if Texas and California both succeeded, Texas' 16 percent tax would be tacked onto the combined 85 percent rate for a total tax of 101 percent. The danger of that threat was intensified by a U.S. Supreme Court precedent that allowed more than one state to successfully assess inheritance taxes against one estate. The addition of either one or both of these two states' valuation powers could seriously scramble the tax picture with huge variations in the estate's taxable base.[9]

I also suspected Dilworth was unimpressed with the competition he saw at the meeting and decided we lacked the legal muscle to mount a serious challenge to his strategy. Harrison was only thirty-two. His experience before joining my office was four years in private practice in the tiny East Texas town of Hughes Springs. His assistant was Bert Pluymen, who had graduated from the University of Texas just two years earlier and was in his first job since law school.

Like most large corporate law firms, Andrews, Kurth was more of a negotiating firm than a litigating firm. Even though he was head of the firm's litigation section, Dilworth had not tried that many cases. The firm preferred negotiating because their heavy involvement in the appointment and election of trial judges gave them an advantage in settling cases before they went to trial. Dilworth's job involved high-stakes bluffing, jawboning, and cutting deals with opposing counsel often cut from the same cloth as him. Lawyers with résumés like Harrison's and Pluymen's generally would be shuffled off to a junior partner, not engaged by a big-time pooh-bah of Dilworth's inflated stature.

Pitting my young lawyers and so-far sketchy evidence against Dilworth and his vast resources and decades of knowledge of the Hughes operation was obviously a lopsided contest. But I had made my reputation in the legal profession by besting opponents who underestimated me, so this mismatch created no apprehension on my part. My first task was to create a special unit under Harrison's leadership, which was uncertain because he had given me notice of his resignation several weeks before Hughes died. He planned to leave the staff two months later.

One of my original hires when I took office in January 1973, Harrison signed on in the fall of 1972 after we met when I made a campaign speech to a regional bar association meeting he was hosting as president of the Cass County Bar Association. He was excited about my plans to invigorate the attorney general's office, so he closed his solo practice in Hughes Springs and joined the staff as assistant chief of the taxation division. I moved him up to chief after the planned retirement of the longtime chief, James Broadhurst.

Harrison was a no-nonsense straight shooter who was offended by the political overtone Bullock added to my office's role as the comptroller's attorney. The irascible Bullock was always looking for opportunities to call attention to himself, brag on his accomplishments, or criticize some other officeholder for not performing according to his expectations. My office would occasionally be targets for these outbursts, which usually were laced with barbed sarcasm regarding our efforts to collect overdue payments from delinquent taxpayers.

I was the beneficiary of these polemics when he railed against my opponent in the election of 1972, so I was able to shrug them off as part of the Austin political scene. But Harrison took the criticisms personally, since his role as my taxation division chief made him the comptroller's lawyer. This discomfort caused him to resign from that position.

Once Harrison announced his intent to resign from my staff, I had made no effort to select his replacement by the time the Hughes case landed at our door. I decided to broach the subject when Harrison and I flew to California for the first hearing on the Hughes estate several weeks later. "You know, Rick, staying and working on this case is a once-in-a-lifetime opportunity," I told him. "You're a fool to give this up. You can always go into private practice later. Is there any way I can talk you into staying?"

"If you'll remove me from being chief of the taxation division and make me a special assistant, just working on this case, I'll stay," Harrison told me. I accepted that offer and appointed Martha Smiley to head the division. Harrison and Pluymen selected four other lawyers and a legal assistant to complete their team.

Their goal was to demonstrate Hughes's lack of intent to select a legal domicile different from Texas, his domicile at birth. That was the basic theme—he intended Texas as his domicile and although he lived elsewhere, he never abandoned that intent. That meant we would have to discern his state of mind—the state of mind of an obsessively secretive man who disappeared from public view for two decades, a man whose family and business managers were intent on maintaining the secrecy he so assiduously contrived. My team was faced with combing through hundreds of thousands of pages of court testimony, Hughes's encyclopedic business files, and government documents in hopes there might be some brief reference to his view of his legal domicile.

The estate lawyers were obviously going to discourage every potential witness in the Hughes empire from cooperating with us. We soon learned they were characterizing us as "the enemy of the estate" to discourage Hughes managers and former colleagues and friends from volunteering any helpful insight into the man and his shadowy existence. Our only consolation was our suspicion that the Hughes lawyers were just as much in the dark about his mental process as we were. They had not seen him in twenty years either.

To give our team trial expertise and a commanding presence in Hughes's home state, I prevailed on a friend from my personal injury litigation days, Florentino T. "Tino" Garza. He was a California trial attorney whose financial success allowed him to work for the comparatively minimal State of Texas wages in part because of his devotion to his Texas roots.

Garza was born in San Antonio to immigrant parents. He and several siblings were orphaned when he was young and were placed in orphanages. An older brother went to New Mexico, established himself financially, and, one at a time, pulled his siblings out of the orphanages and put them through school. About the time Garza was graduating from high school, he joined the army and was sent to Texas A&M for training. The war ended before he completed training, but because he qualified for the GI Bill he went back to the University of New Mexico and majored in English grammar. He then went to UCLA and earned a law degree, only the third Mexican American to do so. He was the first Hispanic offered an appointment to the California Supreme Court, by Gov. Jerry Brown, and he declined it. He was in his early fifties and a legend among California trial lawyers for his smooth but unfailingly effective courtroom skills.

With our team in place, we decided in June that the best way to reconstruct Hughes's frenetic seventy-year lifetime would be to work backward from his death. We needed to eliminate any possibility that his declining health in recent years had prompted him to revisit the issue of his legal domicile.

We took a shot in the dark and queried the attorney general's office in Mexico about Hughes's stay in Acapulco. We discovered that they had sent agents to the Acapulco Princess Hotel in response to rumors that Hughes was gravely ill and found Hughes gone and his aides furiously shredding documents. The Mexican officers ordered the shredding stopped, saving about ten thousand pages of documents. I decided to send Harrison to Mexico City with Tony Cordova, an investigator in our organized crime division and a former state police undercover narcotics officer.

We debated whether to alert the Hughes lawyers to our plans because we were concerned they might try to intercede with the Mexican government. But we decided they would learn about our plans anyway, and public disclosure might forestall any attempt to sabotage our inquiry. We also wanted to send them a message that we were committed to prosecuting this case doggedly. We also hoped to get in print the information about a Mexican doctor who had attended Hughes in his last hours, just to let the Hughes lawyers know that their protective bubble already had some holes in it.

My office issued a news release on June 22 reporting on the Harrison-Cordova mission and our concern over published comments by the Mexican doctor who had treated Hughes. I announced that our investigation would cover the time period that began with his trip to Las Vegas in the mid-1960s and ended with his death. We were going to leave no stone unturned to back up our theme that Hughes never abandoned his intent to claim Texas as his domicile—the home office of Hughes Tool Company, the fountainhead of his wealth. He would have wanted Texas—not California or Nevada—to share in his estate.[10]

In Mexico City, Harrison and Cordova could not believe their good luck. The Mexican officials gave them access to all of the records they had seized from Hughes's Acapulco Princess Hotel room. As they hurriedly opened one manila folder after another and flipped through loose pages of routine correspondence, they noticed a small number of pages with typewritten sequential dates in a column on the left side, time of day in the center column, and notations to the right of each time. The entries often used a code or abbreviation, but they could tell they were daily journals of Hughes's personal existence in his final years.

The logs listed movies he watched, often repeatedly; his location, either bed or chair; and his bodily habits, in intimate detail. They recorded the fact that a barber was brought in to trim his long hair and nails to prepare for a rare meeting with outsiders, this one with Merrill Lynch representatives needing his signature on papers authorizing the sale of Hughes Tool Company when he was in Nicaragua. Harrison and Cordova were not sure exactly what the codes or abbreviations meant, but it was clear they referred to drugs. The Mexican investigators also showed Harrison Hughes's entry visa with a signature they said was not his, raising questions about why he did not sign it himself.[11]

When he was setting up arrangements for the trip, Harrison stumbled upon one of many lucky surprises we would encounter on this case. The woman in Mexico City who was referred to him as a guide and translator, upon learning of his mission, remarked that a relative of hers was a physician in Acapulco who had visited Hughes shortly before he was moved. Harrison flew to Acapulco, where the translator arranged an interview with her doctor uncle. The doctor confirmed that he had examined Hughes the morning the airlift left Acapulco and was shocked that the patient was not in a hospital.

"You're not going to believe what we found," Harrison told me when he returned. Harrison was generally a cool personality, very unemotional and all business. But he was animated and clearly excited as he related his discoveries.

As far as we knew, no other outsiders had seen Hughes's lists and logs. We doubted the Hughes lawyers, who were consumed not only with the estate issues in several states but also with reversing the Hughes empire's downward financial spiral caused by a decade of inept management by his self-serving and often unqualified insiders, were aware of their existence. My heart sank, however, when Harrison told me he had made no copies of the huge cache of documents but instead asked the Mexican government officials to send us copies. I doubted we would ever see a single page from Mexico City.

We decided that this development allowed us to step up our publicity campaign, to again warn the Hughes lawyers they were not dealing with novices when it came to our ability to prove Hughes considered Texas his legal domicile. We filed a request for them to provide us the names and addresses of the nine aides who accompanied Hughes to Acapulco so we could subpoena them to testify.

"We're most interested in talking with the nine aides who were with Mr. Hughes when he arrived in Acapulco Feb. 10," stated my news release issued on June 29. "We will seek to determine why Mr. Hughes was brought to Mexico, his state of health, and why outside medical attention apparently was avoided in spite of his failing health. As far as we can determine, no one except Hughes' personal aides were admitted to the 20th floor of the Acapulco Princess Hotel until shortly before his departure when Hughes was examined by a local physician of Acapulco, who stated that he was suffering 'from lack of care.'" The release also added that a handwriting expert "determined the purported signature of Hughes on his immigration forms was not the real signature of Howard Hughes."[12]

It did not take the Hughes team long to close down our Mexican connection. Five months of pestering Mexico City for the copies finally produced an admission that officials there had yielded to demands from Hughes's Summa Corporation not to allow anyone else to view them. In December, Harrison read an article by Jack Anderson, the Washington-based nationally syndicated investigative columnist, about federal government efforts to investigate Hughes's last days in Mexico.[13] Intrigued at the insider information Anderson demonstrated, Harrison called him and asked if he would share his sources.

According to Anderson, his article reported on events he had orchestrated. He told Harrison that after he learned of Hughes's trip to Mexico, he contacted Treasury Secretary William Simon for help in gaining access to Mexican government officials who could shed light on his quest to determine if Hughes was still alive. Simon, whose IRS agents were also interested in finding Hughes to settle outstanding tax issues, put Anderson in contact with the attorney general of Mexico.

Anderson flew to Mexico City to meet with him but was unsuccessful in convincing him to pursue a raid on the Acapulco hotel. Anderson then suggested a raid would be in order if Hughes had violated Mexican laws. The attorney general agreed to use as a reason for a raid a forged signature on Hughes's entrance visa, which he would determine by comparing the visa signature with one to be supplied by Anderson from government records.

Anderson sent the handwriting sample to Mexico City. His Mexican contact called him April 5 saying Hughes had left Mexico for Texas. Anderson told Harrison he then called Secretary Simon to ask his help in identifying the body as that of Hughes, which the FBI accomplished. When Anderson contacted the Mexican officials for more information, he learned about the seizure of Hughes's documents. His request to view them was denied, but he was told the documents would be turned over to American authorities if they were requested. Anderson then contacted Simon again, who sent agents to Mexico to copy the Hughes papers—the event on which Anderson's article was based. After Simon had obtained the copies, Anderson related to Harrison, he was again refused access because they were private tax documents.[14]

"My question to you," Harrison said Anderson asked him, "is this: what if I could get you copies of those documents, then can I come see them in Texas?"

"If there is a way we can legally let you have access to them, we will do that," Harrison replied.

"Within the next forty-eight hours, Bill Simon is going to call you," Anderson told Harrison, who had just read that Simon was in Moscow and thus thought Anderson was grandstanding. But the next day, Harrison picked up his phone and a voice said, "This is Bill Simon. A mutual friend told me that I have something you would like to have."

"Yeah, that's right, Mr. Secretary," Harrison stammered.

"Well, you know the drill," Simon said. "We have to cooperate with a proper request from the state. You get the governor to request those documents, I am sure we can accommodate that."[15]

Harrison prepared the letter, contacted Governor Briscoe's office, and got his signature that same day. He gave it to Pluymen to hand deliver in Washington.

This was Pluymen's third trip to Washington seeking information on

Hughes. His first was a visit with CIA director George H. W. Bush, who told him the CIA had no files on Hughes. The second was a trip with Bullock to ask the IRS for information on Hughes's tax returns, a trip that also produced no results. At the Treasury Department, Pluymen spent several days being given the runaround before he finally threatened to go to Secretary Simon. The IRS yielded and gave him about twelve rolls of microfilm. Spooked by the cloak-and-dagger aura of the Hughes case—we regularly arranged for a sweep of our offices to guard against bugging devices—and the explosive information he knew he was carrying, Pluymen booked a flight in his own name from Washington to Austin but actually flew to New York under an alias and then flew from New York to Austin under an alias.[16]

Anderson called several days after Pluymen returned and wanted to come to Austin to look at the microfilm, but Harrison had to turn him down. The Internal Revenue Service imposed a confidentiality requirement on us, so Anderson's ploy that gave us a vital head start in our investigation failed in its original intent of providing him with a journalistic scoop.

After viewing each of the ten thousand pages on the films, the Harrison team extracted about sixty pages of the daily activity logs, covering eighteen months near the end of Hughes's life. They detailed Hughes's compulsive behavior such as his germ phobia, his almost around-the-clock movie watching in his room darkened by coverings taped over the windows to prevent daylight or germs from entering, and his dwindling consumption of nourishment. They also recorded ingestion of massive doses of tranquilizers and pain-killing drugs. He was taking up to 170 milligrams of Valium in a twenty-four-hour period, an amount sixty-eight times the recommended dosage, and he did that on a daily basis for the full eighteen-month period documented in the logs. He also was taking large quantities of Empirin Compound No. 4 tablets, which contained codeine, caffeine, and phenacetin, and he was injecting himself with liquid codeine.

They also found a memo from one of Hughes's aides to him revealing the six traveling aides' concern over their legal liability in providing prescription sedatives to Hughes by using phony prescriptions. The memo said his physicians had decided he should deal only with them, and not with the aides, regarding his medications because the doctors "cannot be forced to testify unless it is in a criminal case."[17]

Harrison and I discussed the findings and agreed they would lift our case to a new level. We had accumulated a fairly good paper trail of Hughes citing Houston as his residence, including federal and California income tax returns dating from the 1930s to 1973, state poll tax receipts for 1940–1952 showing a Houston address, a sworn statement from Lummis that Hughes paid poll taxes and registered to vote in Texas until 1966, and Lummis's designation of Houston as Hughes's residence on his death certificate.

Those were important pieces of the puzzle. But they were very small ones in the context of this larger-than-life personality who commanded a dominant role not only in Hollywood and aviation but also the Las Vegas casino and hotel industry, Nevada politics, Department of Defense military contracts, the Central Intelligence Agency, Congress, and the White House. Those feats were the stuff of legends the Hughes lawyers would use to attract the jury to their position that Hughes's legal domicile was Las Vegas. A few signatures on income tax returns and voter certificate applications were not going to counteract the glamour the Hughes team would use to impress the jury. We needed to paint our own portrait of Hughes.

"Juries will turn on your client if they think you're lying or trying to hide something from them," I told Harrison. "If there was ever a group of people who lied and covered up, this Hughes entourage is one of the worst. It won't matter how many Lana Turners they parade before the jury—if we can convince the jurors the Hughes handlers aren't leveling with them, we'll win this case going away."

Hughes's logs gave us the opening we needed to unlock the secrets of his final years, an untold story that was the target of some of the nation's top journalists, law firms, and government investigators. It was the story the Hughes team was well schooled in hiding from public view. It was the perfect antidote to the potent charisma of Hughes's heroic early years. These logs completely stripped away the aura of normalcy nurtured by Hughes's operatives, clearly depicting instead a physically and emotionally spent, mentally unbalanced drug addict being manipulated by his keepers. They allowed us to tarnish the credibility of the Hughes entourage and thereby weaken their ability to discredit our case. Hughes simply lacked the capacity during these final years to abandon or renounce his plans to die with Texas as his legal domicile.

This sad but sensational story was first laid bare in lurid detail to the nation by *TIME* magazine in a cover story in December 1976. The issue included excerpts from a new book by James Phelan, a veteran magazine journalist in his sixties who based his book *Howard Hughes: The Hidden Years* on interviews with two low-level Hughes traveling aides who detailed Hughes's weird existence. The cover illustration was a shocking sketch of one of the aides carrying the helpless, scraggly-looking Hughes to the charter jet that flew him to Houston.[18]

Hughes's Summa Corporation publicists quickly denounced the aides' tales as fantasy, causing the publisher to push Phelan for independent confirmation. Even though Harrison had not yet revealed to the Hughes lawyers the contents of the logs he had obtained from the IRS, his reputation as leader of the only visible government investigation of Hughes's death apparently made him a prospect for Phelan's desperate search for corroboration.

"I just want to know—can you tell me if I'm right or not?" Phelan pleaded with Harrison, whom he tracked down in a bar in Los Angeles. "You're right," Harrison reassured him, producing a sigh of relief from Phelan.[19]

Several months later, in early 1977, Harrison sprang his surprise. During a deposition in California with Howard Eckersley, one of the Hughes travel aides, Harrison asked about Hughes's drug use. The answer was the typical cover-up verbiage used by the Hughes team. Harrison then reached into his file folder and pulled out one of the log pages and introduced it into evidence.

"What's that? Where'd you get that?" asked the shocked Hughes lawyers. Harrison did not have to tell them and didn't. The witness was trapped. Eckersley already had explained how a single aide was the only other person Hughes would allow in his room, so no one but the aide could have prepared the log. He quickly changed his tune, admitting that the log references tracked Hughes's drug usage and identifying the codes they used, such as "BBs" for "blue bombers," the ten-milligram Valium capsules Hughes took by the handful. The log was made simply by inserting a blank sheet of typing paper into an electric typewriter, using tabs to space the columns, and keeping a running account of Hughes medications, foods, and activities. The activities during the 1972–1973 period covered by the logs we had copies of were limited to watching movies, bowel movements, and a rare visit by another staff member.

As incredible a volume of drugs as the logs revealed, we learned in our depositions of the Hughes aides that the logs documented only part of Hughes's intake. In his questioning of Clarence A. Waldron Jr., Harrison asked if he recorded medications only when Hughes instructed him to do so. Waldron said that was correct but that if he happened to be in the room and saw Hughes taking something, he'd add it to the log so that the next person coming in would know.

The aides' attempts to disguise Hughes's drug addiction and declining health were not only part of the Summa Corporation culture but also reflected its concern over legal liability. As the corporate attorneys had suggested in a memo to Hughes that we discovered among the Mexico documents, the Hughes traveling aides were concerned about admitting their participation in the fake prescription scheme used by Hughes's doctors.

The prescriptions were written by Hughes's doctors using the name of one of his aides as the recipient. A regimented routine was followed for deliveries and pickups to mask any Hughes involvement, and only a handful of pharmacies were used. Several of the nine Hughes traveling aides and his three doctors refused to answer questions about drug use, forcing us to go to court to compel them to answer.[20]

Their testimony charted Hughes's growing dependence on sedatives and narcotics over the years to the point that his handlers convinced him to move from the Bahamas to Mexico by insisting that his Bahamas codeine supply was gone but that Mexico assured him an endless supply. This ruse was really part of a power play by one of his executives to forestall Hughes's announced intention to split his business interests between the current managers and a second group to be based in the Bahamas.[21]

This line of questioning in the summer and fall of 1977 naturally caught the attention of law enforcement officials. Harrison and Pluymen were approached by Drug Enforcement Administration investigators. The evidence they had uncovered in their questioning of the Hughes aides led to federal grand jury investigations that resulted in the indictment in March 1978 of Dr. Norman F. Crane, one of Hughes's four personal physicians, and John Holmes, his senior aide, on charges they had illegally supplied Hughes with narcotics for twenty years. In June 1978, another grand jury alleged Dr. Wilbur S. Thain, the physician who had overall responsibility for Hughes's medical care and was given a lifetime consulting agreement by Summa Corporation in 1975 that paid sixty thousand dollars a year, dispensed codeine phosphate to Hughes without legitimate medical reasons.[22]

While my staff's questioning of Hughes's aides was fully implementing our strategy of exposing Hughes's impaired mental acuity fueled by drug abuse, we also were pursuing further examples of his personal expression of legal domicile. We found an unexpected nugget in March 1977, when the Hughes estate complied with a court-ordered search of his vast and comprehensive collection of personal and business records to locate a will.

No will was found, but among the documents retrieved was a carbon copy of a three-page letter Hughes wrote to California tax officials in August 1944 responding to their entreaties that he abandon his insistence on declaring himself a nonresident Californian because his official residence was Texas—where he had not lived in nineteen years.

"I am a Texan and always will be," the letter began, and it continued with characteristic Hughes thoroughness and assertiveness:

> I pay my poll taxes in Texas. I pay all other taxes properly assessed against me there, and pay my federal income tax from there. My home is and has always been in Houston, Texas. I have voted there and expect to vote there in the coming presidential election. I have never voted in any other place. My will is deposited there and the terms thereof will be carried out from there. My bank account is and has always been in Houston. I have no bank accounts in California and never had, except a small account a number of years ago. I am a resident of Texas and have never been a resident of any other place, and would not under any conditions change my residence from Texas.[23]

At about the same time as this powerful documentation of Hughes's intent fell into our hands, we were provided by the estate's attorneys a list of prospective witnesses they planned to depose. The list included many big-name Hollywood stars who had performed in Hughes's movies. We assumed they were chosen not because they had any insight into Hughes's attitude about legal domicile but because they would transport jurors back to the glory days of Hughes's movie making and they could easily say they saw no evidence of Hughes wanting to return to Texas.

Harrison was particularly curious about them listing John Wayne, whose starring role as Davy Crockett in the 1960 film *The Alamo* made him a Texas icon and a sure hit with the jury. Harrison was concerned the Hughes team had tried to turn Wayne against us. He conferred with Garza, and they decided to preempt the estate attorneys by contacting Wayne prior to the deposition to offer our version of the facts. And they decided not only to neutralize Wayne's potential as a pro-Hughes witness but also to convert him to our side by having him vouch for the "I am a Texan" letter in his testimony.

Garza called Wayne and advised him he was on the list for a deposition because the Hughes archives had included five letters he had written to Hughes that he may have forgotten, and he wanted to make sure Wayne would see them before his deposition was taken to avoid any possible embarrassment. "When can you be here?" Wayne asked. "I'm on my way," Garza replied.[24]

Garza and David Deaderick, one of our task force members and a first-year lawyer, went to Newport Beach to Wayne's home. He met them at his front door and bellowed something like, "I know what you are up to, you work for the attorney general of Texas and he is running for governor and this is all politics!"

"Mr. Wayne, I followed you my whole life, your movies and your private appearances. You have always seemed to stand for one thing above all else, and that one thing is fairness. Wouldn't you agree?" Garza asked.

"Well, yeah, I would agree," the surprised Wayne responded.

"You obviously have heard only one side of this story. I just ask you to give me two minutes to tell you our side of the story," Garza continued.

"Well, come on in," Wayne said.

Garza showed Wayne copies of the federal and California tax returns where Hughes had repeatedly and consistently declared his Texas domicile.

"Well, what the hell is all the fight about?" Wayne demanded.

"That's what we'd like to know," Garza replied.

"Why don't they look at these things and quit bothering people like me?" Wayne persisted.

"Well, Mr. Wayne, sometimes when a party has a weak case," Garza responded, "they try to prop it up by affiliating their position with a famous person such as yourself."

"Dammit, I knew that was what they were up to. Why don't you try to get me out of this?" Wayne asked. Garza promised to try.

When Harrison heard Garza and Deaderick's report, he asked the estate lawyers to cancel the Wayne deposition because he did not add anything that wasn't already stipulated to. They refused.

"I'm sorry, Mr. Wayne, we tried our best to talk them out of deposing you, but they are just determined to take your deposition," Harrison told the actor over the phone. "Well, I just really appreciate what y'all have done," Wayne said.

The next morning, Wayne showed the group taking the deposition to a large covered patio flanked by lush greenery and overlooking the Pacific

Ocean. The Hughes lawyers must have realized their Wayne ploy wasn't working as they intended because they had sent a young first-year associate to take the deposition. After she stumbled through Wayne's life history, Garza took Wayne for cross-examination. He asked Wayne if Hughes had always been truthful with him, if Hughes kept his word and his contracts with him, if he thought of Hughes as honest—questions to which Wayne replied in the affirmative.

Then Garza produced the "I am a Texan" letter and had it marked as "John Wayne Exhibit 1." After permitting Wayne to read "John Wayne Exhibit 1," Garza quietly asked, "Now Mr. Wayne, in all of your dealings with Mr. Hughes did he ever do or say anything in your presence that contradicted the statements he made in this letter?"

"No, he did not!" Wayne boomed, and Garza concluded the deposition with a big smile on his face. "John Wayne Exhibit 1" became the first piece of evidence we introduced at the three-month trial that began in Houston on November 14, 1977.

Our search for Hughes's declarations about his legal domicile led us to the dozens of lawsuits that had finally prompted him to flee the country in 1970. Surely, we reasoned, when he testified in those lawsuits, the first question he would be asked after he had stated his name would be a request that he verbalize some indication of the location of his residence. That assumption, of course, failed to take into account Hughes's determination to insulate himself from the reach of lawyers' demands for courtroom appearances. We could find only one instance when he actually appeared in court to testify—a lawsuit filed in 1952 by his movie production studio RKO against a screenwriter.

Hughes, a vocal anticommunist at a time when American concerns over communism were at a high point, had fired the screenwriter, Paul Jarrico, immediately upon learning he had been subpoenaed by the House Committee on Un-American Activities in its investigation of Communist Party activities in Hollywood. Jarrico countersued, contending RKO had violated his contract by refusing him screen credit for a script he wrote for *The Las Vegas Story,* but the judge ruled for Hughes.[25]

Transcripts of the Jarrico trial were long gone from public records. But we tracked down the RKO attorney in the case, Arthur Groman, and asked him if he recalled Hughes's answer to the inevitable question of residency. Yes, he said, he distinctly remembered Hughes's response: Houston, Texas. He also remembered the name of the court reporter who recorded the trial. We tracked down the court reporter and scored a big coup: he found his original notes. By deposing both the lawyer and court reporter, we recreated Hughes's insightful testimony:

> "Where do you live, Mr. Hughes?" asked Jarrico attorney Edward Mosk.
>
> "Do you mean my domicile or my present location?" Hughes responded, listening to Mosk through an earphone his technicians had set up in the courtroom to accommodate his deafness.
>
> "Where do you live?"
>
> "Again, do you mean my legal domicile, or where I am living at present?"
>
> "Where you are living."
>
> "Well, I spent last night at the Beverly Hills Hotel."
>
> "Do you consider that where you live?"
>
> "Not my legal domicile, no."
>
> "What is your legal domicile?"
>
> "Well, I still consider that to be Houston, Texas."[26]

The *Jarrico* case testimony was one of a handful of breakthroughs we enjoyed among thousands of dead ends. We became so accustomed to fruitless searches we almost dismissed out of hand a report we saw in a *Houston Chronicle* gossip column that Hughes's aides had investigated purchase of a condominium in Houston shortly before he died. One of our law clerks called the condominium, the St. James Condominia in the Galleria area west of downtown, and apologized for bothering them with a rumor he assured them was probably phony.

"It's all true," the condominia marketing director assured our surprised clerk, recalling a visit on New Year's Eve in 1975 by a representative of Hughes's Summa Corporation to discuss purchase of the top two floors of the building.[27]

Discoveries such as these were beginning to worry the Hughes estate lawyers. Their initial denigration of us as pickpockets with no legitimate standing in the race for Hughes's estate tax dollars slowly evolved into concern as our evidence of the Texas connections mounted. At the same time, their goal of securing Nevada as the sole domicile based on the testimony of Hughes's inner circle was losing credibility as our depositions revealed these aides to be exploiters of his instability and drug cravings in order to seize control for themselves.

The Hughes team's resources were stretched thin because the Nevada trial on the authenticity of the so-called "Mormon will" was scheduled to begin a week before our Houston trial. And their hopes of avoiding the big 24 percent California estate tax bite also were fading as our success in overcoming low odds to establish domicile ignited California's delayed interest in seeking its spot at the Hughes inheritance tax table.

These factors came together in the fall of 1977 to create a new dimension to our case. A representative of the California state comptroller's office, Jerome B. Falk Jr. of San Francisco, visited me October 21, 1977, to deliver an unexpected message. California, he said, had decided to seek a U.S. Supreme Court ruling to block the Texas probate trial scheduled to begin in Houston on November 14. Their lawsuit would request appointment of a federal master to determine Hughes's domicile.

I was infuriated that California officials, who had mounted no effort similar to ours in state courts to establish Hughes's domicile, would attempt to take a shortcut by going to the Supreme Court now that we were on the verge of winning a state court finding of domicile. They were actually fishing for an agreement to split the estate taxes, and I figured they thought this Supreme Court filing might push us into a compromise. I saw no reason to agree to give them anything. I was as near to being absolutely rude to anyone as I could have been. I told Falk we were not going to stop our process for them, and I chastised him severely for taking what I considered a cheap shot at Texas instead of building their own case for domicile. "We'll see you in the Supreme Court of the United States," I told him as I cut off the discussion and all but threw him out of my office.

A week or so later, Pluymen was questioning an estate witness during a probate court hearing when the witness casually mentioned "an agreement" between California and the Hughes estate. Pluymen was incredulous. We quickly demanded, and were provided, a copy of the agreement. In that document, California agreed to surrender 6 of its 24 percentage points of inheritance tax in return for the estate agreeing to pay California an 18 percent tax if it was found to be the domicile, but only if Texas was *not* found to be the domicile. If Texas was declared Hughes's domicile, California would receive only 2 percent of the estate.

The California comptroller announced the agreement at a news conference on November 11, noting that even if the Supreme Court found the nomadic, reclusive Hughes to be "a resident of no place, we would still get 18 percent. We got a very good deal." He also said he hoped the agreement with the estate would encourage Texas to share the estate taxes with California, quipping that "Texans at times are difficult to negotiate with, but now they may be more inclined to negotiate." Their filing in the Supreme Court was made the same day.[28]

Suddenly we found ourselves fighting a two-front war, in Washington and Houston, against a team of opponents composed of California and the Hughes estate, instead of a single skirmish in Houston against the estate. Supreme Court cases involving disputes between states were a very narrow field of law—this case was designated "No. 76," meaning it was only the seventy-sixth occasion in the court's 188-year history it had considered a dispute between two states. Harrison immediately pulled Deaderick off of the document review group and told him to go to the law library and work exclusively on the Supreme Court case.

Even though we considered the financial arrangements in the California case a naked attempt by the estate to buy its way to Supreme Court adjudication it was barred from achieving on its own, the state could point to a prior Supreme Court ruling that placed its case in a favorable light.[29] Ironically, that precedent from 1939 involved a lawsuit brought by the Texas attorney general seeking to protect its inheritance tax claim from claims by Florida and two other states involving the estate of the son of Hetty Green, the richest woman in American history. In that decision, the Supreme Court accepted jurisdiction, even though the states had not established domicile through court proceedings because the facts demonstrated the combined claims of all four states and the federal government exceeded the value of the estate. The court appointed a master, who established domicile in Massachusetts. That precedent forced us to view the California strategy as a very worrisome development.

Because our trial in Houston began the Monday after the California filing was made in the Supreme Court, their request for court action to stop our trial pending a hearing on their case was made too late to prevent our getting under way. We had barely begun jury selection when the estate attorneys' frustrations of simultaneous trials in Las Vegas and Houston erupted. On the trial's fourth day, after I questioned a potential juror and succeeded in having Judge Pat Gregory dismiss her as prejudiced, one of the estate's attorneys, Frank Davis from Andrews, Kurth, jumped to his feet and moved for a mistrial, complaining that I was "browbeating," guilty of "impropriety," "leading the witnesses," and "putting words in their mouths."[30]

Gregory denied the request and adjourned court for the day. Davis and I hurried out of the courtroom. In the hallway outside, he angrily turned to me and said, "John, I just hope when you go to bed tonight that you just get down on your knee and say a prayer for all the stuff you pulled today."

"Frank, my Momma always told me to beware of loud love and loud religion," I shot back.

"You know that lady could have been fair and you weren't trying to be fair at all," Davis said.

"Frank, I don't need any lectures from you," I retorted and walked away.[31]

A second round of verbal fireworks occurred the next week, when the attorney for two Hughes relatives complained that Harrison was attempting to block a deposition of longtime Hughes aide Noah Dietrich because he feared Dietrich would undermine the Texas case. Davis sought to delay the trial until the deposition could be obtained. I told Judge Gregory they were resorting to "desperation tactics" in a "mad-dog fashion" to delay the trial and allow them to focus on the Las Vegas trial. Gregory later denied Davis's motion.[32]

After those flare-ups, we settled into a tedious trial based largely on introduction of documents and depositions. In our opening statement to the jury, I outlined our case. "We will show that Texas was his domicile of origin and will produce evidence . . . respecting some of the early history of Mr. Hughes's life which will reflect, we believe, facts from which it will be concluded that this was his domicile of origin and that he never manifested any intention during his lifetime to abandon Houston, Texas, as his domicile of origin," I told the jury. "In fact," I continued,

> we will be introducing documents throughout the trial to show that whenever he was called upon . . . during his lifetime to claim a place as home, that he consistently and unequivocally claimed Houston, Texas, as his home; that he never claimed other places as his home; that he never established any permanent home anywhere outside of the state of Texas, and that his lifestyle will reflect that, whether married or unmarried, that he did not claim or maintain a permanent home outside of the state, with the intention of keeping it as his permanent home; that if he ever left, which he clearly did, during his lifetime, California and Nevada, he did so with no intention of returning there to establish a permanent home.[33]

This was our theme. This was our "oak tree." And we repeated it, repeated it, repeated it. That was my way of winning cases.

After participating in the first days of evidence presentation, I turned the case over to Harrison and Garza. Neither side was able to produce any real surprises. The dearth of live witnesses made the trial seem slower and longer than it was.

We completed presentation of our case on January 3, 1978, after introducing almost one thousand documents to support our contention that Texas was Hughes's legal domicile. The estate called as witnesses several of Hughes's Summa Corporation managers, Hollywood friends such as actress and dancer Ginger Rogers and William Randolph Hearst Jr., and Hughes's former wife, actress Jean Peters Hough. All said they had never heard Hughes express any interest in returning to Texas or even refer to himself as a Texan.

Harrison used cross-examination of Mrs. Hough to gently undercut this strategy, asking her if she had ever heard the phrase "Texas handshake type of deal." "Yes," she said, a small smile tugging at the corners of her mouth, "Mr. Hughes used that phrase." Asked what she believed Mr. Hughes meant, she responded, "He meant that as a Texan, his word was his bond, and the deal did not need to be in writing."[34]

None of the witnesses ever heard Hughes denounce Texas as his state of original domicile—once again confirming our "oak tree" position that I continued to teach in a trial training program in my law firm after I left the attorney general's office.

The estate's case was completed on February 13, 1978. I rejoined the trial to hear Harrison's closing arguments the next day. The next morning, the jury reached a unanimous verdict on the first ballot: Hughes was a Texan.[35]

"My staff did just a tremendous job in guiding a very complex matter through to what we thought was the only proper outcome," I told the waiting news reporters.[36]

As sweet as that victory was, we knew another tough challenge awaited us in the U.S. Supreme Court, where the California case was set for hearing March 29. That date was about five weeks before the Texas Democratic primary election, in which I was running against Governor Briscoe. This would be my fourth appearance before the high court to represent Texas, so I was confident the distractions of campaigning would not create any apprehension for me.

Falk, the object of my wrath when he informed me of California's plan to block our initiative, opened the arguments for California by asserting that the case fell within the court's jurisdiction under the *Texas v. Florida* precedent because the combined Texas, California, and federal government inheritance taxes exceeded the value of the Hughes estate, totaling a combined 101 percent. He explained his interpretation of Supreme Court precedents that supported his position, then added, "Another factor I want to mention that brought us here, and I think is important for this Court's exercise in jurisdiction, was our own sense of fairness. To have proceeded independently to litigate the tax claim in our own courts as Texas sought to do, even if we could do so . . . simply did not comport with our notion of a fair and appropriate process."[37]

This bit of grandstanding drew a quip from Justice William H. Rehnquist: "Are you familiar with Lord Canning's statement, 'Save, oh save me, from the candid friend'?"

Falk quickly tried to regroup and repeat his argument, then closed by protesting against our interpretation of the Hughes estate–California agreement. "I think that the suggestion that we are here carrying the bag for the estate, acting for its benefit, is just plainly false as a factual matter," Falk said.

I firmly disagreed with Falk, noting that their stated purpose of the Supreme Court filing was to exclude Texas as an inheritance tax claimant so there would be adequate funds in the estate to pay California's claim. "They said Texas was all that was in their way. . . . I am in their way to try the case, not in their way to assert the claim or the merits of their claim, not in their way to impair their ability to collect on taxes, but in their way to get a favorable settlement of a claim that they are very reluctant to try on its merits. That's what Texas is in the way of," I said. Responding to Falk's "sense of fairness" comment, I said,

> Then why did they wait 19 months after we began our litigation to suddenly emerge into an atmosphere of sweetness and light and fairness? And why didn't they try then, early, to come here, and why, when they come, don't they come on the strength of their own claim, if fairness is their standard?
>
> Why did they come here tendering the limited issue, and the only issue, to this Court, and that is Texas domicile. Now, it's Texas' position that the agreement that was entered into on November 10, 1977, the day before this motion for leave was filed, entered into between the estate's administrators, certain Hughes heirs, and California, amounts really to the estate and the heirs agreeing to pay California in money and services to bring this case, and that, therefore, this Court is

> prohibited, both by the letter and the spirit of the United States Constitution, from entertaining any suit arising in your original jurisdiction concept under these kind of circumstances.

My high-pitched, rapid-fire delivery was stopped in mid-sentence by Justice William J. Brennan Jr. "Is this an argument that in fact California's fronting for the heirs?" he asked.

I lowered my voice level and speed to respond gravely and evenly: "No question that is what's happening."

I closed my argument by admonishing the court, "Never should this court tolerate that kind of a situation. And you would rue the day, if you did, and open the gates for this kind of trading around between high state tax cases, states with weak claims to try to get negative findings against 1 percent states with good claims."

The court ruled three months later against accepting the California case, overturning the *Texas v. Florida* precedent.[38] But the opinions in the case expressed support for allowing the court to help resolve multistate inheritance tax disputes that lacked the triggering issue of tax liabilities exceeding the estate's value, which had been used to accept jurisdiction in the thirty-nine-year-old case.

The opinions suggested the use of a federal court interpleader filing by the Hughes estate to accomplish what California was attempting, and the estate used this guidance to bring the issue before the court several years later to resolve the two states' overlapping claims. Texas, however, was awarded $50 million in that decision, a record amount that remains unmatched, fully vindicating the two years of detective work and courtroom finesse we employed to prove a case that our opponents originally dismissed as frivolous.

I was very proud of the excellent investigation and legal work by my very able staff. It proved we could go up against formidable opposition and win for the citizens of Texas.

(8)

DEFENDING THE DEATH PENALTY

Some Texas attorneys general regarded a U.S. Supreme Court argument as an assignment best filled by subordinates or special counsel. My reaction was the opposite. The prospect of arguing a case before the high court stimulated my competitive instincts as much as the Super Bowl fires the ambitions of a National Football League coach or player. I viewed the challenge of matching wits with—and probing the intellects of—nine of our nation's preeminent legal thinkers for thirty tension-filled minutes as a most treasured opportunity.

I was fortunate to have five such opportunities. They included two disputes with other states—Louisiana, over the state boundary extension into the oil-rich Gulf of Mexico, and California, over the right to tax the estate of Howard Hughes—and three others: a complex natural gas federal regulatory issue, a challenge to our ballot access requirements for minority parties, and the death penalty case.[1]

Although all the cases were important and a privilege to present, the death penalty case posed the most drama and sense of urgency. It was the most significant oral advocacy experience of my life.

The defendant in this case was Jerry Lane Jurek.[2] At stake was not only his life but also the fate of our state's new death penalty statute as well as the fate of death penalty laws in thirty-four other states and the lives of 527 persons sentenced to death in all thirty-five states that had reinstituted the death penalty.[3] The Jurek case was among five the court set for a two-day consolidated hearing with the ultimate purpose of deciding whether to forever outlaw the death penalty in the United States.

The hearings on March 30–31, 1976, occurred at a pivotal time in our nation's uneasy history of capital punishment. Numerous previous court challenges had culminated in death penalty opponents scoring a far-reaching victory in 1972 that unexpectedly wiped all state laws from the books. As a result, when the Supreme Court justices gathered in 1976, no executions had occurred anywhere in the country since Luis Monge entered Colorado's gas chamber on June 2, 1967. In Texas, the last capital punishment had occurred on July 30, 1964, when Joseph Johnson, a black parolee, was electrocuted for murdering a Chinese grocer during a robbery in Houston. The opposition forces gained their historic victory in 1972 when the Supreme Court, after consolidating cases from several states, including Texas, to provide a broad spectrum of death penalty statutes for review, held that existing laws were so arbitrarily applied that they violated the prohibition against "cruel and unusual punishment" in the Eighth Amendment to the U.S. Constitution. The decision resulted in about six hundred death row inmates' sentences being commuted to life in prison, including forty-seven in Texas.[4]

Texas and other states whose statutes had been struck down immediately initiated new death penalty laws to accommodate the 1972 ruling. Approval of the revisions by the high court would represent a major setback for opponents of the death penalty, while freeing the backlog of death row cases would launch a resurgence of executions across the nation. Disapproval would again commute hundreds of death sentences to life in prison and likely forever remove any options for states to enact constitutionally permitted death penalty laws.

To these already weighty ramifications was added the presence of the nation's leading advocate for death penalty opponents, Anthony G. Amsterdam, a law professor at Stanford University who was acting as the primary spokesman for the petitioners. Amsterdam, forty-one, was a brilliant lawyer with impressive credentials. After graduating with top honors from the University of Pennsylvania law school, he clerked in 1960 for Justice Felix Frankfurter, whose own opposition to the death penalty was announced in a dissenting opinion as early as 1948.[5] In private practice, Amsterdam quickly plunged into death penalty cases at a time when Frankfurter's successor, Arthur Goldberg, a Kennedy appointee, was privately pressing the justices to outlaw the death penalty. Goldberg spurred capital punishment opponents to intensify their efforts with an unexpected dissenting opinion in 1963 wherein he urged his colleagues to determine whether the death penalty for rape was unconstitutional, even though the issue was not raised by the defendant's own attorney. Justices William Douglas and William Brennan joined the dissent, offering abolitionists a three-vote head start in their quest for five votes against the death penalty.[6]

The Goldberg dissent helped reinvigorate the offices of the nation's leading advocacy organization for minority rights, the NAACP Legal Defense and Educational Fund (LDF). While its original mission of civil rights litigation had produced tremendous success in the 1950s, including Supreme Court rulings requiring racial integration in universities and public schools, integration litigation was slowing by the mid-1960s. The LDF legal team thus viewed the Goldberg-Douglas-Brennan dissenting comments on the death penalty as a clarion call for their idled litigators. The LDF recruited Amsterdam in 1965 to manage its strategy of arguing that the racial disparity in assessment of the death penalty in southern states violated the Equal Protection Clause in the Fourteenth Amendment to the U.S. Constitution.

That strategy proved short-lived. Federal courts were unwilling to use statistical analysis to void every death penalty rape case involving a black defendant on the basis that a disproportionate share of capital punishments fell on blacks. The LDF team, accustomed to measuring their courtroom results in broad public policy victories, was now gripped by the gut-wrenching realization that failure meant that a human being would die in the gas chamber. Amsterdam and his team expanded their search for constitutional hooks beyond the Fourteenth Amendment, began circulating legal briefs with a menu of constitutional issues to attorneys representing death row inmates, and expanded their scope beyond black southerners to include any execution-bound defendant.

They carefully began steering toward the Supreme Court cases that offered the best chance of adding to the Douglas-Brennan-Goldberg votes—with the Goldberg ballot having been replaced by newly appointed justice Abe Fortas, a likely LDF supporter. Their chances and spirits were also buoyed by President Johnson's appointment of former NAACP general counsel Thurgood Marshall as the first black man to serve on the court.

The LDF's first case, in 1968, was an appeal from Arkansas involving a black man sentenced to death for rape. It almost produced a stunning victory. The justices initially voted 8 to 1 to declare Arkansas's death penalty unconstitutional. But by the time their various approaches were put in writing in 1969, opinions had shifted and Justice Fortas's resignation from the court removed the necessary fifth vote from a majority opinion, causing the court to set the case for re-argument.

The subsequent loss of Chief Justice Earl Warren in 1969 left the LDF lawyers with only three likely supporters—Marshall, Douglas, and Brennan—and the rehearing of the Arkansas case produced no expansion of the court's use of constitutional provisions to void or limit death penalty statutes.[7] The next two LDF cases, from California and Ohio, challenged the constitutionality of two trial procedures: using a single trial to establish guilt *and* to assess the death penalty and allowing juries a wide choice of punishments, including the death penalty, without imposing any standards to achieve uniformity. The Supreme Court ruled against LDF in 1971 in both cases on votes of 6 to 3.[8]

That devastating news was followed a month later by a lifeline that gave LDF a shot at their ultimate prize—an opportunity to argue that the death penalty, by its nature, violated the Eighth Amendment's prohibition against "cruel and unusual punishment." The court reviewed nearly two hundred pending capital cases before selecting three to frame the issue, including one from Texas involving a black man who raped a white woman.[9] The cases were consolidated as *Furman v. Georgia*. All three defendants were black and their victims, white.

The vague admonition against extreme criminal penalties provided in the Eighth Amendment when enacted in 1791 ("Excessive bail shall not be required, nor excessive fines imposed, nor cruel and unusual punishments inflicted") embodied a history so well established in English law that it functioned with little judicial interpretation through the nineteenth century. In 1910, however, the Supreme Court infused the provision with new potency in modern criminal law by citing it as the reason for voiding a fifteen-year prison sentence assessed an American by a court in the Philippines, finding it disproportionate to the crime of falsifying a government record.[10]

From that modest beginning grew an expanding acceptance of the Eighth Amendment as a dynamic and changing guideline that should reflect contemporary attitudes toward punishment. The court fleshed out this concept and gave it an enduring catch-phrase in 1958 in a decision overturning a sentence revoking the American citizenship of a World War II deserter, declaring the Eighth Amendment "must draw its meaning from the evolving standards of decency that mark the progress of a maturing society."[11] The LDF's challenge was to align its racial disparity arguments with evidence of declining public support for the death penalty, load this package onto the "evolving standards of decency" vehicle, and convince five of the nine justices to buy it.

Amsterdam and the LDF, in fact, appeared to benefit from recent trends away from the death penalty. In 1969, New Mexico became the fourteenth state to abolish capital punishment. New York, Iowa, Vermont, and West

Virginia had outlawed or severely limited it in 1965.[12] President Johnson's Commission on Law Enforcement and the Administration of Justice condemned it in 1967.[13] The number of executions in the United States declined from 105 in 1951 to 7 in 1965.[14]

In his argument before the court on the *Furman* case in January 1972, Amsterdam contended that the use of the death penalty was protected from public outrage by its infrequent use, concluding that "when a penalty is so barbaric that it can gain public acceptance only by being rarely, arbitrarily and discriminatorily enforced, it plainly affronts the general standards of decency of the society." His co-counsel, Jack Greenberg, pointed to Texas statistics showing that blacks had a 78 percent chance of being sentenced to death while nonblacks had a 22 percent chance.[15]

The contrary argument in the Texas rape case that became part of *Furman v. Georgia* was made by one of the nation's preeminent constitutional scholars, Charles Alan Wright.[16] A member of the faculty at the University of Texas School of Law, Wright was selected by Atty. Gen. Crawford Martin after being informed that Chief Justice Warren Burger had expressed an interest in Professor Wright's views on the issue.[17] Wright dismissed Amsterdam's concern over the infrequency of death sentences, terming it one, but not the only, element of unusualness. "Some punishments would be prohibited even if applied frequently," Wright told the court. "Insofar as discrimination is raised by these cases, race may have been a factor in past sentences, but, if so, it was a factor in all criminal sentencing—not just sentencing in capital cases."[18]

Amsterdam won the day. His focus on the arbitrariness of the death penalty's use found a compelling advocate in Justice Potter Stewart. He noted that while a multitude of defendants in America were convicted of rape and murder in 1967 and 1968 at the same time these three defendants were found guilty and that while many of the other defendants' offenses were as reprehensible as these, "the petitioners are among a capriciously selected random handful upon whom the sentence of death has in fact been imposed." In what quickly became a pithy synopsis of the lengthy and diverse opinions that produced the court's landmark decision in *Furman,* Justice Stewart said, "These death sentences are cruel and unusual in the same way that being struck by lightning is cruel and unusual."[19]

Stewart was joined by Justice Byron White in finding the operation of the existing death penalty statutes—but not the death penalty itself—in contravention of the Eighth Amendment. They were the two critical votes Amsterdam needed to build on the reliable Douglas-Brennan-

Marshall opposition. Those five votes awarded Amsterdam and the LDF their long-sought goal of moving their challenge of the death penalty beyond the difficult-to-use Fourteenth Amendment's equal protection standard to the more clear-cut "cruel and unusual" test.

The *Furman* opinions, which consumed more printed pages than any case in the court's history and ran to seventy-six thousand words, were a conglomeration of intense personal revulsion toward the death penalty; history lessons dating to the eleventh century; a chronicle of the adoption of the Eighth Amendment; a bibliography of literature and academic studies on criminal law and the death penalty; and a thorough deconstruction of Supreme Court decisions involving the Eighth Amendment, the court's obligation to follow precedent, and dozens of related issues.

Most of the rhetoric carried readers through the thickets of legal, academic, and social science trails that led up to the historic decision but offered no guidance as to what the next step should be. Despite their role as the deciding votes that forged a majority, Justices Stewart and White stated only what they thought *not* permissible, leaving state legislators to guess what the two judges thought *was* permissible.

Only Chief Justice Burger, one the four appointees of President Nixon who dissented from the majority opinions, looked beyond these three cases to address the criminal law revisions mandated by the ruling. He lamented that "the future of capital punishment in this country has been left in an uncertain limbo." In his opinion, Burger wrote,

> Rather than providing a final and unambiguous answer on the basic constitutional question, the collective impact of the majority's ruling is to demand an undetermined measure of change from the various state legislatures and the Congress. . . . While I would not undertake to make a definitive statement as to the parameters of the Court's ruling, it is clear that if state legislatures and the Congress wish to maintain the availability of capital punishment, significant statutory changes will have to be made.
>
> Since the two pivotal concurring opinions turn on the assumption that the punishment of death is now meted out in a random and unpredictable manner, legislative bodies may seek to bring their laws into compliance with the Court's ruling by providing standards for juries and judges to follow in determining the sentence in capital cases or by more narrowly defining the crimes for which the penalty is to be imposed.[20]

The court's ruling was issued on June 29, 1972, several weeks after Texas voters in the Democratic primary cleaned house in reaction to the Sharpstown banking scandal, selecting a new governor, lieutenant governor, attorney general, and half of the legislature. A special legislative session by a bevy of lame duck officeholders to address the death penalty was out of the question.

The revamped state leadership took office in January 1973 with strong support for reinstating capital punishment. Newly elected governor Briscoe included reinstatement as a top priority in his inaugural address to the legislature.[21] The House acted first, voting 102 to 33 on May 8 to mandate the death penalty for anyone found guilty by a jury of murdering an on-duty police officer or firefighter; killing for hire; killing a jail or prison guard while attempting to escape; or intentionally committing murder in the course of committing or attempting to commit kidnapping, burglary, robbery, forcible rape, or arson. The existing penalty range of two years to life in prison was retained for other types of murder. An amendment to substitute life in prison without parole for the death penalty attracted only 29 votes from the 150 House members.[22]

The Senate rejected the House version on a vote of 20 to 9 and replaced the House's mandated death sentence with a provision allowing a judge to impose either death or life imprisonment based on the recommendation of the jury that found the defendant guilty. The jurors' recommendation would be based on a separate post-trial hearing to consider up to eight aggravating and seven mitigating circumstances, reflecting the approach proposed by the American Law Institute's Model Penal Code.[23] Before voting 28 to 3 on May 23 to pass the bill, the Senate also added to the list of death penalty offenses bomb murderers, killers of reform school guards, and anyone who hired someone to kill another person.[24]

The House rejected the Senate changes, sending the bill to a House-Senate conference committee. The House conferees prevailed on the listing of death penalty offenses, dropping the Senate's three additions. Both chambers' versions of the punishment provisions were rejected by the conferees. They agreed with the Senate's contention that mandatory death sentences with no other option would fail to meet the demands of *Furman*. But they replaced the Senate's proposal for the Model Penal Code's list of aggravating and mitigating circumstances with a compromise procedure mandating a life sentence if the jury failed to unanimously answer "yes" to three questions:

1. Was the murder committed deliberately with the reasonable expectation that death would result?

2. Is the defendant likely to constitute a continuing threat to society?

3. Was the murder an unreasonable response to provocation?

"Yes" answers to all three questions would mandate that a death sentence be imposed by the judge.[25]

On the final day of the legislative session on May 28, the compromise bill passed the House on a vote of 114 to 30 and the Senate by 27 to 4.[26] Governor Briscoe signed the bill on June 14 with a pen last used by a young deputy sheriff gunned down in February during a routine traffic stop. The law took effect immediately.[27]

The new law began its voyage through judicial review just two months later, when a twenty-two-year-old school dropout in Cuero named Jerry Lane Jurek killed the ten-year-old daughter of a police officer after abducting her from a community swimming pool and driving through town with the little girl screaming in the bed of his pickup. In one of his two confessions, Jurek said he killed her after she rebuffed his sexual advances. He was indicted for killing her in the course of committing kidnapping and forcible rape, thus triggering the death penalty law. He was convicted and sentenced to death on February 2, 1974.

Jurek's case offered Amsterdam and the LDF their first opportunity to challenge the new Texas law. They filed a friend of the court brief on Jurek's behalf when the case reached the Texas Court of Criminal Appeals for oral argument in November 1974. The court, one of only two states' supreme courts devoted exclusively to criminal cases, ruled against Jurek on April 16, 1975. Unlike the overwhelming support the new law had registered in the legislature, the highest criminal court of the State of Texas approved it by only the slimmest of margins, a vote of 3 to 2.

In the majority opinion, Judge W. A. Morrison noted that the new law was enacted "in response to *Furman*. The question before us is whether these statutes are valid under that holding. Do they provide effective guidance to the jury? Do they adequately limit the discretion of the jury? Do they guard against the arbitrary and standardless imposition of the death penalty? We hold they do."[28] The legislature's decision to limit the death penalty to a small group of narrowly defined and particularly brutal offenses, Morrison's opinion said, "ensures that the death penalty will only be imposed for the most serious crimes. It also insures that the death penalty will only be imposed for the same type of offenses which occur under the same type of circumstances." The legislative decision to limit the jury's decision on punishment to life imprisonment or death, in contrast to the previous range of two years to life imprisonment or death, Morrison concluded, further "limits the standardless imposition of the death penalty." And finally, Morrison praised the requirement that the jury must respond affirmatively to two or three questions that direct and guide the jury's deliberations, he said, and "channel the jury's consideration on punishment and effectively ensure against the arbitrary and wanton imposition of the death penalty."[29]

Morrison refuted Amsterdam's argument that the absence of a list of potential aggravating and mitigating circumstances available for jurors' consideration during sentencing created a fatal vagueness. "The fact that an exhaustive and precise list of factors is not specifically included does not indicate that the jury is without adequate guidelines," he wrote. "We are inclined to believe that the factors which determine whether the sentence of death is an appropriate penalty in a particular case are too complex to be compressed within the limits of a simple formula." Morrison indicated that Texas juries could consider aggravating factors and mitigating circumstances during sentencing and offered these specific examples: "whether the defendant had a significant criminal record[,] . . . the range and severity of his prior criminal conduct[,] . . . the age of the defendant and whether or not at the time of the commission of the offense he was acting under duress or under the domination of another[, and] . . . whether the defendant was under an extreme form of mental or emotional pressure."[30]

He went on to dispute Amsterdam's argument that the sentencing process allows juries too much latitude, contending that "some discretion is inherent and desirable in any system of justice, from arrest to final judgment. . . . To eliminate all discretion on the part of the jury would be to risk elimination of that valuable element which permits individualization based on consideration of all extenuating circumstances and would eliminate the element of mercy, one of the fundamental traditions of our system of criminal jurisprudence. If discretion in the assessment of punishment under a statute can be shown to be reasonable and controlled, rather than capricious and discriminatory, the test of *Furman* will be met."[31]

The dissenting judges, Wendell Odom and Truman Roberts, disagreed with the majority's finding that the new law granted jurors discretion in sentencing. The law's directives regarding the sentencing process, Odom said, used the word "shall" instead of "may" at all critical points, "allowing no discretion in determining the punishment to be received by a defendant who is guilty of capital murder." Judge Odom also found that the law's lack of specific factors to be considered in sentencing did not produce the desirable flexibility praised in the majority opinion: "The fact that discretion is 'inherent and desirable' does not render a vague statute any less vague. The majority have erred in mistaking the vagueness of this mandatory statute for discretion."[32]

Judge Odom was particularly troubled by the legislature's requirement that the jury determine whether

> there is a probability that the defendant would commit criminal acts of violence that would constitute a continuing threat to society. . . .
>
> What did the Legislature mean when it provided that a man's life or death shall rest upon whether there exists a "probability" that he will perform certain acts in the future? . . . We may say there is a twenty percent probability that it will rain tomorrow, or a ten or five percent probability. Though this be a small probability, yet it is some probability, a probability, and no one would say it is no probability or not a probability.
>
> The statute does not require a particular degree of probability but only directs that some probability need be found. The absence of a specification as to what degree of probability is required is itself a vagueness inherent in the term as used in this issue. Our common-sense understanding of the term leaves the statute too vague to pass constitutional muster.[33]

Judge Roberts complained that the provision was unconstitutional because "it is impossible to prove beyond a reasonable doubt or to a moral certainty that a person will act in a certain manner in the future."[34]

The court denied a motion for rehearing on May 7, 1975, passing this emotionally charged issue to me to defend in the Supreme Court of the United States.

The Supreme Court, however, was in limbo on the death penalty issue. Although Amsterdam and the LDF had obtained Supreme Court review of North Carolina's new mandatory death statute as the first post-*Furman* test, with arguments scheduled for April 1975, a stroke suffered by Justice Douglas delayed the matter until the case lost its significance when the North Carolina legislature revised the law.

Douglas's retirement in November and the confirmation of John Paul Stevens as his successor in December freed the court to schedule a broad review of the post-*Furman* sentencing schemes. At that juncture, the court selected *Jurek v. Texas* and murder cases from Georgia, North Carolina, and Florida as representative of the thirty-five new state laws designed to comply with *Furman*. Arguments were promptly scheduled for March 30, 1976.

The loss of a bedrock supporter through the retirement of Justice Douglas was only one of several dispiriting factors facing Amsterdam and the LDF in preparing for the arguments in March 1976. The declining public support for the death penalty that had caused Justice Brennan in *Furman* to conclude that "contemporary society views this punishment with substantial doubt" was now replaced by increasingly robust backing.[35] In California, for example, where the state Supreme Court's ruling abolishing the death penalty in 1972 added impetus to the pending *Furman* decision, supporters forced a ballot vote nine months later to authorize death penalty legislation, which passed by a 2-to-1 margin.[36] Nationwide Gallup Poll results showed death penalty support increased from 50 percent in 1972 to 65 percent in 1976 while opposition percentages dropped from 42 to 28 percent.[37]

Those auspicious trends failed to comfort Bert Pluymen, the second-year lawyer assigned to brief the case for my office. Significantly, the highest criminal court in our conservative state only narrowly approved the new death penalty statute despite overwhelming legislative support that no doubt reflected public opinion. In addition, his research revealed the existence of no other state law that took the hybrid Texas approach of combining a guilt or innocence trial involving specific acts of murder with a separate sentencing hearing that asked three generalized questions whose answers would mandate a life or death sentence. Most states either totally removed jury discretion by mandating the death penalty for defendants found guilty of certain crimes or created a separate sentencing hearing in which juries weighed evidence relating to a specified list of aggravating and mitigating circumstances.

Like the dissenting judges on the Texas Court of Criminal Appeals, Pluymen quickly focused on the sentencing questions posed to jurors after they convicted a defendant, for instance, of intentional murder in the course of a kidnapping, robbery, burglary, or rape. How could that same jury then find, in answer to the first sentencing question, that the murder was *not* deliberate and intended to kill? In his brief to the U.S.

Supreme Court, Pluymen attempted to refute Amsterdam's position that the jury's guilty verdict indeed rendered the first sentencing question irrelevant: "Even if this were true in a given case, it would not be illogical to rephrase substantially the same question another way before imposing the death penalty, given the infinite variety of human conduct and the imprecision of the English language," Pluymen wrote. "It is a way to reinforce that the killing was in fact the calculated elimination of a human being, in the absence of mitigating factors, at which the imposition of the death penalty in Texas is aimed."[38]

As to the second sentencing question mandated by Texas law, Amsterdam would likely ask, "How could the jury fail to find that the person they had just declared guilty of a calculated murder would *not* likely constitute a continuing threat to society?" Here Pluymen noted that the Texas Court of Criminal Appeals cited a list of specific mitigating circumstances that Texas juries could consider in answering this question, thereby giving a jury "access to information at the sentencing phase which it did not have at the guilt or innocence phase."[39] One obvious example of this is when a defendant declines to testify prior to conviction because of trial strategy but chooses to testify at the sentencing hearing.

To take the focus away from all the abstract legal arguments and toward the gory human reality the law was intended to punish and prevent, Pluymen added a long footnote describing the handiwork of some Texas death row inmates. "Unquestionably, the Texas capital punishment statutes hit their mark," Pluymen's footnote began, then listed six heinous examples that concluded with Robert Kleason's death sentence in 1975 for murdering two Mormon missionaries at his house and then using a hacksaw to cut up their bodies for disposal.[40]

But his most telling point, and the one that became a compelling component of my oral argument, was a revealing examination of the new law's actual working results. Amsterdam and the LDF were determined to convince the court that the death penalty fell disproportionately on minorities and that the law created too much discretion at every step of the process, from the prosecutor's decision to bring a capital murder charge to the possibility of a plea deal to the jury being given questions at the sentencing hearing whose answers arbitrarily allowed some defendants to escape death. Such arguments could be refuted only by statistics that showed how the law, in fact, was applied.

In February 1976, the Texas Judicial Council, created in 1929 by the legislature to study and report on the organization and practices of the

Texas judicial system, sent questionnaires to all felony prosecutors seeking data on every jury-tried capital murder case arising after the new law took effect on June 14, 1973. Reports came in from 119 prosecutors, covering all of the state's 254 counties, on 74 capital murder cases tried in 31 counties.

"Petitioner's argument that the submission of these questions is a guise under which juries permit the 'erratic escape' of other capital murderers is resoundingly rebutted by the statistics," Pluymen could now jab at Amsterdam. "In the fifty-eight cases to date in which the first question has been submitted to a jury, it has been answered in the affirmative on all but three occasions, and all three of those times the second question was also answered in the negative. In the twenty-seven cases in which question three [whether the murder was an unreasonable response to provocation] was submitted, it was answered in the affirmative on every occasion."[41] Indeed, the jury's answers were remarkably consistent, not arbitrary as contended by Amsterdam.

Where Amsterdam argued that the "continuing threat to society" question could hardly be answered in favor of the defendant, Pluymen could cite the Judicial Council study to show that juries returned "no" answers to this question in fifteen capital murder cases. And, significantly, the law's color-blindness was confirmed by the fact that the fifteen convicted murderers who were not considered a continuing threat included eight blacks, six whites, and one Hispanic-surnamed defendant.

Amsterdam's second criticism of the "continuing threat" question was that it granted juries an impermissible and impossible power to predict future behavior. Pluymen responded that this argument "strikes at the heart of our system of justice. Judges and juries time and time again make assessments in both criminal and civil cases concerning events which are likely to occur. . . . When the need to protect society through incapacitation is considered a legitimate goal of the death penalty, why should it be impermissible to ask the jury to determine that issue directly in an individual case so that the punishment may indeed be tailored to fit the criminal?"[42]

When we received notice from the Supreme Court of our scheduled argument, I was slated to follow Amsterdam's opening argument in the first spot for the respondent states, despite the fact that the combined five cases were styled *Gregg v. Georgia*. I made arrangements to fly with Pluymen to Washington on March 29 so we could spend the night before the argument reviewing the case. After a preliminary discussion on the plane, we spent two hours in my hotel room weighing Amsterdam's points, rehashing the *Furman* opinions, recreating the legislature's steps, and groping for a strategy that would secure five favorable votes from these learned minds. "Let me try this argument on you," I would say to Pluymen and then launch into an impassioned defense of our law, culminating with the statement that it protected our citizens from "the worst of the worst."

"You can say that, but don't forget—our law only applies to murderers who kill in the act of committing another type of crime," Pluymen would remind me. "A mass murderer can't be sentenced to death unless he also kidnaps, robs, or rapes one of the victims."

Around and around we went, with me retracing the blind alleys he had just spent six months researching and backing out of and he gently reminding me when I overlooked a subtle but critical point certain to be used by a questioning justice to puncture my argument. We called it quits without deciding on a game plan. My legal note pad was filled with pages and pages of scribblings, but they were insights, thoughts, and random jottings, not any sort of cohesive outline.

The next morning over breakfast we resumed our give-and-take, with me still searching for a clear path leading to five justices nodding in assent to my indisputable logic, Pluymen still warning me of the underbrush clogging my hoped-for path. My trial lawyer instincts pushed me toward reduction of the complexities, to simplify my audience's job, and toward hyperbole, to implant a vivid image of my argument that would upstage Amsterdam's performance in my listeners' memories when they later formulated their ruling. But the complexities were almost irreducible, and the hyperbole potential was dampened by the muddy realities of the issues.

Finally, I looked at Pluymen over our empty coffee cups on the hotel restaurant table and said, "I'm just going to take my cue from Amsterdam." Pluymen stared at me blankly. His mouth dropped open and only said "Okay," but I could tell he was thinking to himself, "My God, he's going to wing it—one of the most important cases in decades, and he's going to *wing* it before the Supreme Court of the United States!" We silently put our notes and briefs in our briefcases and headed toward the Supreme Court building.

Milling death penalty demonstrators, pro and con, joined television news cameramen, reporters, tourists, and security guards on the long, wide stairway leading up to the entrance of the building. When we entered the cathedral-like quietness of the chamber, it was packed with people who had waited in line for hours to get a seat. Pluymen and I took our seats at the counsel table next to the podium.

This occasion was a reunion for Amsterdam. He had clerked for the court in 1960, argued the *Furman* case and several others before the court, and was among the elite, highly regarded legal scholars who also were at home in appellate advocacy. His success in leading the death penalty abolition movement's steady ascent made him almost a cult figure among many constitutional scholars and law faculties. A slender, wiry man with a rapid delivery signaling his impatience to demonstrate his facile grasp of the intricately intertwined legal issues at stake, Amsterdam enjoyed the full respect and attention of the nine justices. I was enthralled with the presence he carried so easily and the opportunity to test my skills against such a legendary advocate before this most demanding tribunal.

Because he spoke on behalf of all the petitioners, Amsterdam was allotted one hour of time. His task forced him to begin his argument with a ten-minute history lesson, categorizing and analyzing the thirty-five different state approaches to rewriting laws to comply with *Furman,* before he could delve into his impassioned rationale for challenging their constitutionality.

The justices, who frequently start bombarding attorneys with questions before they can fully launch their argument, listened to his history lesson without interrupting. But Amsterdam's first move toward asserting his misgivings about the state laws drew an immediate question from one of the *Furman* dissenters, Justice Harry Blackmun, an appointee of President Nixon.

"The death penalty at this point in time is therefore characterized in this country by elaborate *winnowing* processes," Amsterdam said in a soaring voice, "involving a selective screening of cases potentially subject to the death penalty, and an array of off-ramps for avoiding the actual use of the death penalty—either by the second stage penalty proceedings in which aggravating and mitigating circumstances are either balanced or adjudicated, or else by definitions of the capital crime, which narrow the capital crime and set it off from others along often intangible and impressionistic lines. The contrast is, I think, striking between capital punishment as it is authorized by these statutes, and the next most severe penalty known to our law, life in prison."[43]

"You don't think," Blackmun interjected, "this is compelled by the holding in *Furman?*"

"The contrast I'm seeking to make," Amsterdam replied, "is between life imprisonment statutes which exist in 52 jurisdictions in this country, for 408 crimes, without all of these elaborate post-hoc justifications, special circumstances, trials, the aggravating and mitigating circumstances, and the very narrow roster of capital crimes, all encrusted with, and surrounded by, procedures which permit selective application, and, the bottom line, wholesale evasion of the provisions of the death penalty statute."

"Of course," Blackmun persisted, "selective application is what you argued before—twice. And, you can't have been surprised, if you read the opinions of 1972, because this kind of thing was forecast, at least in one opinion."

Amsterdam plowed ahead, arguing that the selectivity incorporated in the new laws "is indicative of something less than a broad-based acceptance of the death penalty in our society" and asserting that the new systems' discretionary features failed to meet the concerns of Justices Stewart and White in *Furman*.

Asked by White if "you're going to tell us why you think so," Amsterdam immediately criticized the Texas sentencing procedure in the Jurek case, where the evidence to support a finding that Jurek would be a continuing threat to society took the form of four Cuero residents called to testify on Jurek's reputation in the community.

"Even on the absurd basis on which this jury condemned this defendant to die—four hearsay statements that the defendant's reputation is bad—how can I say that the evidence is, or is not, sufficient to establish that there is a probability that the defendant may engage in future criminal conduct that may be a danger to the community?" Amsterdam asked. "The question is devoid of intelligible meaning, and the answer is unchallengeable, and, Mr. Justice White, that is one of the reasons why this statute is exactly where we were in *Furman*. . . . No less free, no less unfettered, no less arbitrary than prior to *Furman*."

As I scribbled Amsterdam's comments, I underlined his criticism of the four character witnesses who testified to the community's perception of Jurek. I needed to rebut that in my argument. Justice Stevens then pressed Amsterdam on the extent of his "unfettered discretion" argument, asking whether it applied to a limited area of crime such as air piracy, for which the death penalty was provided in federal law.

"Even the narrowest capital crime would be assailable on this ground if there were total discretion within it," Amsterdam responded. "However, I could see one who rejected that argument nevertheless saying perhaps a statute like killing a guard by a prison inmate while under a life sentence—that may be so narrow in terms of the group that it hits that you might allow something in that kind of a case that you wouldn't allow for punishment for all first degree murders."

I made a note of that—Stevens's question had exposed a weakness in Amsterdam's argument that I could exploit.

Amsterdam's concluding thrust attempted to move these five cases, and the impact of the *Furman* decision, away from a discussion of the fairness of the procedure in individual cases and toward a discussion of the fairness of the overall system. The effect of *Furman,* he said, was to force the weighing of any one defendant's death penalty against all similarly situated defendants' punishments, determining that "the imposition of that death penalty on him was cruel and unusual in a constitutional sense because he was being selected out of an indistinguishable group for no reason, to suffer a penalty inordinately greater than that suffered by others. This arbitrariness defeated the penological justifications for capital punishment, this arbitrariness made the death penalty unusual in a constitutional sense." His pronouncement swept through the courtroom like a sonic boom, signaling a quantum leap in the speed of his reasoning power. He was pushing too far, too fast, I thought as I furiously scratched out fragments from his insistent and intense delivery. Justice Stewart agreed.

"Doesn't your argument prove too much?" Stewart interrupted. He listed all of the forms of discretion in our system of adversary criminal justice, from the prosecutor, to the trial judge, to the jury, to the appellate courts, and added, "If a person is sentenced to anything as the end product of that system, under your argument his sentence, be it life imprisonment or five years' imprisonment, is a cruel and unusual punishment because it is a product of this system—that's your argument, isn't it?"

Amsterdam insisted it was not:

> Our argument is essentially that death is different. If you don't accept the view that for constitutional purposes, death is different, we lose this case—let me make that very clear. . . . The decision is different, the discretion is different, and the result is different, Mr. Justice Stewart, in a death case than in a case where lesser penalties are an issue because, as the history of capital punishment under the discretionary system struck down in *Furman* shows, the death penalty has become so repugnant, so abhorrent to those who must actually apply it in particular cases, as distinguished from the abstract question of having it on the books, that in order for a jury and a judge and a prosecutor and a governor to condemn a defendant, an intense *ad hominem* condem-

> natory judgment has to be made which is very different from the kind of judgment applied when it's a five- or ten-year question, which is a judgment which is uniquely difficult to control, uniquely difficult to rationalize or regularize.

As I rose to replace Amsterdam at the podium, I sensed from the nine faces looking at me that Amsterdam's final burst of intellectual emotion pushed him out on a limb that might not hold the weight of the majority of the justices. To accommodate and respect Amsterdam's consummate performance, I began on a deliberately low-key plane, talking slowly and softly. But I also wanted the justices to know from my first words that my argument was not going to be a recitation of our brief or a scripted scholarly appellate law presentation. It was going to be a head-on challenge to everything they had just heard. They were going to hear a jury speech.

"To Mr. Amsterdam's first point, that the system of selectivity such as was condemned in *Furman* still exists, we would say certainly, as applied to the Texas statutes—and I hope I will be able to demonstrate this before I am done—that is not a correct statement," I began. "And, that the system of selectivity condemned in *Furman* does not presently exist in the Texas statute, either in theory, or, in the best evidence, actual practice."

Calling up and embracing Justice Stewart's statement of misgivings, I disputed Amsterdam's concerns over

> prosecutorial discretion, jury discretion, discretion on behalf of our chief executives of our state. That type of discretion, no statute obviously can cure that, nor should it. As Justice Stewart observed, his argument indeed does prove too much. It would be an anomaly, to say the least, if we were to condemn today in this country as unconstitutional the very procedures that our Constitution created, the same Constitution that created the cruel and unusual punishment provision relied upon by Petitioners. It would be an anomaly to say that we cannot constitutionally carry out a sentence today of death in this country, solely because it is being carried out under the very constitutional procedures that created this country, and upon which it is founded. Indeed, that argument proves too much, and I am sure it will be summarily rejected by every Justice.

At that point, I decided my introductory comments had achieved their purpose of providing a transition from Amsterdam's heated and academic rhetoric. Now, it was my turn to step up the pace. To isolate Amsterdam's argument, I decided to emphasize its disregard for the reality at work in criminal prosecutions:

> Now, as to the proposition that the execution of the death penalty in this country, regardless of the circumstances, regardless of the crimes that are selected out by the states for which it's to have application, in the wisdom of state legislatures, regardless of the procedures that are used, regardless of how careful one may be, regardless of the time spent in selecting a fair and impartial jury, regardless of the impartiality of the prosecution, regardless of the facts, regardless of the circumstances of the crime, regardless of affording all the due process for which this country is noted, regardless of all of that, Mr. Amsterdam would tell us that the execution of the death penalty in America is cruel and unusual punishment, even in those events, and must be condemned.

I paused to allow all that repetition to take hold, then added, my voice rising, "Need one today say more to this Court than that statement stands without any legal precedent? He stands utterly alone! The unchallenged law of this country as I speak is to the contrary. Indeed, he should carry a very heavy and compelling responsibility to ask the Court to overturn everything that has ever been said by this Court, and other courts in this country, to the effect that the infliction of the death penalty in the United States of America today is not unconstitutional per se."

I added emphasis to this point by noting that while some Americans strongly believe the death penalty should no longer be used for any purpose, "that, of course, is not the issue. This Court is not a super-legislature. This Court is not the keeper, any more than Mr. Amsterdam is, of the social values and the conscience and moral standards of the people of this country. That's why we have a federal system of government. That's why we have a republican form of government. That's why we entrust decisions of this type, subject always, of course, to review on constitutional standards, to the state legislatures."

Moving to the Jurek case, I mocked Amsterdam's depiction of our case: "He tells us that, really, what has happened here in Texas is nothing more than that we just decided that there was a person that was a reprobate and that he killed a young girl whose father happened to be a policeman and that we decided he ought to die."

At that point a Shakespearean taunt from my debating competition days popped into my head, and I thundered to the justices, "Now, upon what meat can anyone feast to grow so great as to say that about this case in view of this record?"[44] I answered my question, saying, "It's the same thing as conceding, in response to questions from Justice Stevens, that in his view, there could be narrowly defined circumstances, narrowly defined crimes by a legislature, which might even meet his constitutional standards. He illustrated with one, that is, a lifer in a prison who takes the life of someone working there."

Then I launched another repetitive characterization of Amsterdam's isolation, my pitch and volume again rising:

> The theory seems to be, let *me* say what this case is about, let *me* say what the Texas case is about and what the facts are, and let *me* say where we draw the line, let *me* determine what offenses should come within the purview of capital punishment in this country, let *me* decide what constitutes proper social goals, let *me* decide where retribution is possible and proper and where it isn't, let *me* decide when, if ever, the death penalty will deter and thus serve a legitimate social function, and let *me* decide where and when incapacitation of a defendant is justified.
>
> Now I say to all of that, may it please the Court, and it's run through both the *Furman* presentation and through this presentation, the basic fallacy is of asking this Court to blindfold yourselves to any viewpoint other than that expressed by the petitioner, to blindfold yourselves to any data or evidence or experience, other than that to which they point, and the standards for which they have arbitrarily established as the guidepost in this case.

Justice Stevens brought me up short. "Mr. Attorney General, I wonder if that is really a fair statement of his argument," Stevens interrupted. "He has two separate arguments, of course. But the first argument as I understood it was that under the Texas system, there is total discretion in the jury to return a verdict other than the one that requires the death sentence. And as I understood his argument, he says that the first and third of the three aggravating questions that are submitted to the jury in the punishment hearing have already been answered by the jury, and therefore there really is no standard guiding those. Do you have a response to that argument?"

I responded by reciting cases in which jurors found a defendant guilty of capital murder but, through answers to the sentencing questions, assessed a life sentence. One involved an armed man attempting to free prisoners from the Beaumont jail and, in the melee that ensued, the death of a police officer. Because the police officer was killed accidentally by a jail guard and not by the defendant, the jury's "no" answer to the question of deliberate conduct causing the police officer's death required a life sentence. Then I recited the Texas Judicial Council study to demonstrate how juries used the discretion offered in the new law to make allowances for mitigating circumstances that spared the defendant from execution.

Stevens then asked me to respond to Amsterdam's argument that, "if this case [regarding Jurek] is typical, that the evidence supporting an affirmative answer to question number two consisted of nothing more than the offense itself plus four hearsay statements by local citizens [that] they did not approve of this man's reputation, that that question really is kind of an escape hatch by which the jury may exercise leniency?"

"No, sir, not at all," I replied. "I have cited first twelve instances in which the jury found—I recited the one instance of the killing of the policeman, that I believe is a case in point—where there was absolutely no evidence other than the crime itself which would have indicated recidivism, and the crime itself was not, in the jury's mind, of such a heinous character under the circumstances described as to justify a 'yes' answer."

Grateful to Stevens for giving me an opening to recount the gruesome tale of Jurek's crime, I left out few details, particularly not the race of the murderer and victim, because the racial disparity in death sentences was an unstated but well-understood concern in *Furman:*

> Mr. Jurek, a 22-year-old white man, kidnapped a 10-year-old white girl, where her grandmother had taken her for a two-hour swim and had left her in the custody of the pool people, put her in the back of his pickup truck, ran her through the city of Cuero with her screaming at the top of her voice "Please help me," had already told people he was going to "get that girl" or one like her, that "they weren't too young to have sex with," and he intended to have it. Took her to Hell's Gate Bridge, got her out of the truck, undertook to have sex with her, choked her until she fell into unconsciousness and threw her in the river and left her to die, which she did almost immediately, went back with his friends and his beer, with no remorse, came back by the bridge with his friends looking around in the river to see what he could see.

Then I turned to Amsterdam's dismissive comments about the evidence used to prove that Jurek was a likely repeat offender and explained that "the only way we prove bad character in Texas in these cases is by hearsay. You cannot get up on the witness stand in Texas in a courtroom and say 'I believe this person is bad from my experience.' It has to be from the person's reputation within the community. So this quick pass off that it was hearsay testimony doesn't do justice to this record. These were four fine citizens of Cuero that testified that his general reputation in the community for being a law abiding and peaceful citizen was bad."

I could not resist dropping another inflammatory tidbit to further impugn Amsterdam's disparagement: "I don't know how much credence the jury gave to the two questions by the prosecutor that 'did you know that he had done the same thing to a girl in Louisiana and one in Cuero before.' I don't know whether that had any probative force or not."[45]

After another exchange with Judge Stevens about evidence used to demonstrate a defendant's continuing threat to society, I was ready to recount the legislative give-and-take that had produced our new death penalty law when I was interrupted by Justice Thurgood Marshall. One of the court's two firm anti–death penalty justices, Marshall was well known for his pithy questioning of lawyers appearing before the court. He lobbed a totally unexpected demand to me, insisting that "if they had given them life in prison, you wouldn't have to worry about recidivism, would you?"

Chief Justice Burger tried to rescue me, interjecting, "Except for guards, and other inmates and employees of the prison, I suppose that's always a possibility, isn't it?"

"Well, of course, we had a lifer who escaped, and you might have read about it," I said. "We just lost two women as hostages in the course of it. I guess life for them was rather important and to their families, and he was the lifer, what did he have to lose? Under the cloud the Court put us under, because we didn't know whether we had a statute . . ."[46]

But Justice Marshall was not through with me. "There are all kind of cases where if it was actual life in prison, you wouldn't have to worry about recidivism, unless you want to get some way-out case someplace?"

"Well, but to that victim, . . ." I began to answer, but Justice Marshall cut me off again. "Do you think that the mere fact that a man is subject to commit another crime entitles him to be killed, just to prevent him from committing another crime? Why don't you pick him up the first time and kill him?" Marshall blurted out.

I was losing ground and time—the court used a red light on the podium to advise attorneys when their time expired, and I was fast approaching my thirty-minute deadline—so I tried as graciously as possible to accept the judge's admonition and restart my argument. "I think the public is entitled . . . I think, Mr. Justice Marshall, that the legislatures of the states on behalf of the people they represent are entitled to make that judgment," I explained.

Chief Justice Burger again tried to steer the discussion back to my case, asking for clarification on the need for the jury's answers to the sentencing questions to be affirmative to each of these three questions, and to be unanimous.

I used the exchange with Marshall and Burger about recidivism to transition into a rebuttal of Amsterdam's criticism of the death penalty as a deterrent: "The question of recidivism, it seems to me, is the same as the question on deterrence. Mr. Amsterdam himself, it seems to me, acknowledged the significance of deterrence when he said that if given a choice, these defendants would choose the life sentence, when he was debating about whether or not they should have a choice during the sentencing process. And of course, that just is simple recognition by him of this intuitive instinct of human nature to seek to sustain our own lives, the life that we all know is important to every individual."

From that beginning, I again resorted to repetition to emphasize the court's obligation to recognize the deterrent value of the death penalty:

> And if that be so, then why isn't it, and why shouldn't it, be allowable as a deterrent, as a social goal of deterrence, to prevent a lifer in a prison from taking life with immunity? Why shouldn't it be a deterrent, to prevent someone who had a small child that he intends to rape or kidnap, to have not the incentive of his own life to return that child? Why shouldn't we permit a law in our states such as in Texas? . . . Why shouldn't there be a deterrent for a person who goes in a convenience store and undertakes to take someone's life, not to have the deterrent of his own life when he is snuffing out the only eyewitness to that crime in most instances?

I reassured the justices of our legislature's struggle to apply the *Furman* opinions in drafting a new law, providing information not included in the court record or the briefs:

> Under our prior Texas statutes that you condemned, we could put people to death for rape alone. . . . In our old statute, we could put people to death for lying in a death penalty case. We could put them to death for armed robbery. . . . We could put them to death for treason. We had all kinds of randomness and differentials between our capital murder treatment.
>
> Now, we have changed that. Our Senate sat down on the one hand of the aisle and they wrote a statute down in Texas that put all of the code materials in about mitigating circumstances and extenuating circumstances and aggravating circumstances. Our House sat down, on the other hand, and wrote a statute like North Carolina's that said "guilt: death." We compromised. We went to a House conference. I went over and worked, we tried to pore over *Furman,* we tried to understand it—what did Justice Burger say, when he said he might not like a mandatory sentence? What was the right thing to do?

I recited the law's specified capital murders to which the death penalty was assigned, concluding with the killing of a police officer or firefighter while on duty. I used that example to also reassure the court that the new system was not producing racially discriminatory results: "In that particular category of cases under our statutes, we have had three whites kill policemen. Two of them received death, one of them received life. We had one Spanish surnamed defendant kill a peace officer—hung jury. We had nine blacks in cases involving police officers, six death penalties, two lifes, and one hung jury. There is no evidence that once our system began that there is racial discrimination."

And that's as far as I got in my argument, because it ended on an almost humorous note with several of the justices trying to help me answer a question posed by one of them. "Is there a requirement under Texas law that the defendant has known that the victim was a police officer?" Justice Stewart asked.

I paused for a moment, then confessed, "I frankly don't know."

Justice Marshall, now trying to help me, injected, "They were in uniform, am I right?"

I replied, "I think what Justice Stewart may be asking, Justice Marshall, is if someone is impersonating or perhaps you just simply are not aware—he is a plain-clothes officer. You are not aware that he is in the course of duty. I'll check it for you."

Hoping to wedge in the remainder of my racial statistics, I wrapped up quickly: "My impression is that 'knowingly' would be involved. Now, in those armed robbery cases, we had 23 blacks that were tried. Ten of them received the death penalty. We had 20 whites tried for that same bad crime, and ten of those received the death penalty. We had nine Spanish surnamed defendants commit that horrible crime and six of those received the death penalty and one of those has gone back on remand."

At that point, the warning light on my podium went dark, meaning my time had expired. "I'm sorry, my light is off, I could go on to show without any question that not only in theory does the Texas statute meet all of the criticism, by having these narrow categories with questions that deal with recidivism and incapacitation and deterrence and retribution, but also that in practice, and in actual practice, it has met those standards and is working constitutionally in our state," I concluded.

As I was leaving the podium, Justice Blackmun addressed me: "Mr. Attorney General, just to save you the trouble, I think I quote from your code, 'the person murdered was a peace officer or a fireman that was acting in the lawful discharge of an official duty and the defendant knew was a peace officer or a fireman.'"

"I appreciate that very much, Mr. Justice Blackmun," I responded, adding with a smile, "I tried to prepare very diligently for this matter and I didn't do a one hundred percent job."

Three months later, the Supreme Court issued its ruling in the five cases known as *Gregg v. Georgia*. The Texas, Florida, and Georgia laws were approved on a vote of 7 to 2. The North Carolina and Louisiana laws, which provided for mandated death sentences for specified murders, were disapproved on a vote of 5 to 4 because of their lack of discretion in sentencing.

Here is the relevant opinion of Justices Stewart, Powell, and Stevens regarding our new law: "The Texas capital-sentencing procedure guides and focuses the jury's objective consideration of the particularized circumstances of the individual offense and the individual offender before it can impose a sentence of death." And most importantly, "The Texas law has thus eliminated the arbitrariness and caprice of the system invalidated in *Furman*." The justices added that Amsterdam's "contentions to the contrary are without substance. His assertion that arbitrariness still pervades the entire Texas criminal justice system fundamentally misinterprets *Furman*. Petitioner's contention that the second statutory question is unconstitutionally vague because it requires the prediction of human behavior lacks merit. The jury's task in answering that question is one that must commonly be performed throughout the American criminal justice system, and Texas law clearly satisfies the essential requirement that the jury have all possible relevant information about the individual defendant."[47]

Amsterdam and the LDF continued to press the Supreme Court to chip away at death penalty laws, achieving a few successes. But the Texas law approved by the court in *Jurek* remained in effect, with only minor changes, for at least thirty years.

(9)

Managing the Reform of Prisons and Youth Detention Schools

When I included in my death penalty argument before the Supreme Court of the United States a reminder to the justices they were not a "super-legislature," I was referring to more than just Texas' death penalty laws, and I was referring to more than just the Supreme Court. I was also expressing my frustration and concern over federal judges' newfound eagerness to expand the U.S. Constitution to justify substituting their personal vision in place of our legislature's judgment on how a government agency should operate.

The source of that frustration was federal court litigation attacking our state's four largest programs involving institutional care: the prison system, young offender facilities, mental hospitals, and facilities for the mentally disabled. Any one of these cases would have been a massive litigation load—the prison case by itself became the most comprehensive civil action suit in correctional law history.[1] To have four of them hit my office at the same time was an unprecedented call on the resources of the attorney general's office.

The goal of these cases was to establish a new constitutional right. The people who were the intended beneficiaries of this legal right were criminals sentenced to prison time or committed to mental hospitals, juveniles committed to state facilities by a juvenile court judge, and persons suffering from mental illness or congenital mental disability who were committed by civil courts to state facilities. The new right being sought was a right to treatment, a right that would impose on institutions housing these people a level of care to be established by judicial decree.

Determining what level of treatment to provide inmates historically was the province of our legislature. An institution created by the legislature would have its mission defined by law, its operation reviewed each legislative session as part of the budgeting process, and its governing board members held accountable through the confirmation process when the Texas Senate reviewed a governor's appointees. That is the way the system had operated since our legislature began establishing these facilities 120 years earlier.

The notion that criminals, juvenile offenders, and people with mental deficiencies could demand a certain type or level of treatment or care from the government was, to most adult Americans in the 1960s, unthinkable. It conjured up the humorous aphorism "the inmates are running the asylum," which expressed the generally held belief that people being confined in any sort of government facility were not entitled to any say in how the institution was operated. Any constitutional rights they enjoyed before incarceration were believed to be severely limited when they entered the institution, and they were not expected to enjoy free contact with the outside world. Prison wardens and superintendents of juvenile and mental facilities censored incoming and outgoing mail and telephone calls, limited visitors' access, and filtered news available from newspapers, radio, or television. Books with information about the laws governing their condition could be viewed only in the library.

Texans, through their elected legislators and other officeholders, accepted—as did most Americans—these restrictions as necessary components of a system designed to isolate criminals, juvenile delinquents, and mentally unstable people. However, like the ambivalence in most of our public policies, Texans and Americans were repelled by the notion of these outcasts being physically abused. Keep them locked up, yes, but don't take advantage of their defenseless status by torturing or beating them.

To this unstable balancing act were generally added two other admonitions: minimize the costs and prevent escapes. On top of those layers of self-protective public sentiment was added an even more ambivalent commandment that derived from our religious and enlightened cultural heritage—rehabilitate these confinees, help them overcome their weaknesses.

Unfortunately for the managers of these institutions, that last commandment was put into written law, while the public's sentiments were not. Our legislators and state government leaders on one hand wrote into the law a caring and humane vision. But when it came time to spend public funds on facilities to house these unfortunates and on staff to carry out the law's demands, the message was "keep costs low."

It was this gap between lofty ideals in the law and the grubby reality of applying the law that created an opportunity for a small group of lawyers eager to add their causes to the growing list of Supreme Court cases expanding constitutional rights. The goal of these lawyers was to convert broad constitutional "thou shalt not" proscriptions into excruciatingly detailed "thou must" prescriptions enforced by a federal judge.

Instead of providing a broad mission to these institutions and allowing them freedom to devise the means to that end—"go create a prison system to rehabilitate convicts"—these lawyers demanded a court-imposed mandate that specified both the means *and* the end—"go create a prison system with cells of such-and-such a size, with guards who have this level of education, with educational programs teaching the following information and skills" and on and on, for as far as they could keep narrowing management's options.

This thinking repelled me on a personal level because it was based on a fundamental mistrust of the people running our government. My family upbringing, my education, my religion, and my professional experience all assumed most people generally acted in good faith and with good intentions when they were presented with the facts of a situation.

I was not ready to condemn our government and its employees by assuming the worst of them, even though that was an attitude that took a beating because of the Watergate scandal, which forced President Nixon to resign in 1974. On a professional level, I found this approach lacking in common sense and practicality, and I considered it an affront to my grasp of our nation's theory of government built upon control vested in the hands of people elected by the citizenry. But I also was torn by the obvious failures of our state government in recent years to keep pace with our society's evolving and expanding expectations on a wide range of issues—from pollution control to youth detention facilities to consumer protections, among others. As a proud leader of our state government, I was resentful of implications that we were incapable of fixing the broken parts of our system without a heavy-handed and punitive demand from a federal judge.

Yet, the truth was, many of the changes these federal judges forced us to attempt were long overdue. The only way I knew to resolve this dilemma was, as I told a group of legislators who wanted me to defend their dubious reapportionment plan, "I will represent you, but I'm not going to prostitute myself for you." I sought to adjust my defense of state agencies by tempering the vigor of my staff's support for questionable practices to force them to face their flaws.

Despite my misgivings about the federal courts' sledgehammer approach to beating state governments into conformity with fast-changing standards of performance, I recognized that it was gaining favor among our nation's legal scholars and leading judges. The Supreme Court's paradigm shift initiated in the *Brown v. Board of Education* decision of 1954 ordering school desegregation forever changed our nation's limited view of constitutional power. Applications of this new vision of the Constitution came in the 1960s with such cases as *Baker v. Carr* in 1962, which mandated a "one man–one vote" standard in designing legislative districts, and *Miranda v. Arizona* in 1966, requiring law enforcement officers to inform suspects of their constitutional protection against self-incrimination.

Expansive interpretations of constitutional rights that had occurred at a glacial pace through the eighteenth, nineteenth, and first half of the twentieth century now were flying out of the Supreme Court in a torrent. When Richard Nixon campaigned for president in 1968 on a platform that included criticism of the Supreme Court for hampering law enforcement and when he appointed Warren Burger to replace retiring Earl Warren as chief justice in 1969, many believed the Supreme Court's eagerness to second-guess state legislatures would diminish.

Many were mistaken. The Warren court's momentum was impossible to divert or significantly reduce. The Nixon appointees to the court were more conservative in their use of judicial power, but that conservatism also led them toward caution when asked to reconsider issues decided by the Warren court. As the Supreme Court's groundbreaking decisions trickled down to circuit and district judges over time, the entire federal judiciary became more comfortable with using the Constitution to modernize state governments that generally were resistant to change and still dominated by officials from rural areas.

Texas government was an inviting target for these federal judges. The societal and cultural upheavals in the 1960s that painfully wrenched American institutions out of the paternalistic and racially segregated 1950s ethos generally failed to penetrate our rural-dominated legislature, our constitutionally handcuffed administrative branch of state government, or our elected judiciary, in which conservative big-city law firms controlled state and local judgeships. Legislative apportionment laws kept urban areas vastly underrepresented, producing a one-party law-making body with no black faces and only a few Mexican Americans.

For example, Texas' population was 15 percent Hispanic in 1960, but the Senate's lone Hispanic accounted for 3 percent of its members and the

House's six Hispanics were 4 percent of its members.[2] Three-fourths of Texans lived in urban areas in 1962, but the state's limit of one senator per county left such cities as Houston and Dallas with the same single Senate seat in 1960 as they could claim in 1880.[3] Federal judges forced a redrawing of House and Senate district maps in the 1960s, increasing the four largest cities' Senate representation from four to twelve of the thirty-one senators and creating inner-city House districts in urban areas that dramatically increased the representation of racial minorities and the political minority—Republicans.

Of the federal judges who aggressively embraced the new activism spawned by the Warren court, none was more aggressive or successful than William Wayne Justice of Tyler. His quick action on a rural East Texas school desegregation case a year after his appointment in 1968 convinced Department of Justice lawyers to select his court to file a statewide desegregation case, *United States v. Texas,* in 1970. The case directly concerned nine small rural school districts that perpetuated segregation by manipulating district boundaries to exclude black communities. However, Justice seized upon the role of the Texas Education Agency in overseeing the schools' boundaries to justify including in his ruling a demand that the agency halt all discriminatory school district boundary changes statewide and develop a plan to desegregate all Texas schools.[4]

The desegregation case illustrated four strategies Judge Justice utilized in future years to produce a succession of major cases challenging broad government policies. First, he assured plaintiffs top-flight talent and plentiful investigative resources by allowing federal attorneys and advocacy group lawyers to participate as parties or intervenors. Second, he transformed isolated incidents into a platform for much larger cases. Third, his order detailed with precise specificity the changes he required, micromanaging vast state agencies. Fourth, his order gave him continuing control to assure compliance, a strategy that sometimes stretched his control for a decade or more.

Through his long career on the bench—he took senior status in 1998—Judge Justice repeated this uncanny deftness at turning routine cases into exhaustive decisions that overturned state laws and state agency regulations. These decisions redefined government responsibilities in providing bilingual education, conforming legislative and congressional districts to his concept of equality, assuring public school access for noncitizens, and a dozen other examples. Outrage by state government leaders and editorial writers greeted every opinion, but his success rate in surviving review by appeals courts left his many critics stymied.[5]

Partly because most Texas federal judges were slow to embrace the Supreme Court's activism and partly because of Justice's reputation as a fearless reformer ready to challenge any government institutions found deficient, the judge's court became a magnet for lawsuits filed or promoted by advocacy groups. The success of the NAACP Legal Defense and Educational Fund in overturning public school and university segregation in the Supreme Court in the 1950s provided an impressive example for other special-interest advocates to follow. The court's expansion of the scope and size of targets for groups of disaffected citizens created a vacuum quickly filled by a wide variety of new organizations devoted to challenging the status quo.

Staffed by a generation of law school graduates fired with the law's promise for redressing societal and government shortcomings—not to resolve personal or commercial disputes as I and my classmates had been trained in the 1940s—these highly focused forces aligned themselves with political movements to bring a litigation-lobbying-publicity combination to bear in their quests. The government joined this effort, creating a nationwide legal services program in 1974 to promote access to the legal system for low-income Americans.

My office was engaged by these groups on cases involving the state's programs for juvenile offenders, felons, the mentally disabled, and the mentally ill, but the only cases to go to trial while I was attorney general involved our youth offender schools and our prisons. The advocacy group involved in challenging our programs for young offenders was the Youth Law Center (YLC) in San Francisco. It was contacted by Steven L. Bercu, a young El Paso civil rights lawyer employed by a public interest legal services organization supported with federal funds. His investigation of newspaper articles revealing that an inordinate number of El Paso teenagers were confined in state facilities convinced him there was widespread abuse of the juvenile justice system. He believed that officials were accommodating frustrated parents by shipping their unruly kids off to state custody.[6]

Bercu found that El Paso judges were not following one of the U.S. Supreme Court's 1960s expansions of civil rights, *In re Gault*. This ruling in 1967 extended protections for juvenile offenders, requiring legal counsel, the right to confront witnesses, and the privilege against self-incrimination.[7] Parents with troublesome children often found judges willing to commit them to state detention facilities if local detention centers failed to quell a rebellious nature.

Bercu spent several months in the fall of 1970 filing applications for writs of habeas corpus to release twelve of the El Paso children committed without a hearing or an attorney. He also won court approval to interview them. In January 1971, he and a YLC lawyer from San Francisco, William P. Hoffman Jr., selected students at the Gainesville State School to interview first because the facility was located in Justice's jurisdiction, while some of the other children were in facilities located in West Texas, outside Justice's reach. At the Gainesville school, they were denied private conversation with the children because school officials routinely required the superintendent to participate in any outsiders' meetings with students. They encountered similar restrictions at the West Texas schools in Gatesville and Brownwood.[8]

The interviews produced the signed agreements Bercu and Hoffman needed to assume legal representation of the children. They made a second trip to Gainesville on February 10 and again were denied private meetings with their clients. When they reported this to the San Francisco office of the YLC, Bercu and Hoffman were told to immediately use the denial of access as the basis for a lawsuit filed in Judge Justice's court. Two days later, they followed their instructions, seeking an injunction against the schools' restrictive practices and also filing a class action lawsuit to require Texas state juvenile judges to meet requirements of *In re Gault* in committing minors to state detention facilities.[9]

In July 1971, Judge Justice's first step in preparing for this lawsuit to be tried in his court was ordering a letter sent to all 2,500 inmates in the six institutions of the Texas Youth Council, as it was then called—schools for boys in Giddings and Gatesville, and schools for girls in Brownwood, Crockett, and Gainesville—asking whether their commitment resulted from a court hearing in which they were represented by an attorney. The results showed that one-third of the 2,300 respondents were committed at a hearing in which they were not represented by counsel, while 280 were committed without a hearing or counsel. Further development of this information and negotiations with state lawyers produced agreed orders in October and December 1972 that armed Bercu to successfully request state judges to order the release of all juveniles in state facilities committed without attorneys and/or hearings. About 500 to 1,000 youths, or one-fifth to one-third of the state's incarcerated minors, were sent home.[10]

The survey responses also provided an unexpected bonus that gave Judge Justice his first hint of a lawsuit much larger than one about requiring representation by counsel. About fifty of the respondents volunteered that they were abused by TYC staff members. Judge Justice held a hearing in September 1972 to explore these abuse complaints. Testimony of ten inmates from Gatesville and Gainesville convinced Judge Justice to grant, over strong opposition from state attorneys, a request by Bercu and Hoffman to have all TYC inmates interviewed. More than one hundred law students from the University of Texas and Southern Methodist University participated in the interviews during the first several months of 1972.[11]

Judge Justice also rejected state objections to approve, on December 14, 1972, a "participant observer" team, composed of psychiatrists, two masters of social work, and a doctor of psychology, assigned to live on site for a week or two at the Gatesville and Gainesville schools and record their observations for court testimony. In his order, Judge Justice termed the idea "perhaps extraordinary" and added, "yet this is an extraordinary case . . . . When important civil rights are in issue in complex litigation of widespread concern, a court must make every effort to enhance the fact-finding process for both sides."[12]

Bercu and Hoffman's successor from YLC, Peter B. Sandmann, filed amended pleadings to expand the class action lawsuit to challenge the constitutionality of the state's disciplinary actions against incarcerated juveniles. To provide them the investigative and litigation resources they lacked, Judge Justice called one of the Justice Department attorneys in Washington, D.C., whom he had met during the Texas school desegregation case, David J. W. Vanderhoof, to gauge his interest in tackling the TYC case. A positive response led Judge Justice to grant Bercu's motion in May 1972 to add the Justice Department as a participant in the case.

If Bercu and Sandmann were to demonstrate the state's failure to meet its obligation to rehabilitate the TYC juveniles with learning or other developmental deficiencies, expertise from the mental health field would be required. To provide that expertise, Judge Justice approved the participation of the American Orthopsychiatric Association, arranged through a major advocacy group in that field, the Mental Health Law Project, of which the association was a client.[13]

The following month, Judge Justice decided to see firsthand TYC's operations. On June 6, he began a two-day tour that took him to two institutions in Gatesville, about forty miles west of Waco—Gatesville State School, with about 1,100 students on a seven-school campus, and Mountain View State School, a maximum security lockup with about 360 juveniles—and to Crockett State School in East Texas between Huntsville and Palestine, with 126 girls, all of whom were black.

He chose to accompany him one of the experts who would testify in the trial, Dr. Jerome Miller, director of the Illinois Department of Children and Family Services. As would anyone unfamiliar with institutions charged with caring for unruly juveniles, Judge Justice found the experience deeply unsettling and discouraging.[14]

I was unaware of the massive amount of evidence being accumulated by federal investigators and lawyers assisting the plaintiff attorneys during 1972 until I was advised of the case after I took office in January 1973. My housecleaning at the attorney general's office left only one of the state lawyers who had been handling the TYC case for my predecessor. When the TYC board visited my office to brief me on the case, I assured them I was providing them the best litigator on my staff—my first assistant, Larry York. I knew he was top notch because I had tried cases against him while in private practice. I had recruited him from one of Houston's leading law firms, Baker & Botts, which he joined upon graduation from the University of Texas law school in 1964.

When York and I discussed the case, I reconfirmed to him that my goal was not only to present a credible defense to confirm my commitment to rehabilitating the image of the attorney general's office within the legal profession and among political leaders. I also wanted to acknowledge the client agency's deficiencies as demonstrated by the evidence. I was not willing to defend practices that I believed failed to meet the demands of the law and the expectations of our citizens.

That philosophy was especially difficult to maintain in this case because it was one where our job was far greater than merely attempting to fix a problem. It was about imposing profound unknown obligations on a state agency without regard to the ability of the state to adjust to the expanded financial and administrative burden. This navigating through an uncharted legal landscape to determine how much protection the Constitution should offer a youthful offender, and what demands the Constitution should make on the institution confining the juvenile, added enormously to our burden.

We were haunted by the old adage "bad facts make bad law." The facts in this case were a huge negative and the law the plaintiffs were attempting to make promised to be far reaching. The destructive facts we inherited were the by-product of a state agency with leadership mired in the 1950s. Like most state agencies, the TYC was insulated from the governor's reach by a governing board with overlapping six-year terms that required a governor to stay in office six years before controlling a majority. Two of the

TYC's three board members, a seventy-four-year-old semiretired banker from Houston as chairman and a fifty-nine-year-old Central Texas auto dealer, began their service when the agency was created in 1957. The man they originally chose to manage the system, James A. Turman, was still the director.

Turman insulated himself and the TYC from any meaningful oversight by his rubber-stamp board members or the legislature, where his close alliance with House Appropriations Committee chairman W. S. Heatly of Paducah stonewalled any legislative probing. Heatly's twelve-year chairmanship of the committee had started in 1959 and quickly developed into one-man rule of the entire state budget. His brother, Maurice, a medical school graduate but not certified by the American Board of Psychiatry and Neurology, was hired by Turman as a TYC psychiatric counselor in 1963.[15]

Turman's appointment of a Heatly friend, House chaplain Clinton Kersey, to a new deputy director position in 1970 was bitterly criticized by the chairman of the Senate Youth Affairs Committee, Senator Criss Cole of Houston. He found Kersey's qualifications as a former parole officer for TYC far short of the "necessary educational background" required to "develop the necessary programs" that TYC lacked and that it needed to implement in order to improve its performance.[16]

Cole's committee was a new one created by Ben Barnes, the state's youngest-ever lieutenant governor and a protégé of Gov. John Connally. Like his mentor, Barnes was committed to moving Texas' backwater approach to government into the modern era. Barnes had formed the committee, and a nine-member citizens' advisory committee, in 1969 to investigate TYC operations after parents' complaints of brutality to their children at Mountain View led a House committee to send six of its members on an unannounced inspection trip to the facility.[17] TYC also was becoming a target for investigative journalists, including a nationwide broadcast on NBC about juvenile justice.[18] Barnes's efforts foundered, however, when House Speaker Gus Mutscher, a protégé of Heatly, rejected a plan by Cole's committee for a comprehensive review of TYC by the National Council on Crime and Delinquency.[19]

TYC was not only on the wrong end of the national trend toward comprehensive rehabilitation programs instead of a strict disciplinary-based incarceration mission but also losing its inmate population base to modernizing influences. In addition to the five hundred to one thousand juveniles released from TYC following Justice's order requiring court hearings with attorneys for all TYC commitments, TYC was on the verge of losing an even larger number of inmates due to legislative changes enacted in 1973.

The new Family Code, with an effective date of September 1, 1973, prevented "status offenders" such as runaways from being committed to TYC. Under the new code, TYC would be able to accept only juveniles convicted of a crime such as theft or burglary. At the time, 18 percent of TYC's boys and 65 percent of its girls were status offenders. Another law passed in 1973, with an effective date of August 28, 1973, changed the age of majority from twenty-one to eighteen. About two hundred TYC inmates were age eighteen or over and would be released under the new law.[20]

The week before *Morales v. Turman* went to trial in Judge Justice's court in July 1973, York attempted to dilute Justice's impact by invoking a federal law limiting to three-judge court panels any action involving an injunction against a state official in the enforcement of a state law or regulation. My office had succeeded in invoking this law in a case involving the prison system because the court held that the lawsuit challenged the prison system's rules, which met the law's definition of "regulation." But Judge Justice ruled against us because TYC's schools operated almost autonomously and without any regulations established and enforced by the central office. In his opinion ruling against TYC, he decried the "ephemeral, mythical, and indeed, almost non-existent character of the central policy of the Texas Youth Council."[21]

Unfortunately for us, Judge Justice's demeaning observation was irrefutable. The root cause of TYC's problems was Turman. He allowed each superintendent almost total freedom in operating the institutions. Local legislators filled that leadership vacuum, considering the institutions part of their political domain and the superintendents as available to hire their friends and promote their political campaigns. Even when a superintendent produced progressive programs, such as Ron Jackson's at the Brownwood School for Girls, Turman would make no effort to spread those ideas to other institutions because of concern over invading a superintendent's local turf.[22]

Turman's superficial understanding of how his campuses operated left us unprepared for the barrage of excruciatingly detailed testimony documenting mental and physical abuse of TYC inmates, minimal to nonexistent meaningful rehabilitation programs, and a variety of other shortcomings. York and his team of lawyers—Joe Dibrell, Max Flusche, Tom Choate—and Bob Salter, the TYC attorney, realized their worst fears about their overwhelming challenge when they appeared at the final pretrial hearing. The files of evidence prepared by federal government and plaintiff attorneys for the trial covered several big conference tables, and they were stacked three feet high on each table.[23]

When the plaintiff attorneys began introducing their testimony and witnesses in the trial's opening days in early July 1973, the state's attorneys attempted during nightly after-trial meetings to persuade Turman to consider taking the witness stand to offer reassurances that reforms were contemplated by TYC. But Turman flatly refused. He adamantly protested that TYC was one of the best systems in the nation and the complaints were unjustified. He prided himself not only on building TYC into a major state agency but also for playing a key role in drafting legislation creating TYC. He had drafted that legislation during a seven-year stint as a clinical psychologist for the predecessor Texas Youth Development Council, which had been managed by the state's Welfare Department.[24]

Turman's attitude troubled York and his staff. When York, who was thirty-two and new to the give-and-take in the government world, shared his frustrations, I sympathized but urged a measured response: "I do know what you're talking about, Larry, and I do know we need to make some changes. I know you've got some problems there, but let's just be patient. I mean after all, we can't fire people. We're not in that business," I said.

I was a little older and I also knew Turman socially. "Don't be too hard on Turman and Heatly because they're just victims of their generation," I told him.

The cumulative effect of the evidence presented by Bercu, Sandmann, the Mental Health Law Project attorneys, and the Department of Justice lawyers during the five-week trial was devastating to Turman and his superintendents attending the trial.[25] Even discounting the exaggeration and fabrications likely in stories told by troubled juveniles struggling to cope with abusive families, learning deficiencies, and other problems, the mirror held up to TYC by the plaintiff attorneys, the participant observers, and juvenile corrections experts reflected an image few of them recognized.

The plaintiffs' final witness was Jerome Miller, the Illinois correctional facility director who had accompanied Judge Justice on his tour of TYC facilities. He testified that large institutions such as those under TYC "do not work" and allow brutality to persist for years "without administrators knowing about it."[26]

Joe Dibrell opened our case with a conciliatory statement, referring to a brief appearance I had made earlier in the trial. At that time I had reassured Judge Justice that "every person in the sound of my voice and in this courtroom is dedicated . . . to trying to have the most enlightened and progressive approach to that problem."[27] Dibrell said the state's lawyers were "just as interested in seeing that any problems are corrected, and I'm sure this is the feeling of the Youth Council as well . . . [P]roper changes need to be made, [and] we're as interested in implementing these changes as anyone else. . . . [W]e are all hopefully striving with differences of opinion as to how this should be achieved to provide the best kind of care for children who are in need of care because of obvious delinquency."[28] Turman was so incensed at Dibrell's olive-branch approach that he tried to have him fired from the case.[29]

Our defense consumed only a week. We were fighting a rear-guard action, attempting a strategic retreat because we had no ammunition to stage a counteroffensive. We offered testimony from several TYC administrators and consultants and a TYC board member, W. Forrest Smith of Dallas, who had served with Judge Justice in the National Guard and was the lone reform proponent.

While Judge Justice and his law clerks began drafting the sweeping order he would release four weeks later, Governor Briscoe was finalizing an appointment to the TYC board that would dramatically change our case on appeal. The TYC problems were of great concern to Briscoe and his wife Janey, a fixture in the governor's capitol office and considered a knowledgeable and important informal advisor to the governor. They had demonstrated a high-profile interest in juvenile issues earlier in the year when they pushed for closure of Artesia Hall after reports of abuse of juveniles at the privately owned East Texas facility for troubled youths.

Briscoe's chief of staff, Dallas attorney Charles Purnell, sent word to his friends in Dallas during the summer that Briscoe wanted to replace a member of the TYC board. The member's term would expire August 31, and the governor wanted to bring a voice for reform to the beleaguered agency.[30] Louis M. Henna, a suburban Austin Chevrolet dealer who was one of the original TYC members appointed by Gov. Price Daniel in 1957, was an unquestioning Turman backer. He was also a contributor to Briscoe's campaign in 1972 and expected to be reappointed to another six-year term. He was surprised when he was not.[31] Briscoe obtained an agreement from Patsy Ayres of San Antonio, a thirty-nine-year-old mother of two teenagers and wife of businessman Robert M. Ayres Jr., to take the appointment.

One of the first calls she received after the announcement of her appointment was from W. Forrest Smith. The forty-four-year-old Mobil Oil attorney and Dallas civic affairs activist told her of his frustrations in four years on the TYC board. During his first two years, he had supported Turman. But Smith wanted to be an active board member. He began visiting TYC institutions by himself, meeting with the staff and inmates. He came to doubt the justifications presented to the board to absolve staff in inmate abuse cases investigated by state police, and he feared Turman was covering up serious deficiencies.

When one of the youths he met at a TYC school contacted him in early 1973 to report a beating he received, Smith arranged with a friend in a Dallas law enforcement office for the boy to undergo a lie detector test. When he passed the test, Smith brought the issue before the board. Turman and the two other board members refused to consider his evidence and angrily told him he had violated protocol by circumventing TYC staff. Ostracized at future board meetings by the other two members and Turman, Smith decided Turman should be replaced.[32] The appointment of Ayres offered Smith the required second board vote to make the change.

If Ayres needed any convincing of Turman's deficiencies, the evidence flew off the pages of the order Judge Justice released on August 31 and the pages of newspapers reporting on TYC inmates' rampages in the weeks that followed. "Riots" was the most common word in headlines above news articles describing events at the Gatesville and Mountain View schools starting September 6 and ending only after Governor and Mrs. Briscoe and I rushed to Gatesville on September 12 to bring the situation under control.

Judge Justice's twenty-nine-page order of August 31 directed TYC to, among a long list of prohibited practices, stop using corporal punishment by physical force unless necessary for self-defense, defense of a third party, or to restrain escapes or prevent substantial destruction; stop using tear gas except to control a riot threatening life or property; stop segregating on the basis of race, age, or sexual orientation; and limit the use of solitary confinement.

His thirty-two-item list of TYC deficiencies included the use of tear gas on a Mountain View inmate who was locked in his cell for failure to work. Justice stated in the document that "Mountain View's history has been one of brutality and repression. Its reputation has in no small part been a function of ineffective leadership of a staff unqualified by education, experience or personality to effect the rehabilitation of delinquents." The superintendent and his top assistant resigned immediately after the order was issued.[33]

Turman was incensed, as were his school administrators and their staff. An operating environment in which local superintendents ran their schools with minimal oversight from Austin, and guards and other staff often were given wide latitude on disciplinary decisions, was faced with a rigid set of requirements designed to empower their wards and limit their ability to respond. What caught the eye of school administrators was the threat of imprisonment if they were held in contempt for failing to comply.

Once the order was posted in the schools on September 6, the delicate balance of power within the boys' institutions quickly shifted. Sensing their keepers' frustration and disgust, the students celebrated their victory in various ways. All campuses but the Mountain View school were unfenced, and students vastly outnumbered staff, so a number of boys from the Gatesville school decided to leave together. Boys at Mountain View engaged in miscellaneous destruction. Residents in Gatesville and surrounding communities grew concerned at the prospect of bands of escaped juvenile delinquents roaming their countryside, prompting floods of calls to local law enforcement officers.[34]

The disturbances continued intermittently until September 12, when students at the seven dormitories of the Gatesville school began a widespread campaign of destruction. When the TYC board convened for its quarterly meeting that afternoon, Turman said of the Gatesville situation, "We have a state of siege."[35] Salter called me from Gatesville and requested that I fly there to help TYC restore order without violating Judge Justice's order. I agreed to come, and Governor and Mrs. Briscoe also went to Gatesville, going by helicopter.

When we arrived at Gatesville in the late afternoon, we discovered that the combination of Turman's efforts to blame the disturbances on Judge Justice's order and his lax supervision of the campuses had created so much confusion, the staff was looking to me and Governor Briscoe for guidance. About 140 of the school's 900 students were unaccounted for. District Judge Byron McClellan joined us and decided to call Judge Justice at home for clarification. He did so and then put Briscoe on the phone to talk to Judge Justice, who assured him TYC was not restrained from keeping order.

I also called Judge Justice to verify my understanding that his order allowed TYC to use force to stop these disturbances. "Judge, we have a bad situation down here," I told him. "I can look out the window and see these kids running around through these fields around the school property. We need to pick them up and bring them back in, and I want to be sure that you haven't foreclosed that," I told him. He reassured me his order did not preclude returning the runaways to the school.

Salter and I visited the administration building, where the escapees picked up by the sheriff had been confined in sixty lockup rooms that were heavily damaged. Governor Briscoe ordered state police to assist TYC in restoring order, resulting in thirty-two state troopers and four Texas Rangers being sent to Gatesville.[36]

The aftermath of the September 12 events increased Turman's vulnerability to dismissal. Smith told the *Dallas Times Herald* on September 14 that the Gatesville school staff could have used force to prevent the riots and "if they did not, I want to know why not." He told the *Houston Post* on September 16, regarding TYC complaints about Judge Justice's order, "Are we saying we can't run a school without force, without fear, brutality and repression? If so, we shouldn't be running a school." Governor Briscoe blamed the riots on TYC's "misinterpretation" of Judge Justice's order.[37]

When the TYC chairman, Robert Kneebone, called an emergency meeting of the TYC board in Gatesville for the following week to consider a set of reforms Turman had belatedly produced, Smith decided to push for Turman's resignation. He called Mrs. Ayres and obtained her agreement. The afternoon before the meeting on September 21, he called Salter and asked him to alert Turman to his plan and sound him out on resigning so the board would not have to fire him.

He then called Ron Jackson, the thirty-three-year-old highly regarded superintendent of the Brownwood School for Girls to ask him if he would accept an appointment as interim director. A Turman protégé—Jackson's adoptive father was a friend of Turman's through his job as superintendent of the Valley Boys Ranch in Harlingen, and Turman had helped Jackson move through the TYC ranks to his job after he graduated from the University of Texas—Jackson regretted seeing his mentor forced out of office but was eager to rise to the challenge posed by Judge Justice's order.[38]

Turman agreed to resign. He announced it immediately prior to the opening of the TYC board meeting. Kneebone then resigned, saying he refused to serve if he would not be included in decisions. Smith was elected chairman, and he and Mrs. Ayres appointed Jackson interim director. "It's a new ballgame," Smith told the news media. "We've had secrecy, but now we will have an open system."[39]

York tried to use the positive changes at TYC to moderate Judge Justice's ruling, but the judge refused to reopen the case. "A reopening would entail further delays, with the need for more discovery, trial, and briefing. The defendants had a great deal of time to prepare for this case; they were on notice from a very early date of the practices the plaintiffs were protesting and had, in the opinion of the court, ample opportunity to alter them prior to trial, if they had been so inclined," Judge Justice wrote in his final ruling, issued a year later on August 30, 1974.[40]

The massive changes required by Judge Justice in his seventy-five-page order found a receptive audience in Smith and Jackson. Despite the financial and administrative costs imposed by the order, the two men helped convince the legislature in 1975 to initiate funding for the community-based programs requested in Judge Justice's order.

My lawyers pursued appeals to the Fifth Circuit twice, finally winning a significant reduction in Judge Justice's order with a ruling in 1977 that rejected his effort to create a "right to treatment" under the Constitution. Acknowledging the TYC's success in accomplishing reforms under Smith and Jackson, the appeals court said TYC deserved a hearing before Judge Justice to be afforded

> a full opportunity to present proof of such changes. . . . A brief examination of a few of the major reforms alleged to have been made indicates, if true, a new attitude on the part of TYC and suggests that a fuller investigation of these claims would be useful. . . . Consideration of additional evidence is especially important here as we are dealing with a significant federal intrusion into a state's affairs, and we should refrain from interference in state affairs unless necessary. . . . Hence, if Texas has brought its detention facilities up to constitutional standards, we should be reluctant to impose additional restraints.

In a rebuke to Judge Justice for the excruciatingly minute remedies listed in his order, the court concluded its opinion with words that were particularly gratifying to me: "Finally, even if some form of right to treatment doctrine exists, the minimum requirements established by the District Court are excessively detailed. A court is not in a position to monitor day-to-day changes that affect rehabilitation programs. New treatments and testing techniques will inevitably develop. A rigid set of requirements for the state will not enable the TYC to adequately adjust to these changes. The passage of time will render obsolete many of the requirements found in the District Court opinion."[41]

The appeals court decision forced the plaintiffs to retreat from their extensive demands, allowing negotiations between the attorney general's lawyers and the plaintiff attorneys that continued past my administration. A settlement was reached in 1984.

The improvements Smith and Jackson initiated in TYC, and the Fifth Circuit opinion, gave me a great sense of accomplishment. We were able to prevent the scary unknown of a constitutional right to treatment that would have provided an open-ended opportunity for endless litigation and confusion in our state's attempt to rehabilitate young offenders. Yet many of the changes Judge Justice rightly demanded were adopted by the TYC leadership and implemented as their own. I could not have wished for a better outcome.

My hopes for repeating that process in subsequent litigation involving the prison system proved elusive. There were many similarities in the two cases. Both were coping with increased scrutiny from the federal judiciary as a result of Supreme Court expansions of civil rights. Judge Justice was again in command, carefully crafting a behemoth class action lawsuit based on constitutional constraints. Both involved treatment of inmates. Both attracted aggressive participation by the Department of Justice and reformist advocacy groups. Both overwhelmed our office with an avalanche of discovery demands and evidence, involved lengthy trials and multiple appeals, and consumed years in follow-up negotiations and monitoring activity.[42] Both attracted nationwide attention in their respective fields of juvenile and criminal law.

There also were many differences. While TYC's performance was viewed with increasing dismay by legislators, the agency managing our prisons, the Texas Department of Corrections (TDC), enjoyed strong support from the legislature. While TYC suffered from unimaginative and insular leadership, TDC's legacy of reform dated to 1947, when Gov. Beauford Jester's leadership produced a progressive new warden, O. B. Ellis, who served until 1961 and was succeeded by George Beto, who continued that trend for another eleven years.[43] While TYC could claim some national recognition, TDC's stability and low rates of inmate violence and escapes easily made it the envy of other large state prison systems that were generally suffering riots and constant strife.[44] While Turman was a weak leader, Beto and his successor, W. James Estelle Jr., were strong leaders with broad political support.[45]

Major differences were the inmates' ages and backgrounds and the size of the operations. TYC's $19 million annual budget supported a six-campus system housing about twenty-five hundred juveniles in 1973, while TDC spent $26 million a year to house fifteen thousand inmates in fourteen prisons.[46] While TYC had a few hard-core murderers, rapists, and other high-risk juveniles in one fenced unit, all TDC units were fenced and most contained dangerous adults.

Another difference was the lead attorneys. While York was an amiable young litigator from a big-city law firm, the lead attorney on the TDC case was Eduardo Idar Jr., a gruff, fifty-three-year-old civil rights attorney. Before joining my staff, he had been with the Mexican American Legal Defense and Educational Fund (MALDEF), where he had tried lawsuits challenging state legislative redistricting plans. While York strove to prevent antagonizing Justice and enjoyed good relations with opposing counsel, Idar feuded openly with both.[47]

I struggled with how to resolve the animosity between Idar and Judge Justice. I decided not to counsel Idar to revise his aggressive style, because I doubted that would be productive. I attempted to discuss the problem with Judge Justice in his chambers during the trial, asking him jocularly, "Judge, do you realize how unfair you're being to my lawyers?" His cool response pretty much ended the discussion. He and I were acquainted through professional and social contacts, but that relationship failed to help on this issue.

Another difference between the two cases was each agency's changes in population and management coincident with the litigation. While TYC's population shrank substantially due to release of juveniles not legally committed and legislation that lowered the age of majority and restricted TYC to accepting youthful criminals, TDC's 660 percent growth while the case was pending created vast overcrowding problems that worsened conditions the plaintiffs were attacking. While TYC's new management embraced many of the reforms sought by the plaintiffs in *Morales,* TDC resisted any broad-scale changes.[48]

The prison case traced its origin to a fifteen-page, hand-printed petition filed in Judge Justice's court in June 1972 by David Ruiz, an inmate with a thirty-arrest rap sheet who was serving a twenty-five-year term for armed robbery. The rambling narrative complained of harassment by TDC staff for inadequate medical care, his lawsuits alleging unlawful solitary confinement.[49] Ruiz was among a group of "writ writers" in prison who began peppering federal courts with petitions after a Supreme Court ruling in 1964 that allowed inmates to bring lawsuits under the Civil Rights Act of 1871 and another ruling in 1972 that ended routine dismissal of inmates' petitions.[50]

In a sense, another event that year also could be said to be part of the origin of the *Ruiz v. Estelle* case. In a speech at a Southern Methodist University Practicing Law Institute seminar, Judge Justice said, "Should prisons not aim to protect the public and to deter and rehabilitate the criminal without abandoning the civilized ideal that we treat our fellow men, even those who have deviated from society's norm, with some dignity and compassion?" The federal judiciary, he said, "would do less than our constitutional duty" by failing to meet this challenge. After hearing another speaker at the seminar reinforce his beliefs, Judge Justice decided to act on his concerns.[51]

True to his convictions, Judge Justice asked his law clerks to categorize by type of complaint the several hundred complaints he had received from prisoners at the two TDC units in his jurisdiction. When the clerks had organized the complaints into four categories—brutality by staff and other inmates, inadequate medical care, lack of due process, and overcrowding—Judge Justice directed them to select a representative petition from each stack. Among those selected was that of Ruiz. Judge Justice finally selected seven petitions for consolidation into a single case to challenge a broad array of state prison practices.[52]

The consolidated *Ruiz* case began life on April 12, 1974, with a thunderclap. In his order combining the cases, Judge Justice also appointed the Department of Justice as *amicus curiae* with full rights of a party, ordering the federal lawyers to investigate the facts alleged in the petitions and to participate in the case "with the full rights of a party thereto, and to advise [the] Court at all states of the proceeding as to any actions deemed appropriate by it."[53]

A month later, he assured the plaintiffs' representation by the man who inspired him to action with his 1972 speech in Dallas, William Bennett Turner from the NAACP Legal Defense and Educational Fund, by appointing another attorney as plaintiffs' counsel until Turner could complete other obligations and join the case.[54] By the end of 1974, Judge Justice had certified the case as a class action lawsuit embracing all fourteen TDC facilities.

Estelle and his staff, along with my staff, were astounded at Judge Justice's blitzkrieg. A federal judge, on his own motion, mounting an exhaustive federal government investigation of a major state agency created an unprecedented federal intrusion into state government. We decided to seek help from appellate courts.

Idar sought in January 1975 to dismiss the Department of Justice as a party, which on February 10, 1975, Judge Justice denied, as we expected he would. That cleared the way for us to appeal to the Fifth Circuit Court of Appeals, complaining that the burdensome discovery in this case created a hardship that warranted removal of the Justice Department's participation. Judge Justice, our brief said, violated fundamental principles involving federal-state relations by allowing the Justice Department to "rampage through the Texas prison system in the hope of finding unconstitutional activities." Our brief also argued that Judge Justice "flagrantly abused" his judicial power by acting as an "investigator and prosecutor of state institutions" and urged the court to order him to "refrain from any further attempts to conduct on its own motion investigation into the activities of state institutions." We said of Judge Justice's actions that "a grosser misuse of judicial power cannot be imagined."[55]

The Fifth Circuit Court three-judge panel unanimously rejected our appeal on July 24, 1975. We asked the Supreme Court to review our request and lost again, but narrowly, on June 7, 1976. Three of the nine justices—one short of the number required to grant review of a case—supported our argument and issued an opinion critical of Judge Justice. The opinion by Justice William Rehnquist noted with surprise that the narrow relief sought by the individual inmates' petitions was contorted by the federal government into an expansive Department of Justice request that Judge Justice mandate a broad set of requirements affecting all aspects of prison operations. This contortion was a turn of events that Rehnquist said clearly met the definition established by the Fifth Circuit in 1965 of a "really extraordinary case" that would qualify for relief.

"The effect of the actions of respondent [Judge Justice] is to pit the United States, as virtually involuntary co-plaintiff, alongside the inmate plaintiffs and against petitioner correctional officials. I think it extremely doubtful there is any authority for those actions," Rehnquist's opinion said. "The legal assumptions on which the District Court acted involve serious and far-reaching questions which have certainly not been settled by any decision of this Court."[56]

The Rehnquist opinion was as close as we were to come to achieving a fair hearing in the *Ruiz* case. The avalanche of interrogatories and discovery motions we feared quickly materialized and kept us overwhelmed and on the defensive. As interviews of TDC officials and inmates and joint visits to prisons steadily built a larger and larger body of evidence, our strategy narrowed to one of arguing that the abuses revealed in testimony were isolated exceptions and not the rule and that they failed to prove TDC condoned a systemwide pattern of brutality and inhumane treatment.

Our last hope for removing Judge Justice from the case was to seek in February 1978 a change of venue on grounds that Tyler lacked housing for prisoner witnesses. That strategy fizzled when Judge Justice granted the order, transferred the trial to Houston, then volunteered to follow the trial to Houston—an offer which the Houston federal judges, already swamped with a busy docket, were more than happy to accept. The trial was set to begin in October.[57]

In June, Idar and his top assistant, Richel Rivers, went to Huntsville to meet with Estelle and his staff to decide whether to entertain settlement offers from the Department of Justice and LDF attorneys. Estelle was at the head of the long conference table, with Rivers and Idar on either side of him, his wardens and other staff filling seats along the sides and opposite end. Idar, then Rivers, explained the pitfalls of accepting the plaintiff attorneys' settlement offers, which were limited to work conditions and sanitation.

Settlement of those issues, they warned, would remove from the trial two areas where TDC's performance was strongest. That would leave for trial only the areas where TDC was most vulnerable. Their best option, they told the TDC staff, was to keep the work conditions and sanitation issues in the trial to balance the brutality and inadequate medical treatment testimony. Even though they knew that the trial would be a public relations nightmare for TDC and that Judge Justice had stacked the deck against them, Idar and Rivers said, the attorney general's staff would mount an aggressive defense if Estelle wanted to endure the ordeal.

After Rivers completed the two lawyers' presentation, the room fell silent. Estelle's flashing blue eyes sent a penetrating gaze deliberately around the table of grim-faced and anxious wardens as he slowly worked the plug of Red Man® chewing tobacco in his cheek. His gaze stopped at Rivers, who was wearing a summer dress and open-toed white sandals. Keeping his eyes fixed on hers, he leaned between the two of them, sent a stream of tobacco juice into the spittoon resting not more than an inch from Rivers's white sandals while her eyes followed the stream into the spittoon, and then returned to his piercing glare. "Okay," Estelle said, breaking the tension, his eyes still fixed on Rivers's. "We're going to trial." That moment cemented a bond between the beleaguered TDC staff and the outgunned lawyers that survived the grueling trial.[58]

From October 2, 1978, to May 2, 1979, the Department of Justice and LDF presented 133 witnesses, most of them inmates.[59] Because the inmates' testimony was unknown to the state in advance and dealt with specific individuals within TDC, Rivers improvised an "incident report" form for them to use to hurriedly note the inmate's name, prison unit, date of the event, and the names of TDC personnel. A separate sheet would be used for each incident; some inmates reported a dozen incidents. While one lawyer was following the witness testimony, another would be furiously completing the incident reports. When trial recessed at the end of the day, the reports would be organized by prison unit and runners dispatched to the unit with a bundle of the reports. TDC personnel would supply the runner with file folders containing records of the events and send them back to Houston, where the lawyers would pore over the files for use in cross-examination.

When one of the state's attorneys was trying to rebut an inmate's allegation of inadequate medical treatment by reviewing all of his visits to the infirmary, Judge Justice interrupted the lawyer. "What are you doing?" he demanded.

"Well, I am questioning the witness, Your Honor."

"Let me see that," Justice said. When the lawyer handed up the thick file to Judge Justice, he glanced through it, frowned, then tossed it off his bench and onto the clerk's table below, the contents scattering, to express his disapproval.[60]

Testimony concluded in September 1979, nine months after I left office. Three hundred forty-nine witnesses had testified. Fifteen hundred exhibits were introduced. Justice's 249-page opinion, with 219 footnotes, was issued December 12, 1980.[61] Several appeals and continued negotiations resulted in an agreement in 1992 that the state would limit the inmate population to 95 percent of prison capacity, separate hard-core offenders from other prisoners, hire more guards, and improve medical treatment. During the nearly thirty years the lawsuit was fought in court, Texas' prison population increased almost tenfold, from 15,700 in 1972 to 145,000 in 2002.

Undoubtedly, Judge Justice set in motion many needed improvements to our prison system. But his vision of very worthy ideals was imposed without regard to real-world conditions. These included a turbulent administration beset with overcrowded prisons; legislative resistance to needed changes; local law enforcement officials determined to pass their own overcrowding problems up to the state by forcing even minor offenders to serve penitentiary time; and the public's desire to "get tough on criminals," which discouraged politicians from modernizing restrictive parole laws that exacerbated overcrowding.

The *Ruiz* case was the largest piece of unfinished business when I left office. It also was one of the most frustrating and gratifying cases of my time in office, both professionally and personally. Personally gratifying, because my close contact with Estelle during the prison siege and hostage killings in 1974 had given me tremendous confidence in him and respect for his integrity and courage. Professionally frustrating, because I never was able to reconcile in my own mind Judge Justice's federal judicial solution to problems I believed our state government was capable of addressing and, given time, should have been allowed to sort out and resolve.

This case, more than any other I had handled, impressed on me the realization that my six years as attorney general constituted a transitional period, a time when our state and federal governments were attempting to bridge a gap between the turbulent 1960s and the promise offered by the 1980s. It was a period of accelerated change in the legal profession and all branches of government. I considered myself fortunate to have won election to an office that allowed me to play a significant role in shaping our state government's efforts to be the initiator, instead of the follower, on many of the most significant issues of an exciting decade.

Appendix 1

Staff Leadership Team in the Texas Attorney General's Office, 1973–1978

First Assistants

John M. Barron, January–March 1973
Larry F. York, April 1973–November 1974
David M. Kendall, December 1974–December 1978

Executive Assistants

Larry F. York, January–March 1973
Joe Bill Watkins, January 1973–July 1974
John Odam, January 1975–June 1976
Jim Bushala, June 1976–December 1978

Administrative Assistants

Jim Bushala, January 1973–June 1976
Lee Clyburn, July 1976–December 1978

Division Chiefs

Consumer Protection and Anti-Trust Division
Joe K. Longley, January 1973–August 1975

Consumer Protection
Phil Maxwell, September 1975–August 1977
David F. Bragg, September 1977–December 1978

Anti-Trust
Lee Clyburn, September 1975–June 1976
Mike Barron, July 1976–December 1978

Bonds and Charitable Trusts

Robert B. Davis, January–June 1973
Mike Willatt, July 1973–March 1975
W. James Murdaugh, April 1975–August 1977
Jim Riggs, September 1977–December 1978

Crime Prevention

Tom Bullington, January 1973–December 1978

Enforcement

Joe Dibrell, January 1973–December 1978

Environmental Protection

Mike Willatt, January–June 1973
Phil Maxwell, July 1973–August 1975
Troy Webb, September 1975–December 1978

Highway

Watson Arnold, January 1973–December 1978

Insurance, Banking, and Securities

Ralph Rash, January–June 1973
John Odam, January–December 1974
Thomas M. Pollan, January 1975–December 1978

Oil and Gas (until 1977, thereafter Natural Resources)

Houghton Brownlee, January–September 1973
Austen H. Furse, October 1973–December 1978

State and County Affairs

J. C. Davis, January 1973–January 1976
Liz Levatino, February 1976–April 1977
Steve Bickerstaff, May 1977–December 1978

Taxation

James Broadhurst, 1960–1975
Rick Harrison, 1975–April 1976
Martha Smiley, May 1976–December 1978

Transportation

Rex H. White, January 1973–March 1976

David Hughes, April 1976–December 1978

Organized Crime

J. Timothy R. James, 1974–1978

Labor

Jack Dies, 1974–1978

Opinions Committee Chairs

David M. Kendall, January 1973–November 1974

Bob Heath, December 1974–December 1978

Appendix 2
Key Dates in the Life of John L. Hill Jr.

October 9, 1923	Born in Breckenridge, Texas, to John Luke Hill and Jessie George Hoover Hill; the family included a sister, Laverne, who was born in 1922
1930	Attended first grade in Wink, Texas, public school
1931	Family moved to Kilgore
1940	Graduated from Kilgore High School; enrolled in Kilgore Junior College and won a national collegiate debate championship with partner Charles Wellborn
September 1941	Enrolled in University of Texas
April 6, 1944	Lost a race for University of Texas Student Association president to Mac Wallace by 7 percent of the vote
May 1944	Graduated from the University of Texas and commissioned as a lieutenant (junior grade) in the U.S. Navy
December 15, 1944	Commanded U.S. Navy landing craft during amphibious landing on Mindoro Island, Philippines
April 22, 1945	Commanded U.S. Navy landing craft during the battle for Mindanao Island, Philippines
January 1946	Completed Navy service, returned to law school
April 4, 1946	Married Elizabeth Ann “Bitsy” Graham in her hometown of Olney, Texas
1947	Graduated from University of Texas School of Law, admitted to the State Bar of Texas, began practicing in Houston with Albert Jones and Shirley Helm
1951	Formed the law firm of Hill, Kronzer and Abraham with two University of Texas law school friends, Jim Kronzer and Frank Abraham
1955	Elected president of the Texas Association of Plaintiff Attorneys

April 1958	Published in the Texas Bar Journal an article entitled "Effective Techniques of Jury Selection and Jury Argument in Personal Injury Cases" that became a classic primer for trial attorneys
April 10, 1962	Won a $250,000 award for a Houston woman whose husband was one of thirty-four persons killed in a 1959 Braniff airliner crash, among the largest jury awards in the nation, vaulting Hill to prominaance as one of Texas' top trial attorneys and earning millions for his law firm for representing other crash victims.
March–November 1964	Harris County campaign manager for Governor John Connally's reelection bid
1965	Left Hill, Brown, Kronzer and Abraham to form a solo practitioner firm
March 12, 1966	Sworn in as Texas secretary of state, appointed by Governor John Connally; served until January 22, 1968, when he resigned to run for governor
May 4, 1968	Lost primary race for governor, placing sixth in the ten-candidate field seeking the Democratic Party nomination; returned to Houston and reopened a solo practitioner law office
February 7, 1972	Filed as a candidate for attorney general in the Democratic primary
May 6, 1972	Won the Democratic primary nomination as attorney general with 50.1 percent of the 1,994,048 ballots cast, defeating two candidates, including the incumbent, Crawford Martin; ran unopposed in the general election.
January 1, 1973	Sworn in as attorney general
November 5, 1974	Won reelection, this time to a four-year term, after running unopposed in the Democratic primary and the general election
November 5, 1974	Argument before the U.S. Supreme Court in a ballot access dispute, *American Party of Texas v. White*

June 18, 1975	Argument before the Texas Supreme Court successfully opposing Southwestern Bell's challenge of his authority to block a rate increase for intrastate long-distance telephone calls
January 19, 1976	Argument before the U.S. Supreme Court, to settle the seaward boundary between Louisiana and Texas
March 30, 1976	Argument before the U.S. Supreme Court, successfully defending the Texas death penalty law, *Jurek v. Texas*
September 19, 1977	News conferences in Dallas, Austin, Houston, and San Antonio kicking off campaign for governor
December 7, 1977	Argument before the U.S. Supreme Court protesting federal energy regulators' efforts to control natural gas sales, *Southland Royalty v. Federal Energy Regulatory Commission;* he argued the case again on April 17, 1978, when the court ordered it reargued
March 29, 1978	Argument before the U.S. Supreme Court opposing California's attempt to claim Howard Hughes as a resident for the purpose of assessing taxes against the Hughes estate
May 6, 1978	Won the Democratic Party nomination for governor, defeating four opponents, including incumbent Dolph Briscoe and former governor Preston Smith, obtaining 51.4 percent of the 1,812,896 votes cast
November 7, 1978	Lost the general election vote for governor to Republican William P. Clements Jr., with 49.9 percent of the 2,369,699 votes cast
January 1, 1979	Joined the law firm of Hughes, Luce, Hennessy, Smith & Castle, renamed Hughes & Hill
May 5, 1980	Won a $19 million federal court judgment for Ross Perot's Electronic Data Systems Corp. against the government of Iran for breach of a computer services contract
November 6, 1984	Won election as chief justice of the Texas Supreme Court
January 5, 1985	Sworn in as chief justice of the Texas Supreme Court
1986	Formed the Committee of 100 to examine judicial selection and judicial campaign financing in Texas

February 9, 1987	State of the Judiciary address to a joint session of the Texas Legislature in which Hill became the first chief justice to propose the state change its system of selecting judges to an appointive system; the proposal was opposed by most other Supreme Court justices and failed to pass the legislature.
August 25, 1987	Announced his resignation as chief justice effective January 1, 1988, with plans to focus his energies on replacing partisan election of judges with a system in which judges are appointed on merit; the dramatic action was widely applauded by newspaper editorial writers who supported Hill's accompanying plea for reform of the special interest group funding of Supreme Court campaigns. He formed an advocacy group, the Committee for Merit Election, and a political action committee, Merit PAC, to support candidates interested in judicial reform.
December 6, 1987	During an interview with Mike Wallace, Hill criticized lawyer-financed judicial elections in a nationally televised CBS *60 Minutes* exposé entitled "Is Justice for Sale in Texas?" that highlighted Texas justices' acceptance of campaign contributions from law firms and litigants appearing before the court. Republican challengers successfully used excerpts from the program to challenge plaintiff attorney–supported Democratic Texas Supreme Court justices in 1988, winning their first three seats in more than one hundred years.
January 1, 1988	Joined the law firm of Liddell, Sapp & Zivley, which was renamed Liddell, Sapp, Zivley & Hill
1988	Announced his support for a Republican, Tom Phillips, in general election balloting for chief justice of the Texas Supreme Court. Democratic partisans vigorously protested his support of a Republican. Phillips, a strong advocate of Hill's proposals for merit selection of judges to replace judicial elections, won his race.
1991	Named a Distinguished Alumnus of the University of Texas
January 2, 1997	Appointed by Governor George W. Bush to the Texas Lottery Commission; served until February 1999

January 1, 1999	Hill's law firm merged with Locke Purnell Rain Harrell, renamed Locke Liddell & Sapp
2003	Formed another judicial reform organization, Make Texas Proud, to promote an appointment and retention process for selecting Texas judges. The Texas Senate approved legislation (S.B. 794) carrying out the organization's goal of gubernatorial appointment of the Supreme Court and Court of Criminal Appeals judges, but the bill died in the House.
April 2, 2004	Dedication of the John L. Hill Trial Advocacy Center at the University of Texas School of Law
August 2005	Retired from Locke Liddell & Sapp
October 2005	Joined the law firm of Winstead Sechrest & Minick
July 13, 2007	Governor Rick Perry, Attorney General Greg Abbott, Texas Supreme Court Justice Wallace Jefferson, U.S. Senator John Cornyn, and University of Texas at Austin President William Powers Jr. were among hundreds of Hill's colleagues, friends, and family to pay tribute to him following his death on July 9, 2007

Notes

Chapter 1. Riding Sharpstown to Victory

1. Deaton, *Year They Threw the Rascals Out,* 4, 10–13; Katz, *Shadow on the Alamo,* 6–7; Kinch and Proctor, *Texas Under a Cloud,* 24–26, 32–36. The Sharpstown scandal was extensively reported in these three contemporary books by two Austin journalists (Deaton and Kinch) who covered the events and a Washington investigative journalist (Katz). None of the officeholders or Sharp wrote about their involvement. Former state attorney general Waggoner Carr wrote a book with Austin author Jack Keever about his successful challenge of federal indictments growing out of the scandal: *Waggoner Carr: Not Guilty!* (Austin: Shoal Creek Publishers, 1977). Sharp's lawyer in the years preceding the bank legislation was Will Wilson, who switched to the Republican Party in the mid-1960s after serving as attorney general and a state Supreme Court justice as a Democrat. He was rewarded with the No. 3 job in President Nixon's Justice Department. Wilson contends, in a memoir he left for publication at the time of his death in June 2006, that he was notified three days before the scandal broke that Nixon was planning to nominate him to the Supreme Court of the United States but that he was hounded out of office by San Antonio's Congressman Henry B. Gonzalez, the House Banking Committee chairman, who claimed that Wilson instigated the federal investigations leading to the Sharpstown scandal. Wilson blames Gonzalez's ploy on Lyndon Johnson, one of Wilson's longtime political enemies. Wilson resigned October 15, 1971, six weeks after Wilson's boss, Attorney General John Mitchell, is heard on a White House tape recording telling Nixon they needed to decide whether to "toss him [Wilson] to the wolves and, uh, get him out of here" (quoted in Barnes, *Barn Burning,* 209–10).

2. "Sharp Turned 'Homey' Ways into Empire," *Dallas Morning News,* Feb. 7, 1971.

3. Katz, *Shadow on the Alamo,* 59–64; Kinch and Proctor, *Texas Under a Cloud,* 32–33, 38–40, 44–51.

4. Katz, *Shadow on the Alamo,* 65.

5. Ibid., 64–67; Kinch and Proctor, *Texas Under a Cloud,* 28–32.

6. Katz, *Shadow on the Alamo,* 62; Kinch and Proctor, *Texas Under a Cloud,* 41–42.

7. "Independent Wallace Wins Presidency Fight," *Daily Texan,* Apr. 7, 1944.

8. Deaton, *Year They Threw the Rascals Out,* 4.

9. In his memoir, Barnes cites White House tapes of Nixon talking about the scandal with Attorney General John Mitchell and Connally, among other sources, as confirmation of his belief that the federal government's probe grew from a

Nixon-led search for political dirt on Barnes to derail his meteoric political rise and thereby help the Republican Party overcome the suffocating LBJ-Connally Democratic Party dominance of Texas politics during the 1960s (Barnes, *Barn Burning,* 209–10, 215, 218).

10. Interview with Lynn Taylor, Jan. 30, 2006 (unless noted otherwise, all interviews were conducted by Ernie Stromberger in Austin, Tex.).

11. "Labor Stays Out of Governor's Race," *Dallas Morning News,* Mar. 5, 1972.

12. Deaton, *Year They Threw the Rascals Out,* 30–40.

13. "Action Watchword of Hill/Martin's Style Attacked," *Dallas Times Herald,* Apr. 19, 1972.

14. "Hill Charges Martin Is Linked to Sharp," *Dallas Morning News,* Mar. 14, 1972.

15. "Hill Makes Strong Pitch for Attorney General Job," *Dallas Times Herald,* Mar. 15, 1972.

16. Deaton, *Year They Threw the Rascals Out,* 17–18.

17. Ibid., 33. Barnes's memoir also quotes Anthony Farris, the U.S. attorney who negotiated the plea bargain that assessed minor punishment for Sharp in return for a promise to testify, as telling a Barnes friend ten years later that Sharp never should have been offered immunity by the Justice Department, that the deal was "politically motivated" (Barnes, *Barn Burning,* 217–18).

18. Deaton, *Year They Threw the Rascals Out,* 36.

19. "Hill Scores 'Affirmative Harm,'" *Fort Worth Star-Telegram,* Mar. 19, 1972.

20. "Hill Promises Legal Leadership," *Dallas Morning News,* Apr. 4, 1972.

21. "Candidate Hill Reveals Holdings," *Dallas Morning News,* Apr. 18, 1972.

22. "Crawford Martin," *Dallas Morning News,* Apr. 23, 1972.

23. "Air Crash Fatal to 34 Is Studied," *New York Times,* Oct. 1, 1959.

24. "Suit's Outcome Due to Fix Blame in Electra Crashes," *Dallas Morning News,* Feb. 20, 1962.

25. "Jury Awards Housewife $250,000 in Crash Suit," *Dallas Morning News,* Apr. 11, 1962.

26. "84 Killed in Crash near Corsicana," *Dallas Morning News,* May 4, 1968; "Pilot Criticized in Crash; Report Issued on Braniff Accident Fatal to 85," *Dallas Morning News,* Aug. 28, 1969.

Chapter 2. Reforming Consumer Protections

1. "Consumer Bill Seems Doomed," *Houston Post,* May 11, 1971; interview with Joe Longley and Phil Maxwell, Jan. 19, 2005; interview with Joe Longley, Feb. 18, 2005; interview with Liz Lacy, Feb. 18, 2005.

2. *Graves v. Barnes,* 405 US 1201 (1972). The U.S. Supreme Court denied an application for a stay of a three-judge court-drawn single-member district plan for House seats in Dallas and Bexar (San Antonio) counties. Harris County's new

single-member districts, which were drawn by the State Redistricting Board consisting of the House Speaker and four statewide officeholders who inherited the job after the legislature's redistricting attempts in 1971 failed, were not challenged in the lawsuit.

3. Black membership from the three largest counties (Harris, Dallas, and Bexar) grew from two in 1971 to eight in 1973, and Mexican American membership grew from two to five.

4. "Consumer Credit Regulation in Texas—The Case for the Consumer," 49 *Texas Law Review* 1011 (1971).

5. Maxwell, "History of the Deceptive Trade Practices–Consumer Protection Act," sec. 2.5 (cited hereafter as Maxwell, "History of the DTPA").

6. Testimony of Liz Levatino, Senate Subcommittee on Consumer Affairs hearing on Senate Bill 75, Feb. 2, 1973, Senate Staff Services transcript, 28, referring to attempts to shut down activities of a pyramid scheme by Glenn W. Turner's Koscot Interplanetary, Inc. The flashy Turner's sales of mink oil–based cosmetics attracted prosecution by more than thirty state attorneys general ("Fast Buck Gospel," *TIME Magazine,* Nov. 21, 1971). After the Texas attorney general's attempt to use state securities laws to stop Koscot was rejected in 1970, first by the Austin Court of Civil Appeals and then the Texas Supreme Court, an injunction was obtained under the Consumer Credit Code. By that time, about four thousand Texans had invested an average of three thousand dollars in the marketing scheme, with all but a few losing the entire investment.

7. "Austin Report/Crackdown on Deceptive Ads," *Dallas Times Herald,* June 7, 1970; "Consumers Go for Protection to State Office," *Houston Chronicle,* Dec. 18, 1970.

8. Maxwell, "History of the DTPA," sec. 2.5.

9. Longley and Maxwell interview.

10. "Consumer Bill Seems Doomed," *Houston Post,* May 11, 1971.

11. Longley and Maxwell interview.

12. Ibid.; interview with Mickey Moore, Feb. 15, 2005.

13. "Consumer Aid Plan Endorsed," *San Antonio Express,* Feb. 8, 1973.

14. Testimony of Attorney General John Hill, Senate Subcommittee on Consumer Affairs hearing on Senate Bill 75, Feb. 8, 1973, Senate Staff Services transcript, 4.

15. "Buyers, Sellers Back Consumer Shelter Bill," *Austin American,* Feb. 9, 1973.

16. "Consumer Protection Bill Approved by Senate Panel," *Houston Chronicle,* Feb. 15, 1975; "Insurance Firms Win Round on Bill," *Dallas Times Herald,* Feb. 15, 1975.

17. Telephone interview with William P. Hobby Jr., Feb. 7, 2005; "Consumer Protection Bill Prompts Hill-Hobby Dispute," *Dallas Times Herald,* Mar. 30, 1973.

18. Longley and Maxwell interview.

19. "Senate Delays Action on Bill Regulating Trade Practices," *Fort Worth Star-Telegram,* Mar. 30, 1973; "Consumer Protection Bill Prompts Hill-Hobby Dispute," *Dallas Times Herald,* Mar. 30, 1973.

20. Maxwell, "History of the DTPA," sec. 2.6; Longley and Maxwell interview.

21. "Consumer Bill Gets Senate Panel Okay," *Austin American,* Apr. 11, 1973; "Hobby Gives Senate Endorsement for Weakened Bill," *Dallas Times Herald,* Apr. 11, 1973.

22. "Senate Votes Approval of Consumer Aid Bill," *San Antonio Express,* Apr. 18, 1973.

23. "Competitive Auto Rates Win Approval of House," *Houston Post,* May 8, 1973; "Consumer Protection Act, Bond Bill Become Law," *Dallas Morning News,* May 22, 1973.

24. "Hill Aide Denies Surveys Ending," *Houston Post,* Nov. 18, 1977; "Schedule D: Fast Cash Was Bait for Victims," *Dallas Morning News,* Mar. 21, 1976; "Hill Suit Accuses Ward of Deceptive Trade Practices," *Dallas Times Herald,* Mar. 12, 1976.

25. "State Wins Ruling against Wehling," *Houston Post,* Feb. 5, 1977.

Chapter 3. Cleaning Up the Houston Ship Channel

1. "TACB Criticized/Industry Raps Clean Air Standards," *Dallas Morning News,* Dec. 10, 1971.

2. One of Governor Connally's appointees to the newly created Texas Air Control Board in 1966 was Merichem Company president John T. Files, the secretary-treasurer of the Texas Chemical Council, a prominent lobby group. Merichem and a subsidiary, Jefferson Lake Sulphur Company, were convicted three times of water pollution between 1956 and 1958 ("On Pollution Complaints/Files Says Firm Turned New Leaf," *Houston Post,* Mar. 2, 1966). Merichem was cited by Harris County's pollution control watchdog, Dr. Walter A. Quebedeaux, as the Houston area's "polluter of the month" in April 1966 because of foul odors emanating from the company's Greens Bayou plant on five days, and it was listed on his "dishonor roll" the following month due to four days of noxious odor discharges. Quebedeaux began the "polluter of the month" feature at the request of *Houston Post* reporter Harold Scarlett, a tireless chronicler of Houston's pollution problems ("Boss on Control Panel/Merichem Firm Polluter of Month," *Houston Post,* May 6, 1966; "Firm's Head Anti-Polluter/Merichem Accused of Dumping Gas in Bayou," *Houston Post,* June 9, 1966).

3. Smith, *Decline of Galveston Bay,* 49–50.

4. "Air Control Man Heats Up/Board Member Attacks Attorney General's Criteria," *Dallas Morning News,* Mar. 26, 1970.

5. “Air Pollution Enforcer Says Pressure Forced Resignation,” *Dallas Morning News,* Mar. 30, 1971.

6. Smith, *Decline of Galveston Bay,* 3–6; Tyler et al., *New Handbook of Texas,* 3:739–40.

7. “Lethargy Ends Abruptly/Federal Visitors Spur Texas Pollution Drive,” *Dallas Morning News,* Jan. 18, 1970.

8. Smith, *Decline of Galveston Bay,* 12–15 (second quote); “Texas Today/Gold for Houston in a Dirty Ditch,” *Dallas Morning News,* Aug. 21, 1969; “Suicidal Pollution,” *Dallas Morning News,* Jan. 21, 1970 (first quote); “Houston Ship Channel among Filthiest,” *Dallas Morning News,* Dec. 18, 1970.

9. “Pollution Official Scolds Houstonian,” *Dallas Morning News,* Feb. 20, 1970.

10. “Interior Attacks Galveston Pollution,” *Dallas Morning News,* Jan. 15, 1970; “Level of Viruses in Water Alarming,” *Dallas Morning News,* Jan. 16, 1970; “Lethargy Ends Abruptly/Federal Visitors Spur Texas Pollution Drive,” *Dallas Morning News,* Jan. 18, 1970; “Texas Pollution Report Distorted, Official Says,” *Dallas Morning News,* Jan. 24, 1970.

11. Smith, *Decline of Galveston Bay,* 82–92; “Showdown Battle Shaping Up over Galveston Bay Pollution,” *Dallas Morning News,* May 11, 1971; “Government and Texas Gird for Battle over Pollution,” *New York Times,* May 11, 1971; “Pollution Parley Unable to Agree,” *New York Times,* June 13, 1971.

12. “35 Felled on Piers in Houston as Smog Again Envelops Area,” *New York Times,* July 12, 1971.

13. “Smog Blankets Houston,” *Houston Post,* Sept. 12, 1972; “Smelly Blanket of Smog Wraps Houston for 3rd Day,” *Dallas Morning News,* Sept. 14, 1972; “City Ozone, Oxidant Alert Levels Topped,” *Houston Post,* Sept. 23, 1972; “Houston Ozone Tops Safe Level,” *Dallas Morning News,* Nov. 10, 1972.

14. “Humble Oil Co. Fined $2,500,” *Dallas Morning News,* Nov. 24, 1971; “State Ready to Try 3 Pollution Suits,” *Houston Post,* Jan. 12, 1973.

15. Interview with Phil Maxwell, Jan. 12, 2005; interview with Mike Willatt, Feb. 17, 2005; telephone interviews with Terry O’Rourke, Apr. 1, 2005, June 20, 2005; telephone interview with Rod Gorman, June 28, 2005; e-mail interview with Gorman, Jan. 26, 2007. Unless otherwise footnoted, all of the events described in this chapter were distilled from these interviews.

16. Quebedeaux would fill a beaker with a polluter’s discharge sample, drop in a small gambusia carp minnow, and record the fish’s demise or survival. By the time the Armco case came to trial in 1973, he had killed more than twenty-five hundred gambusia minnows with effluent collected from Armco’s discharge over a number of years (Gorman e-mail interview).

17. “Pollution Suit Accord Likely, Judge Reports,” *Houston Post,* Feb. 28, 1973.

18. “Attorney General Office Here Uses Ads in Evidence Search,” *Houston Post,* Jan. 31, 1973.

19. "$100,000 Pollution Fine Paid," *Houston Post,* Mar. 13, 1973; "Hill Urges More Out-of-Court Settlements of Pollution Cases," *Houston Chronicle,* Mar. 13, 1973.

20. "U.S. Files Suit against Armco," *Dallas Morning News,* Dec. 10, 1970.

21. "Full Injunction Urged against Armco Wells," *Houston Post,* Aug. 3, 1971; "Firm Told to Halt Dumping," *Dallas Morning News,* Sept. 19, 1971; "Armco Likely to Drop Waste Well Plan," *Houston Post,* Sept. 21, 1971.

22. "Armco Ruling Termed 'an Important Milestone,'" *Houston Post,* Nov. 12, 1971; "Ex-Aide Changes Armco Testimony," *New York Times,* Dec. 23, 1972.

23. Quarles, *Cleaning Up America,* 63–64; "Rep. Reuss Charges Justice Department Cover-Up in Armco Pollution Case," *New York Times,* Nov. 23, 1972.

24. Investigative journalist Jack Anderson was the first to expose the intervention of President Nixon's staff in the case. He revealed a politically damaging Justice Department memo that detailed the White House's efforts to influence the case in response to Verity's protests, even though, in congressional testimony in 1971, the assistant attorney general named in the memo denied any involvement ("The Washington Merry-Go-Round/Nixon Aide Pulled Strings for Armco," *Washington Post,* Nov. 15, 1972; "Court Intervention Claimed/White House Aided Armco, Memo Says," *Dallas Morning News,* Nov. 16, 1972).

25. "Armco Appeals to Nixon," *Houston Post,* Oct. 1, 1971; Keith Ozmore, interview transcript, Conservation History Association of Texas, Oct. 8, 1999, reel 2046, time code 0:42:23 to 0:42:33, http://www.texaslegacy.org/bb/narrators/ozmorekeith.html (accessed May 14, 2005).

26. "Rep. Reuss Charges Justice Department Cover-Up in Armco Pollution Case," *New York Times,* Nov. 23, 1972.

27. Ibid.

28. O'Rourke telephone interview, June 20, 2005.

29. "Water Pollution Suit Settled," *Houston Post,* Apr. 4, 1973.

30. "Armco to Pay Record Fine over Pollution," *Houston Chronicle,* May 25, 1973.

31. "Local Polluters Fined $1 Million This Year," *Houston Chronicle,* Dec. 28, 1973.

32. "Hill Asks Water Board Join Suit against City Pollution," *Houston Post,* Sept. 21, 1973.

33. "Your World/Pollution Persists," *Houston Post,* Sept. 30, 1973.

34. "Construction Curbs Imposed," *Houston Post,* Oct. 24, 1973.

35. "TWQB Again Sidesteps Move against Houston's Pollution," *Houston Chronicle,* Dec. 19, 1973.

36. "Atty. Gen. Holds Off on Houston Sewer Plan Action," *Houston Chronicle,* July 25, 1974.

37. "Water Board Told Houston's Sewage Poses Virus Danger," *Houston Post,* Feb. 26, 1975; "Forcing City to Meet Sewage Deadline Urged," *Houston Chronicle,* Feb. 25, 1976.

38. "Probers Rap Water Board for Polluter Nonprosecution," *Dallas Times Herald,* Jan. 14, 1975; "Law Enforcement/Panel Criticizes Water Board," *Dallas Morning News,* Jan. 15, 1975.

39. "Right to Sue Polluters Urged," *Corpus Christi Times,* Jan. 14, 1975.

40. "Hill Joins Authority in Suit against City," *Houston Post,* July 31, 1976.

41. "Judge Accepts Settlement in Pollution Suit," *Houston Chronicle,* Apr. 14, 1978.

42. "Aquifer Order Split; Suit Hinted," *San Antonio Express,* Mar. 4, 1977.

43. "Court Rules Hill Can Sue TWQB," *San Antonio Express,* June 2, 1977.

44. "Texas Judge Urged to Halt Order Governing Aquifer," *Dallas Morning News,* Aug. 6, 1977.

45. "Judge Drops Hill's Case Challenging Edwards Aquifer Ruling," *Houston Post,* Aug. 31, 1977.

46. "Hill Wants Power to Contest State Agencies," *Corpus Christi Times,* June 14, 1978.

47. *John L. Hill v. Texas Water Quality Board,* 568 S.W. 2d 738, Austin Court of Civil Appeals Case No. 12752, opinion by J. C. Phillips, ruling of district court affirmed, issued July 12, 1978, rehearing denied July 26, 1978; "Atty. Gen. Hill Loses Round," *San Antonio Light,* July 13, 1978.

Chapter 4. Beating the Southwestern Bell Goliath

1. Brooks, *Telephone,* 309; "Bell Probers Question Top Dallas Management," *Dallas Times Herald,* Oct. 27, 1974; "Ma Bell's No Longer Bell(e) of the Ball," *San Antonio Light,* Jan. 19, 1975; "The Troubles Spread at Southwestern Bell," *Business Week,* June 23, 1975.

2. Brooks, *Telephone,* 3–19.

3. "Sen. Wilson Sticks to Charge of Collusion between Council, Bell," *Dallas Morning News,* Oct. 20, 1970; "Bell Controversy Mushrooms," *Austin American-Statesman,* Jan. 20, 1975; "Four Bell Executives to Face SEC Query," *Dallas Morning News,* Jan. 31, 1975; "Senate Panel Report Alleges Phone Firm Overcharging," *Houston Chronicle,* Apr. 28, 1976; Jack Hopper, "Legislative History of the Texas Public Utility Regulatory Act of 1975," *Baylor Law Review* 28 (fall 1976): 785–86; "Old Scandal in Texas Continues to Bedevil Ma Bell's Operations," *Wall Street Journal,* Jan. 17, 1977.

4. Coll, *Deal of the Century,* 52.

5. Brooks, *Telephone,* 309; Kahaner, *On the Line,* 73–74; "Bell Probers Question Top Dallas Management," *Dallas Times Herald,* Oct. 27, 1974; "Bell Brands Libel Suit 'Incredible,'" *San Antonio Light,* Nov. 16, 1974; "Deceitful Practices, Suicide May Be Alleged in Ma Bell Suit," *Houston Chronicle,* Nov. 17, 1974; "Bell 'Cloud' Cited, Allegations Denied, Confirmed," *Dallas Morning News,* Dec. 22, 1974; "Ma Bell's No Longer Bell(e) of the Ball," *San Antonio Light,* Jan. 19, 1975.

6. Coll, *Deal of the Century,* 63–72; Brooks, *Telephone,* 312–16.

7. "Far-reaching Investigation of Bell Set," *San Antonio Express-News,* Dec. 8, 1974.

8. Coll, *Deal of the Century,* 8.

9. Ibid., 46; "Phone Firms Regulation Bill Suffers Setback," *Houston Post,* Apr. 20, 1971.

10. Brooks, *Telephone,*10–13, 135–36, 233–34; Coll, *Deal of the Century,* 58–59.

11. Brooks, *Telephone,*10–14, 47–49, 133–36, 197–98, 233, 237, 252, 255, 300.

12. Ibid., 55.

13. Ibid., 299–300; Coll, *Deal of the Century,* 11–13; Kahaner, *On the Line,* 39, 56, 170.

14. Coll, *Deal of the Century,* 53–62.

15. Ibid., 61–70.

16. "Prober Alleges Note Concealed," *Dallas Times Herald,* Nov. 19, 1974. The lawsuit produced lots of headlines but no financial awards for the plaintiffs. They won a $3 million district court judgment in 1977 after a sensational trial in which Bell called as witnesses several female employees who said they had sex with Ashley and Gravitt in order to earn promotions, but the award was overturned by a court of appeals in 1978; the Texas Supreme Court dismissed the plaintiffs' appeal in 1980 on jurisdictional grounds ("State High Court Dismisses Bell Slander Lawsuit," *Houston Chronicle,* Oct. 23, 1980).

17. "Deceitful Practices, Suicide May Be Alleged in Ma Bell Suit," *Houston Chronicle,* Nov. 17, 1974; "Like Topsy, the SW Bell Probe 'Just Seems to Grow,'" *Dallas Morning News,* Jan. 20, 1975.

18. "The Troubles Spread at Southwestern Bell," *Business Week,* June 23, 1975.

19. "Hill Willing to Probe Bell," *Houston Post,* Nov. 26, 1974.

20. Interviews with Mike Willatt, Feb. 17, 2005, Dec. 5, 2005.

21. *Handbook of Texas Online, s.v.* "Constitution of 1876," http://www.tsha.utexas.edu/handbook/online/articles/CC/mhc7.html (accessed Nov. 11, 2005).

22. *Handbook of Texas Online, s.v.* "Flournoy, George M.," http://www.tsha.utexas.edu/handbook/online/articles/FF/ff119.html (accessed Nov. 11, 2005).

23. Braden, *Constitution of the State of Texas,* 351–52; McKay, *Debates in the Texas Constitutional Convention of 1875,* 163–64.

24. Based on interview with Daniel Goforth, Dec. 5, 2005; Willatt interviews.

25. Willatt interviews; Maxwell interview, Jan. 19, 2005.

26. "Bell 'Cloud' Cited," *Dallas Morning News,* Dec. 22, 1974.

27. "Love Will Resign If Actions Illegal," *Dallas Morning News,* Jan. 19, 1975.

28. "State Blasts Bell Hike," *San Antonio Light,* Jan. 31, 1975; and "Bell to Raise Rate; State to Fight Move," *Dallas Morning News;* "Bell Revising Rates; Hill Planning Suit," *Houston Post;* "Texas Fights Bell's Intrastate Rate Hike," *Dallas Times Herald;* "Long Distance Boost Outlined," *Austin American-Statesman;* "Hill

Plans to Stop Bell from Increasing Rates," *Houston Chronicle,* all published Jan. 31, 1975.

29. "Hill Waits Bell Decision/Hearing Sought on $45 Million Rate Hike," *Dallas Times Herald;* and "Hill Agrees to Wait on Suit," *Houston Post,* both Feb. 1, 1975.

30. "Meets Bell Officials/Hill Agrees to Wait on Suit," *Houston Post,* Feb. 1, 1975.

31. "State Utility Commission Gains Support," *Houston Post,* Feb. 2, 1975.

32. Letter of Feb. 5, 1975, and attached memorandum, "Texas Intrastate Rates, February 5, 1975," from Ford W. Hall, General Solicitor-Texas for Southwestern Bell, to Attorney General John L. Hill (Exhibit 1, *The State of Texas v. Southwestern Bell Telephone Company*, Cause No. 229,447, 167th Judicial District Court, Travis County, Tex.).

33. Ibid., memorandum, 1, 8.

34. Ibid., 2, 8.

35. "Secret 'Shot,' " *San Antonio Light,* Feb. 6, 1975.

36. "Bell Rate Hike Halted," *Dallas Morning News,* Feb. 8, 1975.

37. "Restraining Order Precludes Long Distance Rate Increase," *Daily Texan,* Feb. 10, 1975.

38. "Bell Hearing Set," *San Antonio Light,* Feb. 10, 1975.

39. "House Supports Hill's Bell Suit," *San Antonio Express;* and "Hill's Bell Challenge on Rate Increase Supported by House," *Austin American,* both Feb. 12, 1975.

40. "A Do-Something Attorney General," *Corpus Christi Caller-Times,* Feb. 12, 1975.

41. Goforth interview.

42. "Dismissal Denied in Bell Rate Suit/Injunction Hearing Set," *Austin American,* Feb. 15, 1975.

43. "Judge Denies Motion to Dismiss Hill's Lawsuit; Bell Must Now Justify Proposed Rate Hikes in Court," *Houston Chronicle,* Feb. 15, 1975.

44. Ibid.

45. "Judge Gives Hill Go-Ahead on Bell Case," *Dallas Morning News,* Feb. 15, 1975.

46. *The State of Texas v. Southwestern Bell Telephone Company,* Cause No. 229,447, 167th Judicial District Court, Travis County, Tex., trial transcript, 147–75 (hereinafter cited as *State v. Bell* transcript).

47. *State v. Bell* transcript, 23–24; ibid., deposition of Sam Holcomb, Feb. 17, 1975; Goforth interview.

48. "High Court Rejects SW Bell Bid/Hill's Right to File Suit against Rate Hike Upheld," *Austin American-Statesman,* Feb. 18, 1975.

49. Quotations in this and subsequent paragraphs come from *State v. Bell*

transcript, 146–68; "Expert Raps Bell Rate Hikes," *Dallas Times Herald,* Feb. 19, 1975.

50. *State v. Bell* transcript, 180–86.

51. Ibid., 187–91.

52. Ibid., 192–95; *State v. Bell,* Order Nunc Pro Tunc Granting Temporary Injunction and Overruling Defendant's Motion to Suspend Injunction during Appeal, issued Mar. 26, 1975; "Bell Intrastate Rate Hike Stalled by Court Order," *Austin American-Statesman,* Feb. 20, 1975.

53. "State Judge Enjoins Bell from Increasing Its Rates," *Dallas Times Herald,* Feb. 20, 1975.

54. "Ma Bell Case Argued," *San Antonio Express,* Apr. 3, 1975.

55. "State Case against Bell Is 'Perfect,' Says Hill," *Austin American-Statesman,* Apr. 3, 1975.

56. "'Bell on Third Strike,'" *San Antonio Light,* Apr. 3, 1975.

57. *Southwestern Bell Telephone Company v. State of Texas,* 523 S.W. 2d 67, Austin Court of Civil Appeals Case No. 12301, judgment of trial court reversed and rendered, per curiam.

58. "Will Soon Show Up on Customers' Bills/New Long-Distance Rates Take Effect," *Austin American-Statesman,* May 17, 1975.

59. "Hill Will Fight Reversal of Rule Blocking Bell Rate Hike," *Houston Chronicle,* May 17, 1975.

60. "Higher Phone Rates in Effect, Bell Says," *Houston Chronicle,* May 16, 1975.

61. "Forum/Jon Ford," *Austin American-Statesman,* May 18, 1975.

62. "Utilities Bill to Briscoe," *Dallas Morning News,* June 3, 1975.

63. Quotations in this and subsequent paragraphs are from "SW Bell Accused of Greed," *Houston Post;* "Hearing on Intrastate Calls/Bell Claims Unlimited Rate Right," *Dallas Morning News;* "Calls Actions 'Bordering on the Extortionist'/Hill Hits Bell 'Rate Power Belief,'" *Austin American-Statesman,* all published June 19, 1975.

64. "Davis/Arrogance by SW Bell," *Dallas Morning News,* June 21, 1975.

65. *State of Texas v. Southwestern Bell Telephone Company,* Texas Supreme Court Case No. B-5327, Respondent's Post Submission Brief, 62.

66. *State of Texas v. Southwestern Bell,* 526 S.W. 2d 526, judgment of trial court affirmed and modified, opinion for the court by Zollie Steakley (J. Walker not sitting), July 9, 1975; rehearing denied Sept. 24, 1975.

67. *State of Texas v. Southwestern Bell,* Texas Supreme Court Case No. B-5327, Respondent's Motion for Rehearing, 2.

68. "Bell Agrees to Cut Rate Hike/Hill Cites Savings for Users," *San Antonio Light,* Aug. 9, 1975; "Agreed Judgment Entered in Bell Rate Hike Dispute," *Dallas Morning News,* Aug. 12, 1975.

69. "Bell Rate Hike to 'Save $,'" *San Antonio Light,* Aug. 12, 1975.

Chapter 5. Corralling Maverick Child Care Home Operators

1. "Why Texas Has Artesia Halls," *Houston Chronicle,* July 8, 1973.

2. CDC National Center for Health Statistics, Vital Statistics of the United States 1975, U.S. Public Health Service; Vital Statistics for the United States 1965, U.S. Public Health Service, both at http://www.cdc.gov/nchs/products/pubs/pubd/vsus/1963/1963.htm (accessed Mar. 9, 2006).

3. "The American Family: Future Uncertain," *TIME Magazine,* Dec. 28, 1970.

4. "State Is Blamed for Not Preventing Death of Girl at Controversial School," *Houston Chronicle,* June 17, 1973; "House Welfare Panel Probing Artesia Hall," *Houston Post,* June 21, 1973; Sagstetter, *Don't Give Me Liberty!* 31–33, 170.

5. *Joseph Davis Farrar et al. v. Clarence D. Cain et al.,* Cause No. 75-H-987, U.S. District Court, Southern District of Texas, Houston Division, trial transcript, (hereinafter cited as *Farrar* transcript), testimony of Charles Huey, 2850–52. Huey and all of the still-living participants in the Artesia Hall episode relived the tragic events in slow-motion detail in this six-week federal court trial a decade after the events in question. Waggoner Carr filed for Farrar a civil rights civil lawsuit against five local and state officeholders, seeking $17 million in damages. A jury found the local officials' actions were not the proximate cause of Farrar's financial loss. They found that Lieutenant Governor Hobby's actions deprived Farrar of a civil right, but they awarded no damages. Farrar's son (Farrar died prior to the trial) appealed and won a judgment requiring Hobby to pay $318,000 in attorney's fees and other costs, which Hobby appealed to the Supreme Court of the United States. Hobby won a reversal of the judgment on a 5-to-4 vote in 1992 (*Farrar v. Hobby,* 506 U.S. 103 [1992]; "Justices Say Hobby Lost Suit But Doesn't Have to Pay Fees," *Dallas Morning News,* Dec. 15, 1992).

6. *Farrar* transcript, testimony of Dale Farrar, 159–80; "Artesia Hall Founded in 1970; Alternative to Reform School," *Houston Chronicle,* June 24, 1973.

7. Report of the Subcommittee on Public Welfare, Texas House of Representatives Committee on Human Resources, *The Case of Artesia Hall,* Oct. 1, 1973, 12–13 (hereinafter cited as Subcommittee Report on Artesia Hall); "Controversy Stalks Liberty School for Troubled Youths," *Houston Chronicle,* Aug. 20, 1972; "School Operator Charged with Murder/County Officials Protested Granting of License to Artesia Hall without Avail," *Liberty Vindicator,* June 21, 1973; *Farrar* transcript, Huey testimony, 2853–61; testimony of Clay Autry, 2829–32.

8. *Farrar* transcript, testimony of Debbie Crump, 2884–98.

9. *Farrar* transcript, testimony of Clarence D. Cain, 1319–24.

10. The local rumor mill was fueled daily for four weeks following the Mother's Day incident by one of the three girls taken to the jail, Debbie Austin. While she waited there for her parents to arrive, her shocking tales drew a sympathetic hearing from her jailers ("School Operator Charged with Murder/County Officials

Protested Granting of License to Artesia Hall without Avail," *Liberty Vindicator,* June 21, 1973).

11. Subcommittee Report on Artesia Hall, 13–27; "Attorney Sees Influence in Artesia License," *Houston Chronicle,* June 29, 1973; "Daniel Explains Artesia Hall Role/Use of Political Influence Denied," *Dallas Times Herald,* July 12, 1973.

12. Subcommittee Report on Artesia Hall, 22; *Farrar* transcript, testimony of Lonnie Gruver, 2284.

13. Subcommittee Report on Artesia Hall, 27; *Farrar* transcript, Cain testimony, 1336–40; Sagstetter, *Don't Give Me Liberty!* 76–79.

14. *Farrar* transcript, Cain testimony, 1347.

15. Subcommittee Report on Artesia Hall, 28; "Artesia Hall Closing Tied to 'Pressure,'" *Houston Post,* July 14, 1973.

16. Subcommittee Report on Artesia Hall, 31; *Farrar* transcript, testimony of Jim Sterling, 3704.

17. *Farrar* transcript, testimony of W. G. Woods Jr., 3622; testimony of W. A. Cowan Jr., 1421.

18. *Farrar* transcript, testimony of Virginia Hvolboll, 3309; Linda Menchun, 3233–43; Joy Whitman, 2961–62; and Sharon Jaye, 3522–27; Sagstetter, *Don't Give Me Liberty!* 126–37.

19. *Farrar* transcript, Hvolboll testimony, 3341; Sterling testimony, 3712–13; Sagstetter, *Don't Give Me Liberty!* 114; "5 Officials Not Liable for Damages, Jury Rules in Artesia Hall Case," *Houston Post,* Sept. 26, 1983; "Facility Shut After Student-Abuse Scandal/Jury Upholds Closing Artesia Hall School," *Houston Chronicle,* Sept. 26, 1983.

20. *Farrar* transcript, Sterling testimony, 3712–13.

21. Ibid., 3717–18.

22. "Artesia Hall Director Charged with Murder," *Houston Post,* June 16, 1973.

23. "State Is Blamed for Not Preventing Death of Girl at Controversial School," *Houston Chronicle;* "Trouble Clouds Artesia Hall," *Houston Post,* both June 17, 1973.

24. Telephone interview with William P. Hobby Jr., Mar. 31, 2006; telephone interview with Bill Wilde, May 25, 2006.

25. Office of Lt. Gov. Bill Hobby, news release, June 20, 1973, Texas Legislative Reference Library, Austin.

26. "Welfare Reshuffle Urged by Committee," *Houston Post,* Dec. 2, 1970.

27. *Farrar* transcript, testimony of George Campbell, 3795–3809.

28. Hobby news release, June 20, 1973.

29. Interview with Larry York, Mar. 22, 2006; interview with Randy Pendleton, San Marcos, Tex., Feb. 20, 2006; "Atty. Gen. Hill's Office Looking at Artesia Hall Credentials," and "Farrar and Son Indicted," *Houston Chronicle;* "Jurors, State Officials Prove Artesia Hall Files," *Houston Post,* all published June 22, 1973.

30. York interview.

31. "Anahuac Banquet Slated," *Anahuac Progress,* June 7, 1973; "Lt. Gov. Hobby Reports on Legislative Progress," *Anahuac Progress,* June 28, 1973; *Farrar* transcript, Sterling testimony, 3711–13; and testimony of William P. Hobby Jr., 1487–88; telephone interview with William P. Hobby Jr., Mar. 31, 2006; e-mail interviews with Hobby, Apr. 25, 2006, and June 22, 2006.

32. York interview; Hobby interviews; telephone interviews with Harry Ledbetter, Apr. 28, 2006, and John Whitmire, June 6 and June 28, 2006.

33. "Hill to Seek Takeover of School," *Waco Tribune-Herald,* June 23, 1973.

34. *State of Texas and State Department of Public Welfare v. Aston Educational Foundation, Inc., et al.,* Cause No. 25,499, 75th District Court of Liberty County, Tex., trial transcript (hereinafter cited as *State v. Aston* transcript), testimony of Carolyn Busch, 179.

35. *State v. Aston* transcript, 39–40; "Court Hearing Plea to Close Artesia," *Houston Post,* June 23, 1973; "Top Level State Executives Converge on Liberty County Courthouse," *Liberty Vindicator,* June 28, 1973.

36. "State Takes Over Artesia Hall," *Houston Chronicle,* June 23, 1973.

37. *Farrar* transcript, Farrar testimony, 536–46.

38. "Use of Artesia, Aston for Child Care Barred," *Houston Post,* June 29, 1973; "Judge Clarence Cain Enjoins Temporary Closing of School," *Liberty Vindicator,* July 5, 1973.

39. *Farrar* transcript, closing argument by Waggoner Carr for the plaintiffs, 96.

40. Farrar's murder indictment was dismissed because a change in the penal code in 1975 made crimes of omission dependent on a statutory duty to perform, which did not exist in the Hvolboll death ("Farrar Reindictment Effort Will Be Made," *Houston Post,* Jan. 27, 1976).

41. "Texas, Illinois to Investigate Child Care," *Houston Chronicle,* Aug. 11, 1973.

42. "39 Unlicensed Schools Listed," *Houston Post,* June 30, 1973.

43. "State Asked to Act against Local Home for Girls," *Corpus Christi Caller,* July 14, 1973; "Brother Roloff Came Singing, Saving Souls," *Houston Post,* July 15, 1973.

44. "Home for Boys in Zapata to Be Probed," *Laredo Times,* July 17, 1973.

45. "State Asked to Act against Local Home for Girls," *Corpus Christi Caller,* July 14, 1973.

46. "Claims of Abuse Continue against Corpus Home," *Houston Post,* July 16, 1973; "650 Letters Praise Roloff; Writers Respond to Pleas by Evangelist," *Corpus Christi Caller,* July 24, 1973; "Letters on Roloff," *Corpus Christi Caller,* July 26, 1973.

47. Telephone interview with John Odam, Aug. 8, 2006; interview with Lynn Taylor, Jan. 26, 2006; 510 S.W. 2d 813, *Ex parte Lester Roloff, Relator,* opinion by Justice Denton issued May 29, 1974, ordering Relator discharged, rehearing

denied July 10, 1974, 914; *Ex parte Lester Roloff,* Petitioner, Texas Supreme Court Case No. B-4462, Memorandum of Law by State of Texas, Respondent, in opposition to petition for writ of habeas corpus, 3; "Petition Hits Three Schools," *San Antonio Express,* Aug. 4, 1973; "Child Care Unit Suits Get Settled," *Austin American,* Aug. 6, 1973.

48. According to a book written by Roloff's wife, his strategy was described as "the only way we could keep [the homes] open; otherwise they would have been closed down immediately. Under tremendous duress, Lester signed this injunction in order to buy some time, since at that time we had two hundred girls in our care and most of them had no place to go" (Roloff and Glenn, *Lester Roloff in Life and in Death,* 201). Roloff said the same in testimony before Judge Mathews, when asked by his attorney why he signed the order. "I signed it under tremendous duress and pressure; and I never did intend to get a license. . . . I didn't know it was permanent. . . . They brought it to me on Friday afternoon, and I signed it and it went into effect. I thought we could appeal it for 30 days. 10 days it was permanent" ("Hearing on the Motion for Contempt and Application for Temporary Injunction," before the Honorable Charles D. Mathews, 126th District Court).

49. "Rebekah Reunion Draws Estimated 2,500 Followers," *Corpus Christi Caller,* Aug. 5, 1973; "Roloff Says Rules Could Force Move," *Corpus Christi Caller,* Aug. 8, 1973.

50. "Roloff Says Rules Could Force Move," *Corpus Christi Caller;* and "Bible Guides, Roloff Says of Girls' Home," *Houston Post,* both Aug. 8, 1973.

51. Telephone interview with Gene Palmer, July 29, 2006; Odam interview; "Roloff Extension Still Uncertain," *Corpus Christi Caller,* Sept. 27, 1973.

52. Day, "State Licensing of Religious Child-Care Institutions," 19.

53. " 'Final Rites' for Children's Home Slated," *San Antonio Express-News,* Oct. 14, 1973.

54. Odam, Taylor, and Pendleton interviews; "Roloff Calls to Briscoe and God for Help in Keeping Homes Open," *Corpus Christi Caller,* Oct. 17, 1973; "Roloff Vows No Compromise on Child Homes," *Houston Chronicle,* Oct. 17, 1973.

55. "Roloff Enterprises Found Guilty of Contempt," *Corpus Christi Caller,* Oct. 27, 1973.

56. "Roloff Starts Jail Term," *Corpus Christi Times,* Feb. 12, 1974.

57. "High Court Orders Evangelist Roloff Freed on Bond," *Houston Post,* Feb. 13, 1974.

58. "Stifle Streakers, Not Homes, Roloff Pleads," *Austin American,* Mar. 20, 1974.

59. "Roloff Backers Are Busy," *Corpus Christi Caller,* Jan. 12, 1975; " 'Tightened' Child-Care License Bill Advances," *Houston Post,* May 17, 1975.

60. "Roloff Loses Appeal, Starts Jail Sentence," *Corpus Christi Caller,* June 22, 1976.

61. *Roloff Evangelistic Enterprises, Inc., v. State of Texas,* 556 S.W. 2d 856, Austin

Court of Civil Appeals Case No. 12589, per curiam opinion issued Oct. 5, 1977, affirming judgment issued by 126th District Court, rehearing denied Nov. 2, 1977.

62. "3 Roloff Homes Ordered to Comply," *Houston Post,* Feb. 9, 1978; "Highest Court Rejects Roloff License Appeal," *Corpus Christi Caller,* Oct. 3, 1978.

63. Quotes from this and subsequent paragraphs from transcript of *60 Minutes* segment, "Brother Roloff," broadcast on CBS Oct. 22, 1978.

64. "Roloff vs. the State/'If Bible Is Right, Then I'm Right,' " *Corpus Christi Caller,* Aug. 20, 1975. The article was part of an ambitious and exhaustive six-part series titled "Roloff A to Z" by Kerry North and Steve Blow.

65. *Encyclopedia Britannica Online, s.v.* "McIntire, Carl Curtis," http://www.britannica.com (accessed June 12, 2006).

66. Day, "State Licensing," 17.

67. Clements's biography confirms that the Clements campaign financed the Roloff flyer and notes that Roloff later boasted of delivering 250,000 votes to Clements (Barta, *Bill Clements,* 213, 290).

68. Snowball, *Continuity and Change in the Rhetoric of the Moral Majority,* 61.

Chapter 6. Attacking Corruption in Duval County

1. *Handbook of Texas Online, s.v.* "McNelly, Leander H.," http://www.tsha.utexas.edu/handbook/online/articles/BB/wmb1.html (accessed Nov. 11, 2006).

2. Clark, *Fall of the Duke of Duval,* 22; *Handbook of Texas Online, s.v.* "Boss Rule," http://www.tsha.utexas.edu/handbook/online/articles/BB/wmb1.html (accessed Nov. 11, 2006).

3. *Handbook of Texas Online, s.v.* "Parr, Archer," http://www.tsha.utexas.edu/handbook/online/articles/BB/wmb1.html (accessed Nov. 11, 2006); Lynch, *Duke of Duval,* 11, 12, 17.

4. Lynch, *Duke of Duval,* 40.

5. "Political Rabbit Pulled Out of Box 13," *Corpus Christi Caller,* Apr. 8, 1975; "Ex-Official Says He Stole 1948 Election for Johnson; Most Involved Are Now Dead," *New York Times,* July 31, 1977; "Gives Details of Disputed '48 Race," *Los Angeles Times,* July 31, 1977.

6. Lynch, *Duke of Duval,* 55–57; Clark, *Fall of the Duke of Duval,* 47–60; *Handbook of Texas Online, s.v.* "Stevenson, Coke Robert," http://www.tsha.utexas.edu/handbook/online/articles/SS/fst48.html (accessed Nov. 14, 2006); "Political Rabbit Pulled Out of Box 13," *Corpus Christi Caller,* Apr. 8, 1975. Dudley Lynch reports the added vote total for Johnson as 202, John Clark quotes a contemporary report that gives the number as 200, the *Handbook of Texas* says 201, the *Corpus Christi Caller* uses 202, and articles in 1977 (quoting a participant as saying Johnson was present) used varied totals, with the *Dallas News* using 202 and UPI using 200, 201, and 202.

7. "Pistols, Rangers, Indictments Mix in Old-Time Texas Political Row," *New*

York Times, Feb. 5, 1954; "Parr Power Ebbs in Texas Politics," *New York Times,* Feb. 7, 1954; "Part of Duval's Political History Written in Bullets and Blood," *Corpus Christi Caller,* Apr. 11, 1975.

8. Lynch, *Duke of Duval,* 69–72.

9. Ibid., 80, 82–85.

10. Ibid., 86–98.

11. "Parr Is Convicted of Fraud in Texas," *New York Times,* July 18, 1957; "Parr Sentenced to 10-year Term," *New York Times,* July 31, 1957; *Parr v. United States,* 363 U.S. 370 (1960).

12. Clark, *Fall of the Duke of Duval,* 77–82, 291.

13. John Clark reflects the Justice Department's animus by noting that one of the Supreme Court justices was President Johnson's appointee Abe Fortas, who, as a politically well-connected Washington lawyer hired by Johnson in 1948, was instrumental in obtaining an injunction from Justice Hugo Black to block a Dallas federal judge's investigation of Parr's handiwork in the Box 13 controversy (Clark, *Fall of the Duke of Duval,* 50, 82).

14. Clark, *Fall of the Duke of Duval,* 94–100.

15. Ibid., 290, 292, 297, 298, 306, 310, 315, 328; "George Parr Guilty of Evading Income Taxes," *Corpus Christi Caller,* Mar. 20, 1974.

16. "Mystery Man Manges Vows to Fight Back at Political Foes," *Fort Worth Star-Telegram,* Feb. 6, 1977.

17. "Briscoe Must Go to Court," *San Antonio Express,* Nov. 19, 1974.

18. Lynch, *Duke of Duval,* 119–20. In December 1970, on the eve of O. P. Carrillo taking office, Manges appointed him and Judge Carrillo's brother Ramiro to the board of the First State Bank and Trust Company of Rio Grande City; a month later, Manges paid seven thousand dollars toward the purchase of a Cadillac for O. P.

19. Clark, *Fall of the Duke of Duval,* 86; "Duval County Rulers Have a Way with Law," *Dallas Morning News,* July 24, 1974.

20. Clark, *Fall of the Duke of Duval,* 299.

21. Testimony of Arnulfo Guerra, House Select Committee on Impeachment, June 4–5, 1975, included in "Before the State Judicial Qualifications Commission, Inquiry Concerning a Judge, No. 5, Dec. 5, 1975, Volume II," 6 (hereinafter cited as JQC report).

22. Ibid., 5–9, 37–38, 126–31, 182–14, 269–71.

23. Ibid., 222–23.

24. Ibid., 10–25, 132–41.

25. "Bates Special Prosecutor in Duval," *Corpus Christi Caller,* Mar. 5, 1975.

26. Lynch, *Duke of Duval,* 126–27.

27. JQC report, 32.

28. "Judge: Got Tip of Parr Ambush," *San Antonio Express,* June 17, 1975.

29. JQC report, 30–31.

30. Ibid., 31–34, 94–95.

31. JQC report, Guerra testimony, 35–36, 99.

32. "Tension Heavy as Once-Solid Duval Splits," *Corpus Christi Caller,* Mar. 21, 1975; Lynch, *Duke of Duval,* 127.

33. Lynch, *Duke of Duval,* 127; "Archer Parr Suspended; Tobin New Judge," *Corpus Christi Caller,* Mar. 25, 1975; "Carrillo Wrongdoing Denied by DA," *Austin American-Statesman,* June 5, 1975; "Guerra Grilled at Carrillo Hearing," *San Antonio Express,* June 6, 1975.

34. "George Parr Claims Manges behind Duval Split," *Corpus Christi Caller,* Mar. 26, 1975.

35. JQC report, Guerra testimony, 44–48.

36. "Carrillo, Parr Trade Legal Maneuvers," *Corpus Christi Caller,* Mar. 28, 1975.

37. Clark, *Fall of the Duke of Duval,* 322.

38. Lynch, *Duke of Duval,* 128; "George Parr Skips Court; Arrest Ordered," *Corpus Christi Caller,* Apr. 1, 1975.

39. "State Supreme Court Backs Carrillo in Duval Decisions," *Corpus Christi Caller,* Apr. 1, 1975.

40. "Hill Pledges to Assist in Duval Probe," *Laredo Times,* Apr. 2, 1975.

41. "Hill Says State to Aid Duval County Probe," *Dallas Morning News,* Apr. 2, 1975.

42. Interviews with John Blanton, Nov. 17, 2006, and Jerry Carruth, Nov. 16, 2006; telephone interview with Tim James, Dec. 1, 2006.

43. Clark, *Fall of the Duke of Duval,* 322–23.

44. "Duval County," *Corpus Christi Caller,* Mar. 23, 1975; "Upheaval in Duval 'Story of the Week,' " *Corpus Christi Caller,* Mar. 23, 1975.

45. "Duval Prosecutor Believes His Life in Danger," *Dallas Times Herald,* Apr. 3, 1975.

46. "Parr Considered Murder, Says Deputy/Changed Mind about Political Enemies," *Dallas Times Herald,* Apr. 5, 1975.

47. "Grand Jury Oath Silences Hill," *Corpus Christi Caller;* "Hill Appoints 2 Prosecutors to Study Duval County," *Fort Worth Star-Telegram,* both Apr. 9, 1975.

48. John Blanton, "Inter-Office Communications, Attorney General's Office," Duval County File, May 8, 1975, May 14, 1975, and May 17, 1975 (hereinafter cited as Blanton, "Inter-Office Communications").

49. Ibid., May 25, 1975; "Duval Grand Jury Indictments Public," *San Antonio Express,* May 24, 1975.

50. Blanton, "Inter-Office Communications," May 25, 1975.

51. Record of Proceedings of the High Court of Impeachment, on the Trial of Honorable O. P. Carrillo, Judge, 229th District Court, Twentieth Day (Tuesday, Jan. 20, 1976), 3063–64 (hereinafter cited as Impeachment proceedings); Report, House Select Committee on Functions of Judiciary, 64th Texas Legislature, 1.

After serving four terms as judge of the 79th District Court, Canales himself was removed from the bench in 2003 for sexual harassment of three women in his chambers ("Decision of the Review Panel Appointed by the Supreme Court of Texas, September 4, 2003," appeal to Texas Supreme Court denied Apr. 10, 2004, *In re Terry A. Canales, Judge, 79th District Court of Texas v. State Commission on Judicial Conduct Inquiry No. 84,* Texas Supreme Court Order No. 03-1044).

52. Blanton, "Inter-Office Communications," June 8, 1975.

53. Ibid., June 28, 1975.

54. "Time for Hill to Join Duval Probe," *Corpus Christi Caller,* June 27, 1975.

55. "Action Lively in Duval Cases/Grand Jury Tampering Cited," *Corpus Christi Caller,* July 3, 1975.

56. "Jury Tampering Investigated in Duval," *San Antonio Express,* July 4, 1975.

57. Blanton interview.

58. "Hill Won't Talk after Meeting Duval Jury," *Corpus Christi Times,* July 9, 1975.

59. Blanton, "Inter-Office Communications," July 13, 1975; Blanton and James interviews.

60. Blanton, "Inter-Office Communications," July 27, 1975.

61. Arnulfo Guerra, letter to John L. Hill, July 28, 1975, from files of John Blanton; Blanton, James, and Carruth interviews.

62. Martinez, *They Call Me Ranger Ray,* 142; "New Ways to Pursue Duval Cases Explored," *Corpus Christi Times,* Aug. 1, 1975; Blanton interview.

63. Blanton, "Inter-Office Communications," Aug. 10, 1975; "Carrillo Disqualifies 1 from New Duval Grand Jury Service/Hill's Staff Grills Prospective Members," *Corpus Christi Caller,* Aug. 5, 1975.

64. Interview with Ray Bravenec, Dec. 4, 2006; Blanton interview.

65. Blanton, "Inter-Office Communications," Aug. 24, 1975.

66. Blanton and Bravenec interviews; Clark, *Fall of the Duke of Duval,* 324; "School Records Found in Benavides Office Attic," *Corpus Christi Caller,* Aug. 22, 1975.

67. "Finding School Records Could Be Breakthrough," *Corpus Christi Caller,* Aug. 25, 1975.

68. Blanton and Bravenec interviews; "Deal Starts Couling Talking," *Corpus Christi Caller,* Sept. 17, 1975.

69. Blanton and Bravenec interviews; Blanton, "Inter-Office Communications," Sept. 14 and Sept. 21, 1975. Also present at part of the debriefing were photographers from *60 Minutes*. An exchange between Bravenec and Couling was included on the program's Aughust 1, 1976 segment on Duval County corruption.

70. Impeachment proceedings, 2486, 2487, 2489, 2490, 2494, 2495; Martinez, *They Call Me Ranger Ray,* 140–41; Clark, *Fall of the Duke of Duval,* 276; Blanton, "Inter-Office Communications," Aug. 24, Sept. 1, and Sept. 7, 1975.

71. Clark, *Fall of the Duke of Duval,* 324–25.

72. "State Winds Up Carrillo Case," *San Antonio Express,* July 15, 1976.

73. "O. P. Carrillo Denied New Trial, Sentenced," *Corpus Christi Caller,* Aug. 8, 1976.

74. "House Impeaches Carrillo on 10 Counts," *Dallas Morning News,* Aug. 6, 1975.

75. "Hester Respected for Duval Actions," *Corpus Christi Caller,* Dec. 15, 1975.

76. Clark, *Fall of the Duke of Duval,* 323–24; Martinez, *They Call Me Ranger Ray,* 146; "Hester Holds Action-Packed Session/Jury Challenged for Oscar Carrillo," *Corpus Christi Caller,* Feb. 3, 1976.

77. Martinez, *They Call Me Ranger Ray,* 162.

78. Telephone interviews with John Odam, Dec. 1, 2006, and Liz Levatino, Feb. 18, 2005.

79. Carruth, Bravenec, and Blanton interviews.

Chapter 7. Fighting California and Nevada for Howard Hughes's Estate Taxes

1. Hoffman, *Lions in the Street,* 89–90.

2. "Howard Hughes Dies at 70 on Flight to Texas Hospital," *New York Times,* Apr. 6, 1976; Barlett and Steele, *Empire,* 582; "Hughes' Physical, Emotional Status Cited by Lummis," *Houston Post,* Aug. 21, 1977.

3. "The Washington Merry-Go-Round/Is Howard Hughes Really Dead?" *Washington Post,* Feb. 27, 1976.

4. "Hughes Is Buried in Brief Ceremony," *New York Times,* Apr. 8, 1976.

5. Barlett and Steele, *Empire,* 580–82, 619, 620.

6. "Hughes Estate Fight Seen as Doubts Rise about Will," *New York Times,* Apr. 8, 1976; "Former Aide Says Hughes Wrote Will and Put It in Bank," *New York Times,* Apr. 16, 1976.

7. Interview with Karen Johnson, Sept. 20, 2006.

8. Interviews with Rick Harrison, Aug. 24, Oct. 5, and Oct. 12, 2006; interview with David Deaderick, Sept. 21, 2006.

9. Barlett and Steele, *Empire,* 584; Harrison and Deaderick interviews; recording of arguments of Jerome B. Falk Jr. before the U.S. Supreme Court, Mar. 29, 1978, in *California v. Texas,* 437 U.S. 601, 98 S.Ct. 3107.

10. "State Hopes to Retrace the Last Days of Hughes," *Houston Chronicle,* June 24, 1976.

11. Harrison interviews; Barlett and Steele, *Empire,* 478, 609.

12. Quoted in "Texans to Examine Last Days of Hughes," *Houston Post,* June 23, 1976; "State Hopes to Retrace the Last Days of Hughes," *Houston Chronicle,* June 24, 1976.

13. "Jack Anderson and Les Whitten/Filling Hughes' Shoes," *Washington Post,* June 24, 1976.

14. Anderson's memoir describes his brokering of the agreement for Mexican authorities to release the Hughes papers to Simon (Anderson, *Peace, War, and Politics,* 276–80).

15. All quotes derived from recollections in Harrison interviews.

16. Interview with Bert Pluymen, Dec. 19, 2006.

17. "Hughes Doctor under Suspicion of Misconduct," *Houston Post,* Oct. 12, 1977.

18. "The Secret Life of Howard Hughes," *TIME Magazine,* Dec. 13, 1976; "Hughes' Security Kept Him Virtual Prisoner, Magazine Says," *Houston Post,* Dec. 6, 1976.

19. Harrison interviews.

20. Barlett and Steele, *Empire,* 239–40, 269.

21. Ibid., 20, 579; "Power Struggle Prompted Hughes' Move to Acapulco, Former Aide Says," *Houston Chronicle,* Jan. 26, 1978.

22. Barlett and Steele, *Empire,* 614–15, 619–20.

23. "'I Am a Texan' Letter Backs Hill's Case on Residency Question," *Houston Post,* Mar. 23, 1977.

24. All quotes in this and subsequent paragraphs on the John Wayne encounters are derived from recollections in Harrison and Deaderick interviews and Florentino Garza, telephone interview, Oct. 25, 2006; Rick Harrison, "Personal Notes on Attorney General's Office," provided to Ernie Stromberger on Mar. 28, 2005.

25. "Hughes Testifies on Firing Jarrico," *Los Angeles Times,* Nov. 21, 1952; "Jarrico Loses Suit against RKO over Screen Credit," *Los Angeles Times,* Nov. 27, 1952.

26. "Hughes Quoted As Testifying in 1952 That City Legal Home," *Houston Chronicle,* Dec. 10, 1977.

27. "2 City Penthouses Explored As Potential Hughes Homes," *Houston Post,* June 17, 1977.

28. "Hughes Estate Tax Fight Goes to High Court," *Los Angeles Times,* Nov. 12, 1977.

29. *Texas v. Florida,* 306 U.S. 398, 59 S.Ct. 563, 83 L.Ed. 817 (1939).

30. "Hill, Attorney in Shouting Match over Hughes Case Jury Selection," *Houston Chronicle,* Nov. 18, 1977.

31. Ibid.; Harrison interview.

32. "Tempers Flare, Hughes' Residency Trial Delayed," *Houston Chronicle,* Nov. 22, 1977.

33. *The Estate of Howard Robard Hughes, Jr., Deceased,* Probate Court Number Two of Harris County, Tex., Cause Number 139,362, transcript volume 1, 4–5.

34. Harrison interviews.

35. "Jury's Finding Says Hughes Was a Texan," *Houston Chronicle,* Feb. 16, 1978.

36. "Hughes Texan, Jury Finds/Decision Could Mean $100 Million for State," *Houston Post,* Feb. 16, 1978.

37. Quotations here and in subsequent paragraphs are from the Recording of

Arguments of Jerome B. Falk Jr., and Texas Attorney General John L. Hill Jr., United States Supreme Court, Mar. 29, 1978, *California v. Texas* No. 76, Orig.

38. *California v. Texas,* 437 U.S. 601, 98 S.Ct. 3107, motion for leave to file a bill of complaint denied, June 22, 1978, per curiam with concurring opinions by Justices Brennan and Powell; "Justices Refuse to Hear Hughes Estate Dispute," *Los Angeles Times,* June 22, 1978.

Chapter 8. Defending the Death Penalty

1. The five Supreme Court cases were: *American Party of Texas v. White,* 415 U.S. 767 (1974); *Texas v. Louisiana* No. 36, Orig., 426 U.S. 465 (1976); *Jurek v. Texas,* 428 U.S. 262 (1976); *California v. Texas No. 76,* 437 U.S. 601 (1978); and *California v. Southland Royalty Co.,* 436 U.S. 519 (1978).

2. This case concerned only the constitutionality of Texas' death penalty statute (432 U.S. 1082, 96 S.Ct. 1090, 47 L.Ed.2d 93). Appeals regarding other aspects of Jurek's conviction reached the Supreme Court several times (*Jurek v. Estelle,* 430 U.S. 951, 51 L.Ed.2d 800 [1977]), *Estelle v. Jurek,* 450 U.S. 1014 [1981]) and resulted in the defendant winning retrial of his case, in which he agreed to plead guilty to a count of capital murder in return for prosecutors' agreement not to seek the death penalty; he was sentenced to life in prison ("Case That Revived the Death Penalty Ended Ironically," *Houston Chronicle,* Feb. 3, 2001). When Jurek's execution was scheduled in 1977, a television reporter for KERA in Dallas sued in federal court to gain access to the execution. Judge William M. Taylor Jr. granted the request January 3, 1977, which I successfully opposed in oral arguments to the Fifth Circuit Court of Appeals in June 1977 (*Garrett v. Estelle,* 552 F.2d 1274, 1279 [5th Cir. 1977]), contending the state was empowered to restrict news media access to executions by prohibiting cameras and sound recordings. The Supreme Court refused to consider an appeal of the Fifth Circuit ruling.

3. The estimate of death row numbers is based on a United Press International survey included in "Death Penalty Argued," *Washington Post,* Mar. 31, 1976. The NAACP LDF estimated 364 (" 'Arbitrary' Penalty Fought, Texas Death Sentence Argued in High Court," *Dallas Morning News,* Mar. 31, 1976). Of the national total, about 60 were in Texas ("Texas Opening High Court's Hearings on Death Penalty," *Dallas Morning News,* Mar. 30, 1976).

4. "Executions Called Cruel and Unusual," *Washington Post,* June 30, 1972; Sorensen and Pilgrim, *Lethal Injection,* 1–2; Banner, *Death Penalty,* 244.

5. Meltsner, *Cruel and Unusual,* 79–80; Banner, *Death Penalty,* 239.

6. Meltsner, *Cruel and Unusual,* 28, 32, 33; Banner, *Death Penalty,* 249–51.

7. *Maxwell v. Bishop,* 398 U.S. 262 (1970); Banner, *Death Penalty,* 255–56.

8. Banner, *Death Penalty,* 256–57. The consolidated cases are reported at *McGautha v. California,* 402 U.S. 183 (1971).

9. Banner, *Death Penalty,* 258.

10. *Weems v. U.S.,* 217 U.S. 349 (1910).

11. *Trop v. Dulles,* 356 U.S. 86 (1958); Banner, *Death Penalty,* 236–38.

12. Banner, *Death Penalty,* 244.

13. Opinion of Justice Powell, *Furman v. Georgia,* 408 U.S. 238 (1972), footnote 63.

14. Banner, *Death Penalty,* 244.

15. Meltsner, *Cruel and Unusual,* 277.

16. The Texas case was *Branch v. Texas,* 447 S.W. 2d 932, 933 (Tex. Crim. App. 1969).

17. Meltsner, *Cruel and Unusual,* 277.

18. Quoted in ibid., 278.

19. *Furman,* 408 U.S. at 306.

20. Ibid., 400, 403.

21. Kuhn, "House Bill 200," 420.

22. "House OKs Death Penalty for 8 Types of Murder," *Dallas Morning News,* May 9, 1973.

23. Banner, *Death Penalty,* 269.

24. "Senate OKs Death Penalty Law," *Dallas Morning News,* May 25, 1973; Kuhn, "House Bill 200," 417.

25. Kuhn, "House Bill 200," 419–20.

26. "Lawmakers Reinstate Death for Five Types of Murder," *Dallas Morning News,* May 29, 1973.

27. "Briscoe Signs Death Penalty," *Dallas Morning News,* June 15, 1973.

28. *Jurek v. State,* 522 S.W. 2d at 938.

29. Ibid., 939.

30. Ibid., 939–40.

31. Ibid., 940.

32. Ibid., 944.

33. Ibid., 945.

34. Ibid., 948.

35. *Furman,* 408 U.S. at 300.

36. "Executions Called Cruel and Unusual," *Washington Post,* June 30, 1972; Blackmun opinion, *Furman,* 408 U.S. at 411.

37. Banner, *Death Penalty,* 268.

38. Brief for Respondent, *Jurek v. Texas,* U.S. Supreme Court No. 75-5394, 27.

39. Ibid., 28.

40. Ibid., 27.

41. Ibid., 28.

42. Ibid., 30–31.

43. Quotations in this and subsequent paragraphs are all from the transcript of oral arguments, *Jurek v. Texas,* 428 U.S. 262 (1976).

44. In a famous moment from Act 1, Scene 2, of Shakespeare's *Julius Caesar,* the conspirator Cassius—using his rhetorical skills to persuade a reluctant Brutus to join the assassination plot against Caesar—insists that Caesar is a grasping, selfish mortal whose grand stature is a result of ego and ambition, not true merit: "Upon what meat doth this our Caesar feed, / That he is grown so great?" The quote was familiar enough to persons of my generation that Senator Joseph McCarthy used it in a scathing attack on Adlai Stevenson, the Democratic nominee for president in 1952; it was turned against McCarthy by CBS's pioneering broadcast news reporter Edward R. Murrow in a famous telecast of his *See It Now* program in 1954, which was recreated by a popular movie tribute to Murrow, *Good Night, and Good Luck* (2005) (text of Murrow broadcast from http://honors.umd.edu/HONR269J/archive/Murrow540309.html [accessed Jan. 2, 2007]).

45. Jurek was charged in 1969 with raping another ten-year-old girl, but the case was dropped because the parents decided to spare the child the ordeal of a trial ("Supreme Court Denies Rehearing of Jurek Case," *Houston Post,* Mar. 29, 1977).

46. During the hostage-taking crisis at the state prison in Huntsville in 1974, I was in frequent telephone contact with the director of the prison system, Jim Estelle. In that incident, Federico Gomez Carrasco, a South Texas drug ring leader serving a life sentence for assault with intent to commit murder on a police officer, killed Elizabeth Yvonne Beseda, a teacher, and Julia C. Standley, a librarian, on August 3, 1974, in a failed escape attempt after holding them and others hostage since July 24, 1974 (Harper, *Eleven Days in Hell,* 3, 5, 290, 298).

47. *Jurek,* 428 U.S. at 262, 263.

Chapter 9. Managing the Reform of Prisons and Youth Detention Schools

1. Crouch and Marquart, *Appeal to Justice,* 2.

2. Tyler et al., *New Handbook of Texas,* 2:12, 4:665; Texas Legislative Reference Library, http://www.lrl.state.tx.us/legis/.

3. *Handbook of Texas Online,* http://www.tsha.utexas.edu/handbook/online/articles/CC/ulc1.html (accessed Jan. 15, 2007).

4. Kemerer, *William Wayne Justice,* 116–17, 121.

5. Among Justice's shrillest critics was the *Dallas Morning News,* editorializing after the Texas Youth Commission (TYC) decision, "It is the judge, however, who affronts the Constitution. A federal judge order a state institution closed? Under what authority? Justice has power to order the correction of specified abuses, which, to be sure, should be corrected whether he orders it or not. But if such an institution as state government exists, no federal judge can remold its shape"

("Justice's Injustice," *Dallas Morning News,* Sept. 6, 1974). In 1977, Rep. Emmett Whitehead of Rusk proposed a bill to locate a halfway house for youthful offenders next door to Justice's Tyler residence in retaliation for his order's demand that TYC move to community-based facilities ("Accomplishments," *Texas Observer,* June 17, 1977). Judge Justice's decision expanding state bilingual education programs was criticized in 1981 as "stupid and ridiculous . . . something you'd expect from Justice" by the chairman of the state's Senate Finance Committee; Governor Clements said he "wholeheartedly" disagreed with the order (Kemerer, *William Wayne Justice,* 260).

6. Kemerer, *William Wayne Justice,* 145.

7. Ibid., 145–46. Without the El Paso judge's denial of Bercu's access to youthful clients, would he have grounds for a lawsuit and could this case have been avoided? It is a question that I pondered because my predecessor's staff advised TYC, during a three-way phone call with Bercu and the superintendent of the TYC school at Gainesville, to persist in its insistence that a TYC staff member must be present during a meeting between a lawyer and an inmate. It is easy to second-guess this type of situation, but it was symptomatic of the lost opportunities I saw for my predecessor to help TYC avoid this calamitous lawsuit by refusing to indulge their ill-advised procedures.

8. Kemerer, *William Wayne Justice,* 147–48; Wooden, *Weeping in the Playtime of Others,* 3, 4; *Morales v. Turman,* 383 F.Supp. 53 at 64.

9. *Morales* 383 F. Supp. at 89.

10. *Lockamy v. State,* 488 S.W. 2d 954 (Tex. Civ. App., Austin, 1972); *Morales* 383 F. Supp. at 69; Kemerer, *William Wayne Justice,* 149; "State Schools Face Threat of Closure," *Houston Post,* Aug. 22, 1973; "Class Suit Attacks TYC," *Bryan Daily Eagle,* July 25, 1973.

11. Wooden, *Weeping in the Playtime,* 5; Kemerer, *William Wayne Justice,* 149.

12. *Morales* 383 F. Supp. at 72; *Morales v. Turman,* 59 F.R.D. 157 (E.D. Tex. 1972) at 159; Wooden, *Weeping in the Playtime,* 5; Kemerer, *William Wayne Justice,* 155.

13. Kemerer, *William Wayne Justice,* 150, 151.

14. Ibid., 156, 157.

15. "Heatly's Relatives Get $142,025 in Pay," *Dallas Morning News,* Apr. 25, 1969. Maurice Heatly also had consulting contracts with several other state agencies and the University of Texas. In the latter role, he had a consultation with Charles Whitman just days before his deadly shooting rampage from UT's Main Building tower on August 1, 1966, a fact that UT officials revealed to stunned journalists afterward. During that consultation Whitman had described a plan to use his high-powered rifle to shoot at pedestrians around the tower from the structure's observation deck. Whitman killed sixteen persons and wounded thirty-one.

16. "Turman Appointment Criticized by Cole," *Dallas Morning News,* Feb. 15, 1970; interview with Ron Jackson, Jan. 11, 2007.

17. "Legislators Inspect Gatesville," *Dallas Morning News,* Jan. 5, 1969; "Gatesville Probe Lights Fire under Texas Youth Council," *Dallas Morning News,* May 25, 1969.

18. "Legislators Inspect Gatesville," *Dallas Morning News,* Jan. 5, 1969; "Youth Justice: Graphic Report," *Dallas Morning News,* May 1, 1971.

19. "Turman Appointments Criticized by Cole," *Dallas Morning News,* Feb. 15, 1970.

20. Kemerer, *William Wayne Justice,* 422; "State Schools Face Threat of Closure," *Houston Post,* Aug. 22, 1973.

21. *Morales* 383 F. Supp. at 60, 61. Justice's order was reversed by the Fifth Circuit Court of Appeals, 535 F.2d 864 (1976) but sustained by the Supreme Court, 430 U.S. 322 (1977).

22. Jackson interview.

23. Interview with Bob Salter, Jan. 18, 2007.

24. Ibid.

25. Jackson interview; Kemerer, *William Wayne Justice,* 159, 160.

26. "Child-Care Specialist Says Big Institutions Don't Work," *Fort Worth Star-Telegram,* July 27, 1973.

27. *Morales* 383 F. Supp. at 127.

28. *Morales v. Turman* trial transcript, 4139.

29. Interview with Joe Dibrell, Jan. 19, 2007.

30. Interview with W. Forrest Smith, Jan. 17, 2007.

31. "The Fast Changing of the Guard at State Reform School Agency," *Houston Post,* Sept. 23, 1973.

32. Smith interview.

33. *Morales v. Turman* (E.D. Tex., 1973), 364 F. Supp. at 166, 170; "TYC Blames 'Riots' on U.S. Court Order," *Houston Chronicle,* Sept. 13, 1973.

34. Salter interview; "TYC Blames 'Riots' on U.S. Court Order," *Houston Chronicle,* Sept. 13, 1973; "Some Gatesville Youths Reject Riot Explanation," *Houston Chronicle,* Sept. 14, 1973.

35. "Gatesville Rioting Cools," *Dallas Times Herald,* Sept. 13, 1973.

36. "30 Boys on Loose after Gatesville School Violence," *Houston Chronicle,* Sept. 13, 1973; Kemerer, *William Wayne Justice,* 161, 162; "Gatesville Schools Rampaged by Boys," *Houston Post,* Sept. 13, 1973; Salter interview.

37. "Schools Could Have Used Force," *Dallas Times Herald,* Sept. 14, 1973; "TYC Member Probing Riot-Restraint Effort," *Houston Post,* Sept. 17, 1973; "TYC Head Vows 'New Ball Game,'" *Dallas Times Herald,* Sept. 23, 1973.

38. Smith interview.

39. "TYC Head Vows 'New Ball Game,'" *Dallas Times Herald,* Sept. 23, 1973.

40. *Morales* 383 F. Supp. at 72.

41. Kemerer, *William Wayne Justice,* 170, 172, 173; *Morales v. Turman,* 562 F.2d 993 (Fifth Cir. 1977) at 996, 999.

42. The prison lawsuit, *Ruiz v. Estelle,* finally concluded in 2003, when Judge Justice terminated his oversight.

43. Martin and Ekland-Olson, *Texas Prisons,* 18–20.

44. Crouch and Marquart, *Appeal to Justice,* vii, viii, 3, 117; Martin and Ekland-Olson, *Texas Prisons,* 24, 25, 82; Kemerer, *William Wayne Justice,* 357.

45. Crouch and Marquart, *Appeal to Justice,* 224, 225; Kemerer, *William Wayne Justice,* 361, 362, 454; Martin and Ekland-Olson, *Texas Prisons,* 82.

46. Martin and Ekland-Olson, *Texas Prisons,* 60; S.B. 11, 62nd Texas Legislature, General Session Laws, ch. 1047, 3547.

47. Martin and Ekland-Olson, *Texas Prisons,* 95–96.

48. Ibid., 111.

49. Kemerer, *William Wayne Justice,* 359; Martin and Ekland-Olson, *Texas Prisons,* 92–93.

50. The Supreme Court cases were *Cooper v. Pate,* 378 U.S. 546 (1964), and *Haines v. Kerner,* 404 U.S. 519 (1972).

51. Kemerer, *William Wayne Justice,* 358.

52. Ibid. An eighth petitioner was added in July 1972 (Martin and Ekland-Olson, *Texas Prisons,* 262).

53. Martin and Ekland-Olson, *Texas Prisons,* 93; Kemerer, *William Wayne Justice,* 359–60; *Estelle v. Justice,* 426 U.S. 925 (1976), 260.

54. Martin and Ekland-Olson, *Texas Prisons,* 93–94; Kemerer, *William Wayne Justice,* 359. Justice appointed Turner to the case in November (Martin and Ekland-Olson, *Texas Prisons,* 94).

55. Quoted in Martin and Ekland-Olson, *Texas Prisons,* 96–97.

56. *Estelle v. Justice,* 926–29. Chief Justice Burger and Justice Powell joined Rehnquist's dissent.

57. Martin and Ekland-Olson, *Texas Prisons,* 109, 110.

58. Interview with Richel Rivers, Jan. 10, 2007.

59. Martin and Ekland-Olson, *Texas Prisons,* 139–40.

60. Rivers interview.

61. Martin and Ekland-Olson, *Texas Prisons,* 168; *Ruiz v. Estelle,* 503 F. Supp. 1265.

Bibliography

Anderson, Jack, with Daryl Gibson. *Peace, War, and Politics: An Eyewitness Account.* New York: Tom Doherty Associates, 1999.

Banner, Stuart. *The Death Penalty: An American History.* Cambridge, Mass.: Harvard University Press, 2002.

Barlett, Donald L., and James B. Steele. *Empire: The Life, Legend, and Madness of Howard Hughes.* New York: Norton, 1979.

Barnes, Ben, with Lisa Dickey. *Barn Burning Barn Building: Tales of a Political Life from LBJ through George W. Bush and Beyond.* Albany, Tex.: Bright Sky Press, 2006.

Barta, Carolyn. *Bill Clements: Texian to His Toenails.* Austin: Eakin Press, 1996.

Braden, George D., et al. *The Constitution of the State of Texas: An Annotated and Comparative Analysis.* Austin: Texas Advisory Commission on Intergovernmental Relations, 1976.

Brooks, John. *Telephone: The First One Hundred Years.* New York: Harper & Row, 1975.

Clark, John E. *The Fall of the Duke of Duval.* Austin: Eakin Press, 1995.

Coll, Steve. *The Deal of the Century: The Breakup of AT&T.* New York: Simon & Schuster, 1986.

Crouch, Ben M., and James W. Marquart. *An Appeal to Justice: Litigated Reform of Texas Prisons.* Austin: University of Texas Press, 1989.

Day, Kathleen LaNell. "State Licensing of Religious Child-Care Institutions: A Case Study of Roloff Evangelistic Enterprises, Inc." MA thesis, Baylor University, 1978.

Deaton, Charles. *The Year They Threw the Rascals Out.* Austin: Shoal Creek, 1973.

Harper, William T. *Eleven Days in Hell: The 1974 Carrasco Prison Siege at Huntsville, Texas.* Denton: University of North Texas Press, 2004.

Hoffman, Paul. *Lions in the Street.* New York: Saturday Review Press, 1973.

Hopper, Jack. "Legislative History of the Texas Public Utility Regulatory Act of 1975." *Baylor Law Review* 28 (Fall 1976).

Kahaner, Larry. *On the Line: The Men of MCI Who Took on AT&T, Risked Everything, and Won!* New York: Warner Books, 1986.

Katz, Harvey. *Shadow on the Alamo: New Heroes Fight Old Corruption in Texas Politics.* Garden City, N.Y.: Doubleday, 1972.

Kemerer, Frank R. *William Wayne Justice: A Judicial Biography.* Austin: University of Texas Press, 1991.

Kinch, Sam, Jr., and Ben Proctor. *Texas under a Cloud.* Austin: Jenkins Publishing, 1972.

Kuhn, Michael. "House Bill 200: The Legislative Attempt to Reinstate Capital Punishment in Texas." 11. *Houston Law Review* 410 (1974).

Lynch, Dudley. *The Duke of Duval: The Life and Times of George B. Parr.* Waco: Texian Press, 1976.

Martin, Steve J., and Sheldon Ekland-Olson. *Texas Prisons: The Walls Came Tumbling Down.* Austin: Texas Monthly Press, 1987.

Martinez, Ramiro "Ray." *They Call Me Ranger Ray.* New Braunfels, Tex.: Rio Bravo Publishing, 2005.

Maxwell, Philip K. "History of the Deceptive Trade Practices–Consumer Protection Act and Article 21.21 of the Texas Insurance Code." 2000. Unpublished manuscript.

McKay, Seth Shepard, ed. *Debates in the Texas Constitutional Convention of 1875.* Austin: University of Texas, [1930].

Meltsner, Michael. *Cruel and Unusual: The Supreme Court and Capital Punishment.* New York: Random House, 1973.

Quarles, John. *Cleaning Up America: An Insider's View of the Environmental Protection Agency.* New York: Houghton Mifflin, 1976.

Roloff, Marie Brady, and Bobby R. Glenn. *Lester Roloff in Life and in Death.* Corpus Christi: Family Altar Publishers, 1994.

Sagstetter, Brad. *Don't Give Me Liberty!* Houston: Liberty Publications, 1981.

Smith, Noel, project director. *The Decline of Galveston Bay: A Profile of Government's Failure to Control Pollution in an Endangered American Estuary.* Washington, D.C.: Conservation Foundation, 1972.

Snowball, David. *Continuity and Change in the Rhetoric of the Moral Majority.* New York: Praeger, 1991.

Sorensen, Jon, and Rocky LeAnn Pilgrim. *Lethal Injection: Capital Punishment in Texas during the Modern Era.* Austin: University of Texas Press, 2006.

Tyler, Ron, et al., eds. *The New Handbook of Texas.* 6 vols. Austin: Texas State Historical Association, 1996.

Wooden, Kenneth. *Weeping in the Playtime of Others: America's Incarcerated Children.* New York: McGraw-Hill, 1976.

Index

Photos and illustrations in the gallery following p. 115 are listed by number.

Amsterdam, Anthony G., 166–70, 172–73, 174, 175–77, 179–87, 190
Anchor Home, 105, 107, 108, 112. *See also* Roloff, Lester L.
Anderson, Jack, 149–50, 151, 228n24, 242n14
Armco Steel Corporation, 38, 44, 45, 46, 48–52, 227n16, 228n24
Artesia Hall: abuses at, 92, 104; Briscoe and, 99, 100–101, 103, 104; closure of, 94, 100, 103–104; Farrar and, 91–96, 103–104; grand jury investigation of, 95–97, 102–104; Hill and, 98, 101–3; history of, 91–92; licensing of, 94, 98; news coverage of, 97, 102, 103, 104; runaways and, 90–92. *See also* Farrar, Joseph D.
Ashley, James H. *See* Gravitt-Ashley lawsuit
attorney general: authority of, 1, 52, 57, 64, 119–20; joint official cooperation with, xi; legal opinions issued by, ix–x, 1; legislative control over, 19, illustration 4; power over corporations of, 49, 64–66; representing consumers, 26, 27, 32; representing state agencies, 15, 35–36, 43, 54, 57
attorney general election campaign, 1972, 7–11, 24
Ayres, Patsy, 203, 204, 206

Barnes, Ben, 7, 11, 200, 223n9, 224n17, photo 4
Bentsen, Lloyd, 5, 25
Bercu, Steven L., 196–98, 202, 246n7
Blanton, John, 129–38, 139, photos 11, 12
Blackwell, Tom, 73–81, 82, 86, 87–88
Bode, Mary Jane, 73, 133
Boyle, Jim, 20, 24–26, 32
Braniff, 14–15, photo 3
Bravenec, Ray, 129, 135–36, 137, 138, 139, 240n69
Briscoe, Dolph: 1972 election of, 7, 11; 1975 legislative session difficulties of, 83; 1978 campaign of, 114, 162, 220, illustrations 6, 8; and Artesia Hall, 99, 100–101, 103, 104; death penalty law and, 172; DTPA and, 32, photo 14; Gatesville State School and, 205–206; and Howard Hughes files, 150; Manges and, 122; public utility regulation and, 71, 83; TWQB and, 56
Bullock, Bob: xxii, 83, 145, illustrations 6, 8; Howard Hughes case and, 142–43, 151; Manges friendship with, 122
business influence in government: 1972 elections cause weakening of, 11, 18, 25, 33; and attempt to curb Hill's antitrust powers, illustration 5; and insurance industry, 25–26, 29–32; and polluting industries, 35, 44–45, 55, 226n2, 228n24; and retail businesses, 23; Hill efforts to address, 24, 27–28, 34; public policy strategies pursued in, 23–24; Southwestern Bell and, 59, 62–63, 68, 73; Texas-based companies determined success of, 23

Cain, Clarence, 93–95, 97, 102–104, 233n5
Canales, Terry, 126, 131, 239n51
Carr, Waggoner, xv, 8, 223n1, 233n5
Carrillo, Oscar, 123, 130, 132, 136, 140
Carrillo, O. P., 122, 123; as assassination target, 125, 129; and *Corpus Christi Caller*, 128; court challenge won by, 127; and federal tax law violations, 126; government funds theft by, 122, 130,134, 135, 136–38; and grand jury action, 131, 132, 134; Hill and, 129, 139; and impeachment, 131, 135, 138, 139–40; and Manges, 124, 126, 238n18; Parr local officials' removal ordered by, 125–26; replacements appointed by, 131; state and federal convictions and prison sentences of, 138

Carrillo, Ramiro: conviction of, 140; evidence against, 136, 137, 138; Manges and, 238n18; Parr federal investigation and, 122
Carruth, Jerry, 129, photo 12
CBS *60 Minutes* television news program, 112–13, 221, 240n69
Champion Paper Company, 44–46, 47–48, 50
Choate, Tom, 201
City of Houston, 39–40, 41, 44, 52–55
Clark, John E., 121–22, 128, 238n13
Clements, Bill, 114–15, 220, 237n67, 245n5
Connally, John: 5, 6, 8, 219, photo 4; 226n2
constitutional revision, xiii–xiv, xx
consumer protection laws: 21, 22; 1967 legislation on, 21–22, 225n6; 1969 legislation on, 22; 1971 legislation on, 17, 22–23; 1972 Hill campaign focus on, 8, 9, 24; and 1973 Deceptive Trade Practices Act (DTPA), 24, 25–32, 34, photo 14
Cordova, Tony, 147–48
Couling, Rudolfo, 130–31, 135–38, 240n69

Daniel, Price, xv, 4, 5, 94, 119, 203
Daniel, Price, Jr., 18, 28, 32, 94
Davis, Will D., 26, 29, 30–31
Deaderick, David, 156
death penalty: history of, 166–70; *Furman v. Georgia* and, 165–66, 169–70, 171–72; and 1973 Texas law, 171–74, 175–57, 179–90
Deceptive Trade Practices Act. *See* consumer protection laws
Dibrell, Joe, 201, 202–203, 216, photo 7
Doggett, Lloyd: background, 19–20; and DTPA, 24–29, 31, 32; during 1971 legislative session, 20, 22
DPW. *See* Texas Department of Public Welfare
DTPA. *See* consumer protection laws
Dunham, Walter, 106, 108, 109, 110, 111

Edwards Underground Reservoir, 56
Estelle, W. James Jr., 208, 210, 212, 214, 245n46

Falwell, Jerry, 106, 109, 115
Farrar, Joseph D.: and Artesia Hall, 90–93, 94–95, 98, 99–102, 103–104; civil rights lawsuit filed by, 233n5; indictment of, 95–97, 98, 99–100, 104, 235n40; professional career of, 90. *See also* Artesia Hall
Ford, Jon, 83

Galveston, 38, 39, 40
Galveston Bay, 37, 39, 40, 55
Gammage, Bob, 28, 30, 32, photo 14
Garza, Florentino T. "Tino," 146–47, 155–57, 162
Goforth, Danny, xviii, 77, 84
Gorman, Rod, 42, 44, 45, 46–47, 48, 49–50, 50–51
Graham, Rev. Billy, 113
Gravitt, T. O. *See* Gravitt-Ashley lawsuit
Gravitt-Ashley lawsuit against Southwestern Bell, 62–63, 67, 68, 73, 230n16
Greenhill, Joe, 84–85, photo 5
Guerra, Arnulfo, 123–29, photo 13

Hall, Ford W., 70, 73, 87–88, photo 8
Hall, Ralph, 7, 22, 23, 28, 33
Hancock, Herb, 98, 129, 133
Harris County, 44, 46, 47, 49, 52, 54, 226n2
Harrison, Rick: and columnist Jack Anderson, 149–50; Hughes case and, 143–45, 146, 147–49, 149–50, 150–52, 153–54, 161–62, photo 19; John Wayne deposition and, 155–57; as Taxation Division chief, 143, 146, 216
Haynes, Richard "Racehorse," 103–104
Heatly, Maurice, 200, 246n15
Heatly, W.S., 36, 200, 202
Hester, Darrell, 139
Hill, Elizabeth Ann "Bitsy," xxi, 4, 15, 111, 218, photos 2, 18, 22, 23, 24, 26
Hill, Graham, photos 22, 23, 26
Hill, Jessie Hoover, photo 26
Hill, John L., Jr.: and Connally, 6; during hostage crisis, 214, 245n46; and family, 4, photos 22, 23, 26; parents of, 12, 13, 120, photo 26; and Roloff, xv, 107–8, 111, 113–15; as secretary of state, 6, 9, 19, 219, photo 4; sense of humor of, xxi–xxii, photo 21; student debating skills of, 13, 218, photo 1; as University of Texas student, x, 3–4; World War II service of, 4, 218, photo 2

Hill, John L., Jr., as Attorney General, legislative actions of: and Carrillo impeachment, xx, 139–40; and child care facilities licensing requirements, 110; and legislation to limit antitrust lawsuits, illustration 5; and mobile home buyer protections, photo 15; and new constitution, xiii-xiv, xxi; and 1973 DTPA, 24–34, photo 14; and open records, open meetings, legislative ethics laws, xiv, xx; and polluters, 54–55; and statewide criminal law prosecution powers, illustration 4; and utility regulation, 82–83, photo 9

Hill, John L., Jr., as Attorney General, office management of: and conflict between staff attorney and Judge Justice, 209; and efforts to minimize politics in attorney general office actions, vii-viii; and integrity of legal opinions requested by government officials, ix–x; and "John Hill Rule," photo 20; on news articles quoting the attorney general's office, xx, 133; pollution lawsuits action urged by, 43; and pressure from Armco, 50–51; regional attorney general offices established by, x–xi, 41; and staff quality, xi–xii, xx–xxii, 15–16, 18–19, 66, 88, 98, 141, 199

Hill, John L., Jr., as Attorney General, public appearances of: at Duval County grand jury meeting, 134–35; at Gatesville State School, 205–6;
news media praise for, 53, 71, 75, 137; in state and federal district courts, 48, 52, 55, 73–74, 75–76, 77–80, 102–103, 129, 160–61, 162, 203; in state and federal appeals courts, 56–57, 81–82, 243n2; in state and federal Supreme Courts, xi, xv, xx, 84–85, 88, 163–64, 165, 182–89, 219, 220, photos 10, 19; at TWQB meetings, 53, 54

Hill, John L., Jr., as Attorney General, strategic initiatives of: and expanded role of attorney general, 52, 56–57, 64, 69; on defense of flawed state actions, 56–57, 193, 199, 202, 246n7; on federal court intrusion into state government, 191, 193–94, 214; law enforcement philosophy, ix, xi, xv, 24, 43, 48, 50–51, 63, 113, 129

Hill, John L., Jr., political activities of: 1968 gubernatorial campaign, 6; 1972 attorney general's race, 7–11, 24; 1974 attorney general's race, photo 5; 1978 gubernatorial campaign, 104, 113–15, 220, 237n67, illustrations 3, 7, 8; and Leon Jaworski, 7; and political activities prior to 1968, 4–6

Hill, John L., Jr., professional career of: airliner crash lawsuits won by, 14–15; and commitment to improving legal profession, viii, ix, 13, 162; and father's attitude toward trial attorneys, 12; courtroom skills and strategies of, xi, xx–xi, 12, 14, 178; early law practice of, 12–13; plaintiff's law career choice by, 12

Hill, John L., Sr., 12, 13, 120, photo 26

Hill, Laverne, 3, 218

Hill, Martha, photos 22, 23, 26

Hill, Melinda, 4, photos 22, 23, 26

Hilitos, Los, 139, photo 12

Hobby, William P., Jr.: 1972 lieutenant governor campaign of, 7, 11; 1975 legislative session difficulties of, 83; and Artesia Hall, 97–101, 103; and church-operated schools, 110; and DTPA, 28, 30–31, 32; as potential candidate for governor, illustration 6; and public utility regulation, 59, 71, 82; and public welfare issues, 97

Houston Ship Channel: and 1970–71 pollution indicators, 41; federal pollution hearings, 40; history, 37–39; city of Houston pollution of, 39–40, 52–55; pollution lawsuits won by Hill staff, 46–55

Howard Hughes Estate: Andrews, Kurth, Campbell, and Jones actions for, 141, 143–44, 145, 160–61; other states' tax claims, 144, 158–60, 164; and secret Hughes logs, 148–53; Texas tax claim, 142–58, 159–62, 162–64

Hughes, Howard: death of, 141; Hill investigation of, 142, 143, 146–58; reclusive lifestyle of, 141–43, 151–53; staff logged activities of, 148–53; and youth in Houston, 142

Idar, Eduardo, Jr., 209, 210, 212

Jackson, Ron, 201, 206, 207, 208
James, Tim, 98, 128, 139, 217
Jaworski, Leon, 7
Johnson, Karen, 142–43
Justice, William Wayne: on belief in federal court action to improve prisons, 210; and creating class-action lawsuits, 195–96; media and state government critics of, 245n5; and *Morales v. Turman,* 197–98, 199, 200–201, 203, 204, 205–206, 207; and *Ruiz v. Estelle,* 209, 210, 211–13

Keever, Jack, 223n1
Kendall, David , ix–x, 64, 66, 68, 70, 72, 73, 215, 217

Lacy, Liz, 22. *See* Levatino, Liz
LDF. *See* NAACP Legal Defense and Educational Fund
Ledbetter, Harry, 100
Legislature, Texas: 1967 consumer legislation passed by, 21–22, 225n6; 1969 consumer legislation passed by, 22; 1971 consumer legislation defeated by, 17, 22–23; 1973 DTPA passed by, 28–33, photo 14; 1975 Carrillo impeachment by, 131, 135, 138, 139–40; child care facilities licensing requirements passed by, 110; death penalty law passed by, 171–4, 189; and Duval County district attorney's office, 126; and executive branch, 19; federal court-ordered redistricting on minority, urban membership of, 20, 194–95, 224n2, 225n3; and financial disclosure laws, xiv; and lobbyist registration, xiv; and Hill, xiii–xiv, xx, 54–55, 74, 81, 139–40, illustration 4; mobile home buyer protections passed by, photo 15; public utility commission law passed by, 82–3; and redistricting challenges, xiv, 193, 195; rural interests' dominance of, 20–21, 194; scandal impact on 1973 membership of, 18, 25, 171; and Sharpstown scandal, 1–3, 7, 9–11, 17, 42
Levatino, Liz, 22, 28, 29, 31, 139, 216
Longley, Joe K.: 42, 215, photos 7, 15; background, 8, 19; as consumer lobbyist, 20, 23; and DTPA, 24, 26–29, 31
Louisiana-Texas boundary litigation, xv, xx, 165, 243n1, 220

Manges, Clinton, 122–23, 124, 125, 126, 129, 131, 238n18
Martin, Crawford, 8, 9, 10, 11, 43, 169
Martinez, Ray, 129, 135, 138, 139, photo 12
Mauzy, Oscar, 28, 30, 31, 32, photo 14
Maxwell, Phil, 42, 43, 45, 54, 64, 216, photo 6
Moore, Mickey, 27
Moral Majority, 106, 115
Morales v. Turman. See Justice, William Wayne; Texas Youth Council
Morris, Charles "Lefty," 8
Mutscher, Gus, 3, 9, 18, 23, 200. *See also* Legislature, Texas; Sharpstown scandal

NAACP Legal Defense and Educational Fund, 167–68, 170, 173, 174–76, 190, 210, 212
natural gas royalty litigation, xii
natural gas supply crisis, xii
1973 Texas death penalty law, 172–74, 175–77, 179–90
Norris, Jan, 8, 10
Nugent, Jim, 74–75

O'Rourke, Terence: and Armco, 49–50; background, 41–42; as head of Houston office, 41–43, photo 6; and Houston Ship Channel, 44–52
Oaks, Steve, 97, 100
Odam, John, xviii, 10, 104–107, 109–10, 139, 215, 216, photos 6, 12, 27
open meetings and records laws, x, xiv
opinions committee, ix–x

Palmer, Eugene, 107
Parker, Carl, 32, photo 14
Parr, Archie, 117–18
Parr, Archer: county judgeship, 126–27, 131, 134; and Duval County water district,

128; and federal tax evasion conviction, 122; and Hill investigation, 134, 140; and grand jury investigation, 124, 131
Parr, George: and Box 13, 118; and death of Floyd, 119; convictions overturned by, 119; and feud with Carrillos and Manges, 122–27; Duval County affairs controlled by, 119, 120, 123, 130; and federal income tax evasion conviction, 122; Hill corruption investigation of, 130, 138; suicide, 127
Pendleton, Randy, 99, 104, 109, 110
Pluymen, Bert: background, 144–45; and Supreme Court death penalty case, 175–78; Duval County task force member, 139, photo 12; and Hughes litigation, 146, 150–51, 159
pollution control laws: 1972 Hill campaign focus on, 8, 9; and federal government action, 40, 41, 43, 48, 49; and Harris County action, 44, 46, 47, 49, 52, 54, 55, 226n2; and Hill enforcement, 44–57; city of Houston, 39–40, 44, 52–55; and impact on industry and environment, 35; industry opposition to, 34–35, 44–46, 48–49, 226n2; and state enforcement structure, 43–44; TWQB, TACB enforcement of, 36, 39–40, 41, 44, 52–57
Pope, Jack, 111
Powell, Gene, 137, photo 12
Public Utility Commission, 83, 87, 88, photo 9
PUC. *See* Public Utility Commission

Quebedeaux, Walter, 44, 48, 50, 52, 53, 226n2, 227n16

Rebekah Home for Girls, 104–10, 111, 112. *See also* Roloff, Lester L.
Rivers, Richel, 212–13
Rodriguez, Rudy, 129, 136, 139, photo 12
Roe v. Wade, xii
Rogers, John, 8, 9
Roloff, Lester L.: CBS *60 Minutes* interview with, 112–13; and court order to license schools, 106, 236n48; defends operations at legislative hearing, 106; goes to jail to publicize licensing challenge, 110; and Hill licensing enforcement, 105–106, 107–10, 111–12; and Nueces County attorney investigation, 104–105; offers Hill campaign support, 114; opposes Hill in 1978 campaign, xiii, 113–15, 237n67; radio ministry, 105, 108, 113, 114, 115; refusal to obey court order, 110, 111–12; retaliation against state licensing efforts, 105, 106, 109, 110, 113, photos 16, 17
Ruiz v. Estelle, 210–14. *See also* Justice, William Wayne; Texas Department of Corrections

Salter, Bob, 201, 205, 206
Schieffer, Tom, 106
Sears, Will, 70, 75–81, 84–85, 86, 87, photo 8
SEC. *See* Securities and Exchange Commission
Securities and Exchange Commission, 2–3, 62. *See also* Sharpstown scandal
Sharp, Frank, 1–3, 7, 9–10, 17, 223n1, 224n17
Sharpstown scandal: 1–3, 7, 223n1, 223n9; and 1972 elections, 9–11, 18, 171; and 1973 legislative session, 17, 18, 25, 33
Shepperd, John Ben, 119, 128
Shivers, Allan, 119
Simon, William, 149–50, 151
60 Minutes television news program, 112–13, 221, 240n69
Smith, Preston, 2–3, 6–7, 10–11, 98, 220
Smith, W. Forrest, 203, 204, 206, 207, 208
Southwestern Bell Telephone Company: 58, 59, 62, 68; 1975 intrastate rate increase proposal, 63, 64–87, 88; and AT&T, 58–62; and negative publicity, 68, 85; and PUC 1976 rate increase proposal, 88. *See also* Gravitt-Ashley lawsuit
Spier, Col. Wilson, 95, 100, 103
Steakley, Zollie, 84, 86–87
Sterling, Jim, 95, 96–97, 99–100
Supreme Court, Texas: 57; and Bell, 77, 81–85, 86–87, 88; and Canales, 239n51; and Carrillo, 127; Hill arguments to, 84–85, 88, 220, photo 10; and Roloff, 110, 111–12; and TWQB Edwards Aquifer lawsuit, 56, 57

Supreme Court, U.S.: and Duval County reform efforts in 1940s and 1950s, 119, 121, 238n13; expansion of constitutional rights by, 193–94, 196, 209; Hill concern over expansion of constitutional rights by, 191, 193, 194; history of death penalty rulings by, 165–70, 174–75; Nixon's plans to appoint Wilson as a member of, 223n1

—and Texas confinement cases: and landmark ruling on juvenile detainees' rights, 196–97, 200–201; and landmark 1964 ruling on prisoners' rights, 209; Hill request for dismissal in TDC lawsuit denied by, 211

—Texas death penalty cases in: 1976 appeal to, 165, 175–90; Texas law in 1972 declared unconstitutional by, 169–71; Texas legislature in 1973 rewrites death penalty law to comply with 1972 ruling by, 171–74

—other Texas cases in: and Hobby wins appeal of attorney's fee award in Farrar lawsuit, 233n5; broadcaster's appeal of ruling affirming states' power to prevent televised executions rejected by, 243n2; California seeks to block Texas Hughes estate trial by appeal to, 159–60, 162–64; Hill arguments to, xi, xv, xx, 163–64, 165, 182–89, 219, 220, photo 19; legislative redistricting cases decided by, xiv, 224n2; Roloff appeal rejected by, 112–13

TACB. *See* Texas Air Control Board

Taylor, Lynn, 105–6, 107, 109–10, 111, 112, 113

televised executions, 243n2

Temple, Arthur, 32, photo 14

Tenn-Tex Alloy Corporation, 44, 45, 46–47, 50, 51

Texas Air Control Board, 35, 36, 43, 47, 51, 226n2

Texas Department of Corrections: budget, 209; description, 209; history, 208; and *Ruiz v. Estelle,* 209–13

Texas Department of Public Welfare, 94–95, 97–101, 104–109. *See also* Artesia Hall; Roloff, Lester L.; Vowell, Raymond

Texas Rangers, 129, 135, 136–37, 138, 139, photo 12

Texas Water Quality Board: and Edwards Aquifer, 56–57; Hill staff tactics rebuffed by, 44, 55; history of, 35–36, 43, 51; and Houston Ship Channel pollution, 40, 44, 53–55; pollution lawsuits controlled by, 43–44, 52

Texas Water Rights Commission, 56, 128;

Texas Youth Council: budget, 207, 208; contrast with TDC, 208–209; history, 199–200, 202; legislative criticism of, 200, 208; and *Morales v. Turman,* 197–99, 201–208; reforms, 203–204, 206, 207; school campuses, 197, 198

TDC. *See* Texas Department of Corrections

Truan, Carlos, 106

Turman, James A., 200–206, 208

TWQB. *See* Texas Water Quality Board

TYC. *See* Texas Youth Council

utility regulation, 58, 67, 71, 80, 82, 83, photo 9. *See also* Public Utility Commission

Vowell, Raymond, 98–101, 103, 104–105, 109

Wayne, John, 155–57

Whitmire, John, 100, 103

Willatt, Mike: 216, photo 6; and Bell, 64–65, 67, 68, 81, 84, 86; background, 42; and pollution lawsuit strategies, 45; and TWQB, 53

Wilson, Will, xv, 121, 223n1

Wood, John, 129, 136–37, photo 12

Woods, W.G. "Dub," 95, 97, 101, 102, 104

Wright, Charles Alan, 169

Wyatt, Oscar, xii

York, Larry: 215, photos 6, 7, 27; and aphorisms by Hill, xxi–xxii; Artesia Hall case and, 98–104; Attorney General-elect Cornyn and, xii; background, 98, 199; and Louisiana-Texas boundary litigation team, xx; and *Morales v. Turman,* 199, 201–202, 207, 209